xuxa

Xuxa

THE MEGA-MARKETING OF GENDER, RACE, AND MODERNITY

Amelia Simpson

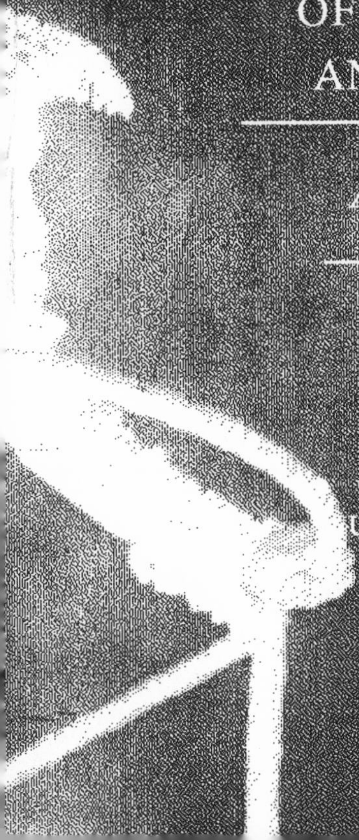

TEMPLE UNIVERSITY PRESS
Philadelphia

Temple University Press, Philadelphia 19122

Published 1993
Printed in the United States of America

The paper used in this publication meets the minimum requirements of American National Standard for Information Sciences—Permanence of Paper for Printed Library Materials, ANSI Z39.48-1984 ∞

Library of Congress Cataloging-in-Publication Data
Simpson, Amelia S., 1952–
Xuxa: the mega-marketing of gender, race, and modernity/by Amelia Simpson.
p. cm.
Includes bibliographical references and index.
ISBN 1-56639-101-6 (cloth : alk. paper).—
ISBN 1-56639-107-5 (pbk.: alk. paper)
1. Television broadcasting—Social aspects—Brazil. 2. Xuxa. 3. Women in television—Brazil. 4. Television and children—Brazil. 5. Brazil—Race relations. I. Title.
PN1992.6.S48 1993
302.23′45′0981—dc20 93-18121

Frontispiece: Xuxa in the Carnaval parade in Rio de Janeiro, 1992 (photo by Antônio Milena/Abril Imagens).

CONTENTS

ACKNOWLEDGMENTS

XUXA'S NARRATIVE CONTINUES TO UNFOLD AS this book goes to press. In keeping with her shift to television markets outside Brazil, the star's debut English-language children's program is being sold in syndication throughout the United States. I am grateful to numerous friends and colleagues for helping to keep me apprised of such developments during the preparation of this book, and for providing invaluable support in the form of materials, dialogue, and encouragement. In Brazil, I want to thank Carlos Hasenbalg and Denise Ferreira da Silva at the Centro de Estudos Afro-Asiáticos for the opportunity to consult with them and use the archives. Sandra Medeiros generously facilitated my access to a wealth of material about Xuxa. Antônio Carlos Secchin's friendship and hospitality were as much appreciated as was his help with research on the book. I am grateful to Cora Rónai, Jane J. Sarques, Aluízio Ramos Trinta, and the Fulbright staff in Rio de Janeiro for their thoughtful comments and kind attention. In the United States, I particularly want to thank Randal Johnson for his readiness to lend an ear and apply his expertise as a Brazilianist. I would like to recognize the very welcome support of many friends in Austin, Texas, and Gainesville, Florida, who showed faith, understanding, and enthusiasm for the project. Finally, I am grateful to my father for encouraging a critical eye, my mother for showing where to cast it, and my husband, to whom I dedicate this book.

Introduction

XUXAMANIA

IN 1980, CARLOS DIEGUES made a movie called *Bye Bye Brazil*. In the film, a tiny band of circus performers travel deep into the Amazon in search of a town or even a village that television has not yet reached. They discover that not a single corner of the nation remains untouched by television. *Bye Bye Brazil* commemorates a kind of turning, or no-turning-back, point in Brazilian history by acknowledging the presence of television as a permanent and pervasive feature of cultural discourse. In Brazil, as in the United States, the shapes that flicker on the television screen, and those missing from it, increasingly describe the form and meaning of the world. In the ongoing debate over the significance of the penetration of that medium in contemporary culture, the case of a young woman named Xuxa (SHOO-sha) is instructive.

Blond sex symbol Maria da Graça Meneghel, universally known as Xuxa, emerged in the 1980s as a mass media figure of unprecedented dimension in Brazil. By the end of the decade, she had become the undisputed *rainha* (queen) of mass culture, "the national megastar."[1] Backed by Brazil's TV Globo, the fourth-largest commercial network in the world, Xuxa has built an empire around a television program that is aimed at children but informs the culture at large about ways of being in society. The ideological impact of the entertainment Xuxa provides is all the more powerful for being projected by the sophisticated Globo network at a population more likely to have a television set than a refrigerator or running water.[2]

Brazil may be unique in the world today in its peculiar combination of a highly developed mass communications industry and an undereducated, needy population that nevertheless watches a lot of television. Brazilians, in fact, are said to watch more television than any other people of the third world.[3] Xuxa's television program, saturated with the confining fictions of the status quo, constitutes what one observer called the "cultural diet of over ten million young television viewers, day after day."[4] The numbers are much higher today than they were when that comment was made in 1989. The "Xou da Xuxa" (Xuxa Show), until very recently a five-hour-a-day, six-day-a-week affair in Brazil, where it first aired in July 1986 on TV Globo, is now broadcast in Latin America in sixteen countries as well as in the United States (on the Spanish-language network Univisión). The English-language version of the program is scheduled to air in the United States in 1993.

30 hours a week

Xuxa arouses endless fascination, sometimes awe, and occasionally hostility. Rarely is she viewed with indifference. The star's presence can be so commanding that people burst into tears at the sight of her. Xuxa tells of miracles that have occurred on the "Xou": a paralyzed child suddenly clapped his hands, and a mute burst out singing.[5] These stories contribute to the cultlike expressions of devotion the star inspires. When she makes her exit at the end of her television show each day, standing at the door to her spaceship throwing kisses and promising to return soon, a plea rises from the crowd below: *"Volta! Volta!"* (Come back! Come back!). As the spaceship begins its ascent, the huge stage model of the famous Christ the Redeemer statue on top of Corcovado Hill in Rio de Janeiro comes into view on the television screen. The two images compete for the small viewing space until gradually the spaceship shrinks and the Christ grows larger. Finally, all that remains is the familiar religious (and touristic) icon, with one small alteration: two pink neon Xuxa hearts on Christ's chest glow in the stage lights. The iconographic figures of Xuxa and the Christ of Corcovado are thus joined in a joyful, moving, transcendent spectacle. The scene not only indicates Xuxa's stature in Brazilian culture but also illustrates the careful manufacture of the star's image. This kind of seemingly transgressive narrative is consistent with Xuxa's irreverent, permissive style, which, examined more closely, reveals a broad strategy to divert attention from her delivery of a set of messages about control.

In his book *Stars*, Richard Dyer points out that celebrity figures are generally considered politically insignificant since they do not wield any real institutional power. "Because of this belief," the author writes, "the ideological significance of stars is masked and discounted. Just because it is so masked," he argues, "its real political power is all the greater for being less easily resisted."[6] Xuxa's image, carefully cultivated to serve the interests of a sponsored medium, is embedded with representations of gender and race as heavily compromised as are her displays of culture and modernity. Xuxa is the embodiment of some of Brazil's deepest contradictions. She also stands for some of its most treasured beliefs and desires. People call Xuxa a Midas, a Sleeping Beauty, a Snow White, a princess, a saint, an idol, a goddess, and a fairy godmother. Her most familiar title is "Rainha dos Baixinhos," or "Queen of Kids," using her special word for children (pronounced by-SHEEN-use). Suspended in a pastiche of labels and associations, Xuxa's image conveys a variety of powerful messages wrapped up in an appealing cloud of sex and drama and fun and money.

According to the *Washington Post*, Xuxa has remarked, "There are children who haven't learned to say 'mommy' or 'daddy' yet, but they know how to say 'Xuxa.' It makes me very happy."[7] Xuxa's huge success, whether measured by such anecdotal evidence or by the numbers, reveals an unusual mass appeal. The rewards of the public's devotion to Xuxa are not inconsiderable. One article calls her "Our Lady of the Industrial Era, saint of the business community," referring to the profits rendered by an array of enterprises spinning off from the "Xou."[8] Xuxa's LPs routinely top the sales charts in Brazil (despite the fact that she admits to possessing little musical talent), her films attract huge audiences, and her name on such items as bicycles, surfboards, toys, thirteen types of Xuxa dolls, a monthly magazine with a circulation of 700,000, clothes, shoes, shampoo, cosmetics, jewelry, school supplies, soup, yogurt, and cookies earns her millions of dollars. For live performances, the star receives the highest fees of any Brazilian entertainer. Xuxa owns a chain of clothing shops, a travel agency, a modeling school, a cattle ranch, a limousine service, and real estate in Latin America and the United States.

The star also shares in the profits earned by the Paquitas—teenaged, blond, Xuxa lookalikes who work as helpers on the show. Now there are also Paquitos, male versions, with their own products. Xuxa's messages are perpetuated through these and other clonelike figures who constitute a text of the future. The fortune she accumulated in just a few years earned her thirty-seventh place on the 1991 *Forbes* list of the world's highest-paid entertainers, accompanied by names like Michael Jackson and Madonna. Xuxa was the first Latin American ever to appear on the list. Only five of the forty *Forbes* slots in 1991 were filled by women. Xuxa's wealth endorses a success myth that contributes to the creation of a larger-than-life figure whose authority in the media marketplace is undisputed in Brazil and whose cultural resonance fills and stretches the imagination.

The clues to deciphering Xuxa's extraordinary projection reside in her image as it is constructed by a variety of media texts. Dyer's discussion of the range of materials involved in the production of film star images applies equally well to Xuxa:

> The star phenomenon consists of everything that is publicly available about stars. A film star's image is not just his or her films, but the promotion of those films and of the star through pin-ups, public appearances, studio hand-outs and so on, as well as interviews, biographies and coverage in the press of the star's doings and "private" life. Further, a star's image is also what people say or write about him or her, as critics or commentators, the way the image is used in other contexts such as advertisements, novels, pop songs, and finally the way the star can become part of the coinage

> of everyday speech. . . . Star images are always extensive, multimedia, intertextual.[9]

Materials such as those that Dyer lists are the kinds of sources used for this study. It is through these texts that Xuxa's image is created—by its consumers as well as its producers—and translated into a narrative of remarkable authority.

Xuxa's image is powerful because it effects a reconciliation of contradictory and incongruous views as it affirms the familiar configurations of the status quo. The Xuxa phenomenon constitutes a tightly controlled, narrowly circumscribed universe of values and attitudes. The star functions as an agent of transcendence, who performs a magic healing of fissures in Brazilian culture by reinforcing a variety of conflicting views of the dominant society, especially those regarding gender and race. Through Xuxa, the public achieves a sense of relaxation of the tensions generated by the gradual but real and public questioning of traditional gender roles, by the deeply troubling and largely denied racism in Brazil, and by the disjunctive experience of inhabiting a society in which the first and the third worlds exist side by side in discordant competition.

Just as in the United States Madonna "raids the image bank of American femininity," Xuxa's stardom draws on reserves of sentiment about gender roles.[10] Her sexually provocative style on television seems at odds with the context of a children's program. Yet the expression of overt sexuality in precisely such a context is fundamental to the star's powerful representation of women in society. Xuxa's mass audiences are drawn to a figure who is able to reconcile views of women that are cherished but as improbable as they are incompatible. The star affirms both the erotic and the domestic roles. Xuxa is the embodiment of the ideal woman, fully dedicated to courting male interest through behavior designed to be sexually stimulating, and at the same time deeply devoted to the task of caring for children. Her caretaker role is enacted literally on the television screen, where she is shown surrounded by adoring children, and symbolically in her role as "Queen of Kids" and national spokesperson for the Brazilian child. Xuxa's erotic performance on children's television maintains the sex symbol image she developed earlier in her days as a *Playboy* model and soft-porn movie actress. By stressing the elements of aggressive eroticism and compliant domesticity, Xuxa's narrative affirms dominant views of gender roles. Her representation of femininity serves the interests of the social hierarchy, perpetuating inequality by working to naturalize the myth of beauty and other mechanisms of disenfranchisement and marginalization.

Xuxa's persistent emphasis on a blond model of beauty is also fundamental to her appeal to mass audiences. She asserts the superiority of whiteness through her own image and its many manifestations, including the blond imitation Xuxas, the Paquitas, who are the envy of virtually every Brazilian girl at one time or another. Blondness is a norm of attractiveness that is inaccessible to most people in Brazil, the country with the world's second-largest number of people of African descent. Yet Xuxa's representation of an all-white aesthetic is symptomatic, not prescriptive. The star's promotion of the white ideal functions only with the complicity of an audience eager to view blond beauty. Xuxa helps Brazilians resolve the conflicting feelings that are naturally aroused by this predilection by continually asserting her Brazilian identity as she celebrates the blond ideal of beauty. Xuxa's six-year, very public relationship with the most famous black man in Brazil, soccer champion Pelé, is also important to the way her image functions to legitimize what is known as the myth of racial democracy. That myth, which dispenses with racism by means of blanket denial, governs attitudes in Brazil despite evidence of profound and widespread racial discrimination. Xuxa is able to endorse the myth of racial democracy in part by continually reminding the public of the symbolic coupling of black and white that her affair with Pelé represents. In her celebration of whiteness, Xuxa not only taps deep and jealously guarded feelings among Brazilians about race but also asserts the validity of a nearly universal ideological construction wherein the blond female is presented as "the most prized possession of white patriarchy." [11]

The consumerism promoted on the "Xou" is another seemingly paradoxical feature of the Xuxa phenomenon, given the realities of life in a country where, as one observer put it, "differences in economic capital are among the greatest in the world." [12] Over 70 percent of working people in Brazil earn 250 dollars a month or less; by the end of elementary school 82 percent of students have dropped out; and the poorest 50 percent of Brazilians share only 2.5 percent of the country's national income.[13] Yet the intensity of the feelings Xuxa arouses is channeled into a first world model of consumption. With its constant and thinly disguised barrage of sales pitches, her program fuels the dream of a profoundly consumer-oriented lifestyle. The central question about television—not What's on? but rather What's not on?—has particularly critical significance in circumstances such as those in which the advertising-saturated "Xou" operates. One of the important functions of television in Brazil is to supplement or replace the formal education unavailable to the thousands who belong, nonetheless, to the "plugged-in classes."[14]

Xuxa's image registers a history of attitudes about gender and race that are not unique to Brazil. These attitudes find expression the world over in a variety of manifestations. In the United States, for example, the Barbie doll, originally a sex toy for adult men, echoes in the imaginations of generations of children.[15] The typical Barbie look is blond and white. The doll's proportions, blown up to human size, would be an anatomically improbable 39-21-33. Yet that representation of ideal femininity, like Xuxa's, has thrived in the promotional environment of consumer culture. Cy Schneider, the man responsible for launching Barbie's ad campaign on television, understood how the doll worked: "Little girls saw Barbie as the young woman they wanted to be someday."[16] The ideals Barbie and Xuxa project, of course, are so far beyond reach that the fundamental lesson learned is about not measuring up. Barbie and Xuxa are icons that play on and feed back a social definition of feminine beauty and perfection. Through television's relentless marketing, Barbie became "the most popular toy in history," and Xuxa emerged as Brazil's "Queen of Kids."[17]

There is some resistance in the United States to Barbie's function as a fashion icon selling images of femininity in the form of commodities and sexualizing the body in the interests of marketability.[18] Susan Faludi tells of a young feminist, for example, who defines herself with the slogan "I am not a Barbie doll."[19] By contrast, the ubiquitous image of Xuxa is rarely challenged in public discourse in Brazil. The consensus of approval of Xuxa expressed among the general public is one of the most striking aspects of the phenomenon. Some seemingly unlikely endorsements suggest that the desire for consensus itself may govern the appreciation of Xuxa and her version of Brazil. A scene captured by David Byrne and included on his video "Ilé-Ayé: The House of Life" (1989), illustrates the case. The video documentary about African religious practices is set in Salvador, Bahia, the center of African-Brazilian culture. The scene in question takes place inside a community based on the model of African village life and organized around a spiritual center called a *terreiro*. The camera follows a small boy as he enters the walled community. He rounds a corner, and we see a group of about twenty young children. There is music playing and the kids are singing and dancing enthusiastically. The music is a Xuxa song.

The juxtaposition of the sounds of Xuxa in the temple of devotion to Africa is strange and puzzling. What the scene means to the members of the *terreiro* and what kinds of inflections other audiences may bring to their readings of the Xuxa phenomenon are questions that deserve consideration. This study attempts to explore the significance of such a scene by approaching the meaning and authority of Xuxa's image in sociological and semiotic terms. The assumption is that, because Xuxa is a star of unsurpassed magnitude in contemporary Brazilian culture, her image is important in relation to the attitudes and values of the society that grants her stature and yields her capital. This analysis examines aspects of Brazilian culture that are reflected in the defining features of Xuxa's stardom: her representation of femininity, her exclusive white aesthetic, and the promotion of an idea of culture and modernity predicated on consumerism. These elements of Xuxa's image are the basis for her acceptance as well as the rare rejection, delineating the preferred reading of her narrative as well as the critical one. Since Xuxa shares a symbolic history with blond sex symbols around the world, her story sheds light on patterns of thinking and feeling in other cultures as well, including that of the United States.

The chapters that follow begin with a look at the origins of Xuxa's image. Chapter One shows how, by a combination of chance and calculation, Xuxa emerged in 1983 ready for television with a set of associations that cater to the ideological configurations of dominant attitudes about gender and race in Brazil. Through her modeling career and her six-year relationship with Pelé, Xuxa's image acquired specific features crucial to the iconographic authority that would later prove so appealing and communicate so effectively to mass audiences on television. Chapter Two examines Xuxa on television. Starting with her program on the Manchete network (1983–1986) and continuing after 1986 in ever more produced and penetrating forms on the "Xou da Xuxa" on Globo, the star's image has saturated Brazil with an insistent narrative reinforcing the attitudes and values of the status quo. The nature of the television show formula, its mechanisms and its Xuxacentric design, are discussed in terms of culture, ideology, and profit. Xuxa's flourishing business empire is the subject of Chapter Three. A product of the intense cultivation of allegiance to the star and her encouragement of consumerism as the fundamental expression of that devotion, the empire markets the same messages as the "Xou." Through Xuxa's records, movies, and many other products, her followers absorb the lessons that inform her projected view of Brazil. Chapter Four examines the "cloning" of the star and places the Xuxa phenomenon in different perspectives to assess some of the possible figurative and substantive meanings it holds for the future of a Brazil now indelibly inscribed with that media-driven model of culture. Finally, Chapter Five considers a critical event in the star's history—the alleged attempt in 1991 to kidnap Xuxa and one of the Paquitas. A turning point in Xuxa's narrative, the episode illustrates the sensitivity of her image as a register of social tensions. The threat to the stability of that beloved and seemingly benevolent sign triggered a national debate about Brazil's idea of itself and hastened the expansion of Xuxa's empire beyond Brazil.

ONE

MYTHS OF BEAUTY AND MYTHS OF RACE

THE EXTRAORDINARY dimensions of the Xuxa phenomenon inevitably pose the question of the origins of such an imposing cultural icon. Besides charisma, Xuxa's ability to harness the emotional energy of a mass public is a product of her representation of specific values and attitudes in Brazilian culture. Xuxa has come to embody her country's complex and conflicting feelings about race and gender in particular. In both cases, Xuxa's strategy as a star has been to uphold dominant views in Brazilian society, using various means to create and highlight consensus and to downplay differences and alternatives. On the role of stars, Barry King provides a description valuable in assessing Xuxa's presence in Brazilian culture:

> Stars have a major control over the representation of people in society—and how people are represented as being in the mass media is going to have some kind of influence (even if only of reinforcement) on how people are in society. Stars have a privileged position in the definition of social roles and

types, and this must have real consequences in terms of how people believe they can and should behave.[1]

Where gender roles are concerned, Xuxa has come to play a fundamental part in setting and reinforcing standards of female looks and conduct. Thousands and thousands of girls and women—like one thirty-seven-year-old Brazilian who, after a liposuction procedure, declared, "I'm not quite like Xuxa, but I look a lot better," —learn to measure themselves against the star.[2] Through Xuxa's public exposure, beginning with a hugely successful career in modeling that preceded her work in television, she established a public image as a compliant, sexually provocative woman with a childlike, innocent quality. That image tells females how to be, and males what to expect.

Through her dissemination of a white standard of beauty, Xuxa also teaches Brazilians about race. The public's awareness of her long affair with black millionaire celebrity Pelé is central to the effectiveness of Xuxa's image. That relationship works to explain and justify the absence of virtually any affirmation of nonwhiteness on the "Xou" or in other manifestations of the star's image. How can she be racist, Brazilians ask, if she was Pelé's girlfriend? Yet it is precisely that relationship that gives her the license to promote an exclusively white ideal. This chapter explores this and other elements that define the origins of Xuxa's iconic authority in Brazilian society. The star's background, as expressed in a variety of media texts, establishes an essential part of the narrative from which Xuxa emerged in 1983, groomed for her debut in television, her image already formed.

In the tradition of stars, Xuxa has been provided with

a discovery myth, embellished by a series of anticipatory strokes including the evocative note of her provincial origins. Santa Rosa, the small town where Xuxa was born on March 27, 1963, enters the star's biography as a nod to rural Brazil and to the nostalgia toward an often idealized past felt by those in her audience who are recent immigrants to urban areas. Not far from the Argentine border, Santa Rosa is in the state of Rio Grande do Sul, in the southern and more European part of Brazil. Xuxa's birthplace and childhood home are featured in her official biographical sketch also because they are important as a way to naturalize a significant element of the star's image. Highlighting her southern origins places Xuxa's atypical looks in the context of the racial continuum that informs Brazil's cultural geography, within which the country is divided into a predominantly white south and nonwhite north. Xuxa's claim to Brazilian identity is made plausible by that measure of belonging at the same time that she displays the features of the coveted other, the blonde that is so often viewed as a symbol of superiority. Thus image management gives Xuxa the flexibility to play on Brazil's mental habit of exalting the blonde while simultaneously asserting kinship with a nation of nonblondes.

The story of Xuxa's discovery is inscribed in the tradition of stars. It is the kind of sequence that plays in the daydreams and fantasies of young girls everywhere. Xuxa's middle-class background makes the story seem accessible, while the privilege conferred by a certain norm of attractiveness is left out of these accounts of her discovery. In 1970, Xuxa's father, a military man, was reassigned, and the family moved from Santa Rosa to Rio de Janeiro. One day when Xuxa was sixteen, the story goes, a man followed her home from school, introduced himself to her mother, and said he worked for Bloch Publishing, one of the largest publishers and distributors of magazines in Brazil. The Bloch people were looking for fashion models, and the man thought Xuxa should be photographed. Her mother listened, and eventually gave him a picture of Xuxa at age thirteen. Two days later, one of Bloch's magazines set up a photo session, and Xuxa's career began.[3]

There are other versions of the discovery myth, in keeping with the tendency for the details of such narratives to multiply with the telling. In one variation, a Bloch magazine talent scout spotted Xuxa at a teen dance.[4] In another variant, Xuxa was simply walking down the street in Rio—like the girl from Ipanema who strolled past the open-air bar where Tom Jobim was writing a song—when a photography editor with Bloch saw her, followed her home, and knocked on the door. He asked Xuxa's mother for permission to put her on the cover of a romance magazine, and her father for his CPF, the equivalent of a social security number, so she could be paid.[5] These stories differ in their details but have in common an emphasis on the mundane origins of Xuxa's stardom. Her fame and fortune today seem to rest on a chance encounter of the past, a notion calculated to touch the deep reserves of hope that sustain people who daily face hardship and poor odds. Destiny and chance are presented as the keys to success, in the spirit of a lottery.

During the five years from Xuxa's discovery—said to have occurred on a Wednesday in November 1978—until her first television show for children aired on the Manchete network in 1983, she developed into one of Brazil's top models. The media texts make her ascent in the fashion world look effortless. Xuxa described her career as a "snowball" that simply started rolling, growing, and gaining momentum. In the beginning and throughout the eighties, media texts linked Xuxa to a passive representation of femininity. These texts generally camouflaged any assertive, mature qualities that could be viewed as challenging the notion of masculine mastery and domination, particularly in the workplace. It was not until a dozen years later, with Brazil's economy in decline and her various business enterprises making heavy profits, that Xuxa's hard-working nature came to be seen as a way to manage an image problem. By then it had become desirable to promote the idea that Xuxa had earned her wealth, so as to avoid her public identification with the privileged and resented financial elite.

As Xuxa's fortune grew, her relative power was also symbolically controlled through a series of media texts that registered the notion of discipline. In her official profile distributed in 1991, her "greatest quality" is listed as "discipline," and "what makes her happiest" are "the results of her work."[6] Another promotional document refers to the "military discipline" Xuxa learned at home as a child. The same source includes a series of testimonials that underline Xuxa's hard-working nature. Her mother declared that Xuxa deserved her success because she earned it through "effort and dedication." Adolfo Bloch, the president of Bloch publishers and of the Manchete television network where Xuxa got her start in television, spoke of her "extraordinary work ethic."[7]

In the nineties, the star also began emphasizing an American Dream type of optimism that supports the status quo in many ways, among them by presuming a level playing field. Xuxa repeatedly argued that she was a good model for children because she was a *vencedora* (winner), downplaying other characteristics many Brazilians associate with great wealth, such as exploitation, egotism, and hypocrisy.[8] Even in the nineties, however, the view of a strong, determined personality, a *vencedora*, was balanced by the assertion of passive femininity through various strategies, including separating the star from knowledge of her financial empire. When asked how much money she makes, Xuxa's standard response throughout her career has been that she has no idea. (In an October 1991 interview, for example, she said: "I swear to God, I have no idea how much money I have; I don't even know where it is.")[9] Central to the star's narrative is the construction of an image of femininity that cannot be seen as threatening to traditional views of gender. By identifying with submission and ignorance and by displaying a narrowly defined beauty and a controlled body, Xuxa reinforces traditional attitudes. She invites male approval in a way that tends to place women in competition with each other and to silence them by encouraging envy and self-contempt.

Xuxa's representation of traditional gender roles emerges in accounts of her early years as a model. Rather than presenting ambition and determination, the media texts emphasize shyness and immaturity. When discussing the first time she performed alone, for example, Xuxa spoke of being terrified and phoning her mother minutes before the fashion show began to ask her to pray and light a candle to a guardian angel. It was a lingerie show, and when the spotlights shone on Xuxa's *bumbum* (bottom), her legs began to shake.[10] The anecdote draws attention to the way the body is valued in the display profession of modeling. The episode is treated as a kind of baptism; Xuxa's tone reveals a mixture of embarrassment and pride.

Other stories from the early years of Xuxa's career underscore the quality of vulnerability. One text describes an incident when she was just seventeen and had been hired to pose for a series of photographs in the United States. Xuxa was dismayed to discover upon arrival that she was expected to provide sexual services instead, and she hastily extricated herself from the situation. The account implies not only Xuxa's vulnerability but her desirability as well.[11] The story also establishes limits in the representation of the ideal female, drawing a line at open prostitution. Another example of this particular method of defining the appropriate uses of sexuality is a story Xuxa tells of how Pelé was restrained from punching an Arab who had placed a wad of dollars in her hand at a party.[12] Here, again, the subject of the open exchange of sex for money is raised and pointedly rejected. The frequency with which that theme is raised by Xuxa (in a reference to her past in a Miami Spanish-language television interview in 1992, for example, she declared, "I wasn't a prostitute") suggests that the issue is important to her image.[13] Xuxa regularly approaches the border between sex symbol and sex worker, but without crossing it—except once, fictionally, in her role as a prostitute in the 1982 movie *Amor Estranho Amor* (Love Strange Love).

Xuxa's vulnerability is highlighted again and again in the representation of her relationship with Pelé, who became her protector. Questions of race as well as gender imaging are interwoven in the story of Xuxa and Pelé. Here, his role in establishing Xuxa's image of femininity will be considered first. Xuxa and Pelé met in November 1980, when she and three other models were invited to pose for the cover of *Manchete* magazine. The soccer star had just been granted a Dominican Republic divorce from his wife of twelve years. The aim of the cover photo on the December 20 issue, in which Pelé, wearing a tuxedo, is surrounded by the four young women wearing come-hither looks and scanty costumes, was to "celebrate" his bachelorhood.[14]

The image of a man announcing his sexual readiness, surrounded by women about half his age displaying themselves in poses of semi-arousal, established the context for the way Pelé and Xuxa's relationship would subsequently be treated in the media. Pelé would be master and she the mistress, protected by a very traditional view of gender roles. It follows that the two should publicly break off their relationship in 1986 at precisely the time when Xuxa was replacing him as the best-known and best-selling entertainment figure in Brazil. Once the role of protector was no longer viable for Pelé, the image of the relationship became untenable.

An account given by Xuxa and Pelé themselves of their first conversation, at the photo session in November 1980, was published in an article in *Manchete* magazine two years later.[15] Here, the messages about gender roles that their relationship conveys were clearly expressed. Xuxa remembers that she was intimidated by the soccer champion but eventually approached him, introduced herself, and told Pelé about a job she had been offered in New York. When he asked who the employer was, however, Xuxa "didn't seem to know," *Manchete* reported. Pelé suspected a shady transaction, and his doubts were confirmed when Xuxa revealed that she had been given only a one-way plane ticket. Finally, Pelé asked Xuxa how old she was. *Manchete* recorded the response: "Xuxa whispered, 'Seventeen.'" The trip was, of course, canceled.

The image of the passive female—someone to whom things happen—is invoked again in accounts of the evening after the photo session when Pelé took Xuxa out to dinner. One report portrays the evening as a type of dream date. In this tale, Brazil's legendary soccer star called Xuxa's home after the photo session to ask permission to take the teenager out to a nightclub and then to dinner. Xuxa's father answered the phone and, when the caller identified himself as Pelé, responded with something on the order of, "Sure, and I'm the queen of England." Xuxa's mother cleared up the misunderstanding, and her daughter reportedly arrived home that night "radiant."[16] The plot reads like an episode from a sitcom, or perhaps a fairy tale, with an ogre-like father and a facilitator mother.

The dream-date motif was elaborated during the next stage of the relationship, which coincided with the most desirable and public of all courtship occasions in Brazil: Carnaval. Xuxa was seen everywhere with Pelé, including the numerous Carnaval balls of the 1981 season. As one magazine put it, "after her Carnaval with Pelé, which the entire country witnessed, Xuxa was famous."[17] It was big news when, at one dance, Pelé deserted Xuxa for a Swiss journalist. But a couple of dances and one Carnaval parade later, the journalist flew home and Pelé showed up again with Xuxa at two prestigious balls on Fat Tuesday. Photographs from the period describe a playboy–plaything relationship of the type typically documented in the social pages at Carnaval time, and Xuxa did not try to dispell the impression. When asked, for example, if their age difference bothered her (Xuxa was eighteen and Pelé was forty), she answered no, "he thinks I'm fun."[18] Xuxa was even selected the 1981 "Queen of the Panthers," a title for which each year's crop of young beauties who come from well-to-do families or work in the display professions compete at Carnaval. Thanks to the attention Pelé generated, Xuxa was able to establish herself quickly in the public eye in a glamour girl–sex symbol role.

In the third phase of their relationship, Xuxa's role is extended to include protégée to the male mentor. She would later call Pelé her "guru" and say that her life was divided into two parts, before and after Pelé.[19] He is sometimes described as a sort of Pygmalion, creating and molding the young woman, a notion that carries to an extreme the idea of female compliancy. The vulnerable female motif surfaces again in Xuxa's account of the first lesson she learned from Pelé. She explains:

> My career was going along fine and then the problems began because I posed nude for some magazines [after she turned eighteen and was no longer a minor]. That's when I met Pelé. [Actually, she turned eighteen four months after she met him]. He taught me that my family could protect me. It was the best thing I ever did in my life. If I had moved out, I don't think I would have made it. It was too much for me to handle alone.[20]

The "problems" had to do with the fact that the Meneghel address in Grajaú, a neighborhood in north Rio de Janeiro, had become public knowledge and the family's life was disrupted by threatening and obscene phone calls.

When Xuxa reports that her bags were packed and she was ready to leave but Pelé persuaded her to stay at home, it is not his lesson for her but hers for all women that is conveyed most persuasively. The feminine ideal of dependence and submission is affirmed by means of this allegorical tale. A photograph of Xuxa and Pelé published in *Manchete* reinforces the image of male control and female subordination.[21] The couple is posed on a beach; Pelé stands facing the camera, bare-chested, in white pants stretched tightly across his hips. The strained fabric puckers in a series of lines that point to his crotch, the focal point of the composition. Pelé's hands are placed on his hips, and his legs are spread in a firm, confident stance. Xuxa, in a bathing suit, kneels on the sand next to him. She has a hand wrapped around his thigh, and her head leans into his hip at a suggestive angle. The photo is a portrait of the hierarchy of gender, a configuration that appears again and again in the media texts from which Xuxa's star image emerges.

Under Pelé's tutelage and protection, by the end of 1981 Xuxa had appeared on more magazine covers in Brazil than had any other model. She had also begun to inspire a considerable amount of resentment among women. Xuxa would later label that resentment envy and on one occasion insist that it was the definition of the devil.[22] She complained about the vicious mentality among women in modeling, and her sentiment was echoed by one journalist who called the industry a "nest of poison pet snakes." In the same article, Xuxa is quoted on the subject: "In the world of fashion and beauty, everybody's out to get everybody else. They'll let you pose with your makeup smeared if you're not on your toes. There are models out there who are way too old and they're afraid, they're really scared, they can't stand our being young."[23]

Women in general had reportedly begun showing a great deal of hostility toward Xuxa. There were accounts of women throwing stones at her car and screaming at her on the street to stay away from their husbands.[24] It was said that men would call the Meneghel house offering large sums of money for a night in bed with Xuxa, but the women would accuse Xuxa of "stealing" Pelé and threaten her with violence.[25] These reports played a useful role in shaping Xuxa's image, since they gave evidence of how effectively she was conforming to the feminine ideal. The desirable results—to divide, and thereby weaken, the female community—were put on display in the media to confirm Xuxa's commitment to the status quo of gender relations.

Xuxa's nude posing in the early 1980s resulted in her emergence in the national media as a professional sex symbol. She boasted about that role in one story about a model who turned to her after a fashion show and said, "You know what the difference between us is? I'm a model who wears clothes. Get it?"[26] The December 1982 issue of *Playboy* featuring Xuxa is a collector's item today. Another example of Xuxa's early imaging is found in her response to a 1982 article in the gossip magazine *Amiga*. The article claimed that she had had cosmetic breast surgery, and Xuxa answered by posing for *Manchete* holding open her blouse to exhibit her breasts. In the caption, Xuxa challenged readers, "Do you think I need plastic surgery on my bust?"[27] This text erases any doubts as to Xuxa's willingness to conform to the sex symbol role.

Another photo published a couple of months earlier in the same magazine prominently displays Xuxa's *bum-*

bum.[28] The picture shows her wearing a twist of cloth around her waist and between her buttocks, which face the camera. She is smiling over her shoulder, next to a caption that elaborates on the photographic representation of the feminine ideal: "Beauty from head to foot. That's why she doesn't need to speak—nor should she."[29] The absence of any acknowledgment in mainstream media texts in Brazil that such a configuration of visual and verbal cues might be demeaning is striking. In later years, Xuxa would defend her nude photo period with calculated disingenuousness, saying that since the human body is a beautiful and natural thing, there can be nothing wrong with displaying it.

In the early 1980s, the media began comparing Xuxa to Marilyn Monroe, a consecrated sex symbol in Brazil as she is all over the world. Walter Hugo Khoury, who directed Xuxa in the 1982 soft-porn movie *Amor Estranho Amor,* called her "the new Marilyn Monroe."[30] Xuxa's representation of the Monroe image of the "sensual/childlike woman who adapts herself to every man's desires but inspires only envy in women," is examined in an article by Maria Rita Kehl published in the feminist magazine *Mulherio* in 1982. Kehl shows how even the prestigious and generally progressive *Folha de São Paulo* "bought" the Marilyn Monroe image, reporting that Xuxa says "unbelievably dumb things," but in "a really cute way."[31] Kehl observes that the Monroe image, by identifying exclusively with what is thought of as male desire, represents a way of denying female identity. According to Kehl, those who cultivate the sex symbol image become caricatures of women, like transvestites.

One way of measuring the degree to which Xuxa's representation of femininity is designed to appeal to the

Transvestites and Xuxa

conventions of male viewing is to examine her somewhat tenuous but nonetheless emblematic connection to the transvestite community. When one of Brazil's most famous transvestites, Roberta Close, interviewed Xuxa on television in December 1984, the event represented a staged performance by two of Brazil's best-known sex symbols.[32] Rebroadcast in 1991, the episode was not a challenge to Xuxa's image, because the transvestite's representation of femininity is ideologically compatible with that of the star. Roberta Close spent years molding a body and tailoring a set of moves to resemble the ultimate in conventional feminine desirability. Close's legitimacy in the straight world derives from the fact that men find the transvestite attractive. Even a group referred to in the mainstream press as "hard-core super machos" attending a Roberta Close lingerie fashion show in Porto Alegre were willing to overlook the implications about their own sexuality in their enthusiasm for the transvestite.[33] The Brazilian *Playboy* magazine went so far as to publish a series of nude photos of Close in 1984.

Feminist Rose Marie Muraro calls transvestites like Close a product of underdevelopment, arguing that more progressive societies just aren't interested anymore in the stereotype of women that Close represents: the eyelash-batting, submissive, sex kitten variety.[34] In any case, the contours of feminine sexuality that Xuxa embodies belong to the same sphere as those of the man-pleasing transvestites. It is common knowledge in Brazil that many transvestites adopt Xuxa's name along with their feminine identity. Transvestites have even died from attempting to emulate her. A rash of deaths occurred in São Paulo in 1983 after a number of men gave themselves lethal injections of silicone to try to acquire a "Xuxa body."[35]

Xuxa's image attracts through the multiplicity of meanings it embodies as well as by the specific nature of each aspect. Alongside the glamour girl–sex object role, Xuxa has managed to convey a childlike, innocent, wholesome quality as well. In 1982 *Veja* described Xuxa as having the "provocative sensuality of a little girl–coquette who excites tropical fantasies."[36] Xuxa injected a hint of innocence in comments to the press about how great it was to go to nudist beaches in Europe where "grandma and mom and the kids and the grandkids all run around naked. They're naked because it's more comfortable that way, in the heat, by the sea. . . . Nakedness, by itself, isn't wrong. But here in Brazil, it's still considered something dirty and immoral."[37] The numerous observations in the media that Xuxa did not drink or smoke and had been a vegetarian most of her life reinforced the view of the model's lifestyle as natural, not nasty. That perspective was further substantiated by Xuxa's parents, who publicly backed her and supported the direction her career was taking. Her mother insisted that "after Xuxa, nice girls can pose nude. She's challenging the prejudice that it's something only vulgar people do."[38] Xuxa reported in a May 1982 article that her father had refused to show the nude photos of his daughter to anyone at first, but that now "he even shows them to his friends."[39] In these various remarks, the apparent defiance of social convention has a liberating, progressive air to it, although what it really stands for, of course, is merely permission to celebrate more openly the dominant attitudes toward the female body.

Xuxa's approach corresponds in many ways to the 1950s *Playboy* "philosophy" in the United States. Dyer describes the magazine's attitude as one "that [saw] itself as socially progressive, taboo-breaking," although essentially "what *Playboy* succeeded in doing was making sex objects everyday."[40] Xuxa contributed to a similar process in Brazil, naturalizing the idea of women as sex objects and masking the constructed nature of that view. Xuxa's "innocent" approach to sexuality coincides with that of a 1950s figure featured in the early *Playboy* years: Marilyn Monroe. When Monroe's earlier nude posing surfaced during her Hollywood star years and threatened to create a scandal, her response followed the same cues as Xuxa's defense after she became Brazil's number one cover girl. Monroe asserted a "naturalness in relation to sexuality" and declared that she was not ashamed of the famous "Golden Dreams" calendar shot, which was used as *Playboy*'s first centerfold photo. Monroe reiterated her view in statements such as this one from her last interview: "I think that sexuality is only attractive when it is natural and spontaneous." Dyer's observations about Monroe apply equally well to Xuxa: Monroe "combined naturalness *and* overt sexuality" in a way that was meant to be viewed as something "new" and "progressive."[41] "Time and again," Dyer remarks, "Monroe seems to buy into the 'progressive' view of sex, a refusal of dirtiness—but that means buying into the traps of [specific] sexual discourses: the playboy discourse, with women as the vehicle for male sexual freedom."[42]

Xuxa sought to exploit the "child-woman" duality that Monroe, with her sexually suggestive and at the same time "childish, vulnerable, innocent, playful air," had expressed decades earlier.[43] The public responded to the captivating image of a Brazilian woman who could defend nude posing as healthy and wholesome on the one hand, and declare that men in her country weren't "ready for eroticism" on the other.[44] At the end of 1981, Xuxa signed a contract to act in *Amor Estranho Amor,* a film that would play an important part in the configuration of Xuxa's image. The movie is set in a brothel, which is housed in an elegant mansion in São Paulo. (To some extent, the movie is a house tour.) The events take place in the twenty-four hours preceding a coup d'etat. Political intrigue is thick as a group of politicians gather at the brothel, while, in parallel fashion, the resident women vie for power among themselves, illustrating how female disunity can serve the interests of a male-dominated (and in this case, male-owned) institution.

The day before the coup, the son of one of the prostitutes, played by a thirteen-year-old actor named Marcelo Ribeiro, arrives unexpectedly at the brothel. So does Xuxa, who plays a prostitute from southern Brazil, hired to seduce a rival of one of the political schemers. Xuxa is placed in a box wrapped like a gift, which is wheeled into a room full of men and prostitutes. She emerges dressed as a bear in white fur, and does a striptease. In a later scene, Xuxa tries to seduce the young boy, who is supposed to be about ten or twelve—"almost a man," but not quite. Xuxa is wearing her teddy bear costume when she approaches the boy. She offers herself to him as a toy, saying "Do you want to play with me? I'm a soft teddy bear. See how soft I am. So soft. So soft." Xuxa utters moans of pleasure as the camera moves in for a closeup of the boy fondling her nipple.

This was the scene that would concern her image managers later on, after the star had assumed the role of children's idol and advocate. Xuxa tried to have the movie withdrawn from circulation in Brazil and, in June 1991, won a judgment prohibiting distribution of the film in video cassette form. The judge refused to award damages for the "vulgarization" of Xuxa's image, however, arguing that she alone was responsible for that.[45] Of course, it was impossible to control public access to *Amor Estranho Amor* entirely. The film is readily available today in U.S. video rental stores, for example, including one of the large chains. Xuxa's lawsuit itself naturally drew attention to the film, leading to the appearance of articles like one in *Amiga* entitled "Sex with Children Is No Longer an Issue with Xuxa," which began, "Xuxa doesn't want to be seen having sex anymore with a 'baixinho.'"[46] Yet it is clear from the media coverage of the controversy that the movie represented less of a threat to Xuxa's image at home than to her plans to move into the international children's television market.

While Xuxa's performance with the boy in *Amor Estranho Amor* attracted attention in Brazil after she became a children's star, she was not censured for it. Her role in the film and her nude modeling in the early eighties seemed to make Xuxa, if anything, more likable. By representing a specific gender role that was under attack by women's movements in Brazil and abroad, Xuxa performed the important function of reasserting the validity of the old-fashioned way. The movie, in particular, stood for tradition because of the cultural context that allowed the scene with Xuxa and the boy to be understood as a familiar initiation rite, one that is customary among Latin men—even at the end of the twentieth century—and usually involves a prostitute, or maybe a maid. Marta

Suplicy, a psychologist and sociologist who specializes in issues of sexuality, observes that there is considerable pressure on Brazilian boys to begin performing sexually at about the age of the boy portrayed in *Amor Estranho Amor*. She explains, "In our culture, it's still difficult to keep boys from going to prostitutes. There is very strong peer pressure—and if by age thirteen or fourteen the boy still hasn't had sex with a woman, his peers and even his father begin to get suspicious." Suplicy challenged mainstream attitudes when she questioned a boy's initiation into sex with a prostitute as "necessary background" for later, more mature relationships.[47] In this cultural context, Xuxa's appearance in the soft-porn movie, rather than provoking fears that she might inspire a precocious sexuality in children or incite child-centered sexual fantasies in adults, became part of the image of femininity that endears her to audience by conforming to, and thus affirming, the validity of familiar gender roles.

Xuxa's representation of femininity is reinforced by her embodiment of the blond ideal of attractiveness. Robin Tolmach Lakoff and Raquel L. Scherr discuss blondness as a quality of passivity that conspires with the common gender stereotype to produce the myth of an ideal "dumb blond":

> The fairness of the hair, eyes, and skin of the perfect blond is parchment, the proverbial *tabula rasa* to be written upon, to absorb and reflect the ideals and illusions of those who look upon her. . . . Blondness is, physically, imprecise: especially in portraits, but in reality too, blond hair merges with the atmosphere to create a sort of haze. . . . The best blond is the one who is the most passive, has the least direct influence on her environment. And that is the "dumb blond," who has

no ideas, no ambitions other than to use her beauty to find a man to support her and, more importantly, to give her the definition she cannot achieve on her own.[48]

Whether or not an archetypal component figures in the meaning of blondness, the value cultures assign to the idea of the blonde clearly has ideological implications. In Brazil, a country where at least half the population can claim African ancestry, race is defined on a complex scale of gradation. More than 120 words describing different shades of skin are used in order to avoid saying "black." Pelé and Xuxa represent the extremes on the scale of black to white. Pelé's features, hair, and complexion are what Brazilians consider truly black, while Xuxa, whose grandparents are from Austria, Poland, Italy, and Germany, is even whiter than the white of Portuguese origin. Xuxa and Pelé's romance reminds Brazilians of the troubling racial issue, but places it in a pleasant, harmless context, dissipating its threatening potential. The couple stands for a meeting of the far ends of the racial spectrum, a kind of ideal union symbolized by two beautiful people.

Xuxa is able to embody a very powerful ideological construct in Brazilian culture, the myth of racial democracy, because of her link with blackness through Pelé. So complex and threatening is the question of race relations to Brazilians that an official ideology was invented to dispose of the problem. According to that vision, which emerged after the abolition of slavery in 1888, the population, through miscegenation, would eventually lose its racial differences and become a "racial democracy." Since the process of miscegenation, however, was originally envisioned by the dominant white class as a process of "whitening," built into the very notion of a society somehow "above" racism is the privileging of lighter skin. It is hard to overestimate the impact of the myth of racial democracy on Brazil's thinking about race and culture:

> Racial democracy's main tenets are the absence of racial prejudice and discrimination, which in turn imply the existence of equal economic and social opportunities for whites and blacks. The foundations of racial democracy are more than a simple matter of faith, the beliefs having assumed the character of commandments: "(1) Under no circumstance should it be admitted that racial discrimination exists in Brazil; and (2) any expression of racial discrimination that may appear should be attacked as un-Brazilian."[49]

The racism that characterizes Brazil relies heavily on the process of naturalization. To naturalize racial discrimination is not to neutralize its effects but rather to make them seem to disappear. Stuart Hall distinguishes between "overt" and "inferential" racism, and makes the point that the latter is, "in many ways, more insidious, because it is largely *invisible*."[50]

The evidence that so many Brazilians subscribe to the myth of racial democracy lies in the fact of pervasive denial. The wish to celebrate a mythical racial enlightenment regularly outweighs the statistical and anecdotal evidence of widespread discrimination. Racism is easily observed in a variety of common situations in Brazil. Blacks, for example, are not seen serving food in restaurants in places like Ipanema and Copacabana. In apartment buildings in those same neighborhoods, blacks have to use the service elevator or risk being stopped by the doorman. Blacks driving after dark may be detained by the police to check whether the car is stolen. Brazilians all know that the expression "good appearance" in a job announcement means "not black." As Muniz Sodré, who heads the School of Communications at the Federal University of Rio de Janeiro, has observed, sometimes "the black himself is racist toward the black," having internalized a status assigned by the dominant society.[51] The classic problems of racism do indeed exist in Brazil, and Xuxa is able to exploit the difficulty the nation has in facing them by invoking a happy vision of the union of black and white. The desire to be rid of the problem and to be absolved of responsibility for it draws Xuxa's public to her symbolic resolution of the issue of race. At the same time that solution allows her audience to celebrate the ideal of whiteness the star represents, which is itself encoded in the myth of racial democracy.

Pelé is a particularly suitable figure for the role he plays in the racial configuration of Xuxa's image. His race lends him the necessary symbolic authority, while his fame and fortune position him outside the condition of being black in Brazil. Pelé himself alludes to this in his reply to an interviewer's question about whether he ever faced problems with racism in Brazil: "It's not particularly useful to ask that of a black man who has become famous in sports or the arts."[52] Almost all of the country's most famous blacks are in the entertainment business or are athletes like Pelé, who has played a fairly conservative role in Brazilian society and has alienated some activists by his lack of participation in the struggle against racial discrimination. Pelé is rarely asked about racial issues, but he did address the question in the interview mentioned previously. His other remarks in that interview are revealingly evasive, contradictory, and diplomatic:

> There is no parallel between the Brazilian view of the issue [of racism] and what happens, for example, in the U.S., in South Africa or in other countries where there is segregation. When [North] Americans are racist, they're open about it. They talk and act like racists. Nobody pays any attention to a black man walking down the street in New York with a white woman. Here [in Brazil], people still stop and stare and make remarks. But the best lesson I've learned comes from the slums where I saw blacks and whites getting along together perfectly. It would be wonderful if that were the case in all segments of our society. . . . Brazilians, thank God, don't have it in their nature to be blatantly racist. So, what it boils down to is, if poor blacks can't get in the door, poor whites can't either. . . . It's a complicated situation, far from easy to analyze, because it's camouflaged.[53]

The camouflage Pelé refers to is supplied by the myth of racial democracy whereby prejudice and discrimination are effectively masked. Popular statements such as "the black does not have a problem," and "we do not have barriers based on color," and "we are a people without prejudice" lend credibility to the myth and show the persistence of Brazilians' willingness to subscribe to it.[54] In a sense, one can see Pelé as someone camouflaged from himself. He is a black man disguised as the "King" of soccer, the national passion.

As a symbol of black success—the exception that proves a rule in which Brazilians have heavily invested—Pelé represents blackness in a nonthreatening way. His frequent depiction in the media as a playboy further suits the role.[55] The media's regular chronicling of Pelé's social life endorses the stereotype of the black male's sexual prowess. When Xuxa and Pelé ended their romance in

1986, his image in the media reverted to that of the bachelor stud. Most of his dates recorded in the social pages were with models or beauty queens, most of whom, like Xuxa, were very young. The gossip magazines ran articles about Pelé's girlfriends such as the one showing Miss Brazil '89, Flávia Cavalcanti, who is pouting in the photograph because she wants to "preserve her virginity at all costs" and the "King" is "getting tired of it."[56] In September 1987, *Manchete* did another cover posed like the 1980 one with Xuxa. Here, surrounded by four different young women, Pelé once again projects the image of a man driven to sexual conquest. In terms of both race and gender roles, Pelé is the ideal symbolic partner for Xuxa because he too signals the dominant attitudes and values to which her image constantly alludes.

Pelé also contributed to the illusion of a country free of racial prejudice by playing another role. At the same time that the media were projecting the Pelé of fickle heart and inordinate sexual appetite, he appeared—often in the very same articles—discussing his presidential aspirations. In 1984, Pelé declared, "I want to be the first black president of Brazil."[57] At Carnaval time in March 1987, a *Veja* article reported the remark by Pelé that in "four or five years" he would be prepared to "assume a political post, perhaps as president of the republic."[58] In 1992 he told the *Folha de São Paulo*, "One of these days, I'm going to have to step in and take care of Brazil."[59] In the media texts about Pelé, he emerges as a figure who, like Xuxa, stands for the resolution of contradictory beliefs. The talk about becoming president of Brazil sustains the myth of racial democracy, while at the same time other views of Pelé present the reassuring image of a man with the harmless ambitions of a playboy.

In 1983, *Manchete* ran two photos under the title "The Would-Be-President Pelé and His Sweet First Lady Xuxa."[60] Here, the verbal and photographic messages transmit clearly the couple's significance. Pelé is shown wearing a brief-style bathing suit and the large gold chain with a cross pendant that appears in most of his photos. He is leaning on a tree against which rests a large sign advertising Pelé health clinics. He holds a bottle of Pelé vitamins in each hand. Xuxa appears in a separate photo, seated on a post. She is wearing a camouflage jacket with the left shoulder pulled down to reveal one naked breast. Xuxa's legs are spread wide and bent at a right angle at the knees, on each one of which rests a hand. Her feet are bare and are stretched into the position they would be in if she were wearing very high-heeled shoes. Behind her is a tangle of barbed wire. Xuxa's is certainly not the portrait of a "sweet first lady." Pelé comes off more as a salesman hawking a brand of body-building snake oil than a presidential candidate. The two photographs effectively undermine the title, making it clear that the couple is not seriously expected to be pictured as president and first lady.

Xuxa's promotion of a white ideal invests the old message of the superiority of whiteness with extraordinary power in the age of mass media. She fits perfectly into a nearly universal mentality of privilege, one that endorses what Dyer calls the "racial hierarchy of desirability."[61] Xuxa's fair skin, blond hair, and blue eyes, and the replication of that look in the Paquitas and in the many products connected to the "Xou," reinforce what most people in Brazil learn about race from the time they are very young. These images circulate in the society at large, but are especially pervasive through the mass media and the advertising industry, which, as Carlos Hasenbalg has observed, "reinforce the negative self-image of Afro-Brazilians who are either invisible or portrayed in stereotyped roles."[62] Anybody who watches Brazilian television for half a day sees that it is dominated by whites and by white images of power, success, intelligence, and beauty. A 1988 analysis of images of blacks in advertising found that in a group of 203 ads from television and a set of mainstream magazines including *Veja* and *Manchete*, blacks appeared in only 9, and 3 of those were government campaigns for military recruitment or measles vaccinations. In the remaining 6, blacks were either presented in crowds, disassociated from the products advertised, as if to avoid "contaminating" them, or shown *"no seu lugar"* (in their place) as the saying goes, namely, as entertainers or manual laborers.[63] This kind of treatment of blacks by the media in Brazil contributes actively to the formation of negative views such as those found in another study. Here, a group of seven- to eighteen-year-old youngsters, half of them black, were asked to attribute specific characteristics to either blacks or whites. The responses need no decoding. The words "stupid," "ugly," "thief," and "pig" were associated overwhelmingly with blacks, while "pretty," "doctor," and "rich" were attributed almost exclusively to whites.[64]

There is a great deal of evidence of racism in Brazil in the modeling and fashion circuits. In Brasilia, in 1988, an eight-year-old girl was disqualified from a beauty contest and had to return her prize because she was "too dark-skinned." The judges had picked her unanimously, but the mothers of the losing contestants, all lighter-skinned, refused to accept the decision.[65] This incident follows the 1986 election of the first black to win the Miss Brazil contest, Deise Nunes de Souza, who had announced her intention to use her throne to draw attention to the problem of racial prejudice. A number of fashion photographers and models, including Brazil's top black model of 1990, Zuleika, have testified to blatant color prejudice in the profession.[66]

Being black does not necessarily exclude one from the beauty industry, but being white offers untold advantages. The mulattas of Brazilian social folklore and samba shows for tourists may be promoted as the most beautiful and sensual women in Brazil, but they are only "second-class sexual objects" compared with the lighter-skinned beauties.[67] Just having white skin, however, is not always enough in Brazil. In a footnote to the article on blacks in advertising previously cited, it is observed that not only is there a notable absence of black female models but white models with dark hair and eyes are also missing: "The number of white, blond, blue-eyed models appearing in [Brazilian] publications makes one think more of Sweden than Brazil."[68] Xuxa is one example. But her association with Pelé enters her biography as a kind of proof of immunity to racism, which then functions as a license to exploit the appetite for the blond and blue-eyed ideal in a country with the largest black population outside Africa.

Xuxa's influence on thinking about gender roles is no less powerful than her effect on views of race. She sets standards of feminity that inspire thousands and thousands of girls and women. Xuxa's modeling school teaches a new generation about the virtues of professional display. Asked about her plans for the future in a 1986 interview, Xuxa answered, "I'm really interested in helping girls who are starting out. . . . Sometimes I see a girl on the street and I tell her, 'You could be a model. Take some photos with such and such a photographer, lose a little weight.' "[69] Directly, through statements such as these, and indirectly, by serving as an example of the ideal, Xuxa conveys the idea that the display of the body is the fundamental characteristic of feminine identity.

One of the effects of sending that message is to reinforce the traditional views about being beautiful that inform Brazilian culture. The anthropologist Roberto da Matta suggests that the cult of the body in Brazil is a legacy of slavery. A good body was important to the survival of both the slave who possessed it and the owner who possessed the slave. A famous poem, "Recipe for a Woman," by Brazil's beloved poet Vinícius de Morais (1913–1980), is often cited as representative of the national attitude: "May the ugly ones forgive me, but beauty in a woman is indispensable" (in Portuguese, *fundamental*). To be female in Brazil, Maria Rita Kehl observes, is to be placed in one or the other camp—that of the beautiful and indispensable or that of the ugly and superfluous, who are invited to forgive the poet but are more likely to be found apologizing for themselves.[70]

The authority Xuxa's image has acquired derives in part from a cultural context in which girls and women, as well as boys and men, internalize such values. As early as 1982, Xuxa was described in the media as representing the new standard of beauty for women everywhere. At the same time, another current in the media texts suggests that elements of the beauty myth, generally associated with the first and not the third world, were at work in the articulation of the Xuxa phenomenon. That instrument to control women and undermine their advancement in the dominant culture is examined by Naomi Wolf:

> The beauty myth tells a story: The quality called "beauty" objectively and universally exists. Women must want to embody it and men must want to possess women who embody it. This embodiment is an imperative for women and not for men, which situation is necessary and natural because it is biological, sexual and evolutionary: Strong men battle for beautiful women, and beautiful women are more reproductively successful. Women's beauty must correlate to their fertility, and since this system is based on sexual selection, it is inevitable and changeless.

As Wolf goes on to explain, "none of this is true." Rather, the beauty myth is a "belief system that keeps male dominance intact."[71] Many of the manifestations of the beauty myth analyzed by Wolf surface in the gender discourse of the Xuxa phenomenon. Media reports of her dissatisfaction with her own looks when, at the same time, the media were presenting Xuxa as the ideal representation of beauty, are suggestive of the erosion of self-esteem stimulated by the beauty myth. Further evidence of the myth's influence is provided by Xuxa's announcment that she intended to remedy the situation by undergoing cosmetic surgery to alter the shape of her nose, make her eyes look bigger, and remove the plump look from her cheeks.

The desire to go to such lengths to satisfy an ultimately unattainable goal of perfection indicates how effective the beauty myth is as a control mechanism. It works through hunger as well: Xuxa's height-to-weight ratio changed over the years from five feet, six inches and 121 pounds at age sixteen to an unnerving five feet, ten inches and 125 pounds at age twenty-eight. Another well-known model and Brazil's "sexual icon" of 1986, Monique Evans, weighed 110 pounds at five feet, seven inches. She had liposuction performed on her buttocks and thighs and two operations on her breasts, to make them first larger and then smaller.[72] The willingness of women—including those who are not professional beauties—to submit to surgery and dangerous diets demonstrates the power of the messages the beauty myth sends.

Xuxa's constant emphasis on the grooming of the female body, through her clothing boutiques for children and teens, her modeling school, her beauty tips, and her fashion-show parade of outfits on the television program, reinforces images of femininity that are not only "physically and psychologically depleting," but expensive.[73] The modern form of the beauty myth is really a first world device aimed at controlling those women who have gained a certain amount of status—precisely the kind of woman Xuxa is, in terms of her professional achievements, but keeps concealed beneath a mask of convention and obedience.

Xuxa's image transmits her allegiance to the conventional terms of femininity elaborated in Brazilian culture, and incorporates the discourse of beauty maintenance as a sign of prestige. Only the well-to-do can afford the first world look Xuxa epitomizes, which is seen on Rio's beaches and exported around the world as a representation of leisure in Brazil. Yet, as Rose Marie Muraro points out, everyone, rich or poor, is "bombarded, principally through television, by the ideology of beauty, vanity and consumerism projected by the ruling class." Muraro argues that rural, lower-class women tend to have more positive feelings about their bodies because they have less contact with the media. Exposure makes the situation of the urban working-class woman more difficult: She finds that "the values sold to her on television are practically inaccessible. She wants to be pretty and appealing, to use this or that product, but all it takes is one glance at the mirror . . . to see how hard it's going to be to achieve."[74]

Yet it is hard, too, to resist the media's messages about ideal femininity. The media's intrusion into the lives of Brazilians is comparable to that in many first world countries: Brazilians watch more television than any other third world people.[75] The nation ranks fourth in the world in the number of television sets (28 million), behind only the United States (154 million), Japan (79 million), and Britain (33 million).[76] A study of television viewing in Brazil's largest city, São Paulo, showed that 95 percent of the population watch regularly during the week. Ninety percent watch television regularly during the weekend, and 26 percent of those are heavy viewers. Interestingly, there is a correlation between heavy television viewing and low educational levels, and there are indications of a connection with low income levels.

The decade of the eighties in Latin America was one of economic decline and, at the same time, one of tremendous growth in the influence of mass communications. The eighties saw what professors Regina Festa and Luiz Fernando Santoro call the development through the media of a "vast network of unprecedented social standardization through which were passed, on a massive scale, information, social values, aesthetic forms, consumer trends, and the systematic and cumulative construction of symbolic modes and social relations."[77] One of the effects of this process was to raise expectations that were much more likely to be frustrated in Brazil than in the similarly media-saturated first world. The average Brazilian's ability to purchase goods or to conform to the ideals projected by the mass media is disappointing. Nico Vink writes that "a contradictory consumption society has been formed in which, for the majority of the population, the images of consumption goods have increased more than the real access to these goods."[78] The media cut across class lines to offer the same dream of happiness—through the purchase of a refrigerator, a pork roast, or a pair of Xuxa sandals—to the rich who can buy them all and to the poor who can afford none.

The dream of perfection set forth for women, on the other hand, is inaccessible in an absolute sense, since it exists to be enforced, not fulfilled. While the cult of the body and the importance placed on a woman's physical beauty are not recent developments in Brazilian culture, changing contexts and the media's power to present these images lend them new meanings. Old and new sometimes combine in startling ways. For example, it goes unchallenged in Brazil when a police officer is portrayed in a major magazine article checking her makeup before she goes on duty because, although "she may face some dangerous situations," she hasn't forgotten "that beauty is (still) indispensable."[79] The allusion is to Vinícius de Morais, whose ideas about indispensable beauty constitute an ingredient of the typical Brazilian's cultural identity. The indispensability theme appears again in the advertising copy for a fashion spread in the mainstream *Manchete* magazine. Here, the text verbally dismembers and exiles the woman who has denied the indispensable:

> Women are being welcomed again fully into society, now that they are no longer ashamed of their natural femininity, and are exhibiting their curvaceous lines once more. At last, heads, trunks, and limbs are reassembled, demonstrating that true independence does not mean denying indispensable attributes, much less copying masculine styles. Respect for one's shape is the consequence of a true respect for one's feminine condition.[80]

This particular assertion of the indispensable-versus-ugly paradigm is a classic expression of the beauty myth. Here, she who is not conscientiously cultivating her curves is alienated from nature, society, her body, and her self. It may be noted here, too, that the ad copy attempts to exert pressure to conform by vaguely invoking a past feminist rebellion—the demise of which is, appropriately enough, announced through fashion—that the majority of Brazilians did not even share. Yet Brazilian women recognize the threat of alienation as one related to the kind of change associated with the first world. One of the reasons Xuxa's image managers take such care to assert conventional gender roles is their wish to distance her from messages about change implied by her otherwise desirable first world associations.[81]

If the advertising business in Brazil is not discreet about the way it uses the female body to sell products, neither is there subtlety in the way it constructs a view of the body itself. A striking example is the cover of the July 26, 1987, Sunday magazine supplement to the *Jornal do Brasil,* intended to illustrate and sell the issue's lead article. The text concerns Rio de Janeiro's first "delegacia de mulher," a police station for women. The first "delegacia" in Brazil opened in downtown São Paulo in August 1985 and was designed to deal exclusively with violence against women. The "delegacias" are staffed by women only, and they offer the victims of rape and other crimes an alternative to the often traumatic and unproductive experience of reporting such crimes at an ordinary police station. The cover of the Sunday supplement from the *Jornal do Brasil* features a plastic female mannequin, photographed against a red background. She is seen from the waist up, nude. Over her breasts are printed the words "A Very Special Police Officer." She is wearing a cowboy hat, bright red lipstick, and heavy eye makeup. A gold, star-shaped badge stamped with the word *Xerife* (sheriff) is stuck to her skin, approximately where such a badge might be worn on a uniform. Her hat and badge are not typically Brazilian, but rather more like props from a North American cowboy movie. The mannequin's skin is white except for a pink blush around the nipples. A small revolver is propped in her unjointed fingers. She stares directly into the camera's eye.

Like the story about the police officer tending to her makeup before going on duty, the *Jornal do Brasil* cover assures the viewer that, although they may have entered the male domain of law enforcement, women will remain fundamentally outside. The mannequin displays her femaleness vividly, since she is naked. Her badge of authority is a toy, and it is pinned, punishingly, directly to her skin. Her fingers cannot even hold her gun, much less squeeze the trigger. She has been disassociated from the role she is supposed to represent so that, instead of an agent of the law, we see a lifeless doll, undressed, painted, and posed as an erotic object.

In 1983, *Manchete* published a seven-page article on women in advertising. Xuxa is given as an example of "sexistication" (a play on the word "sophistication," and, presumably, on "sexist," as well). She appears in a photograph with two other models in lycra bathing suits. They are tying themselves up with a long, black electrical cord, one end of which is plugged into Xuxa's mouth. The article ends with a statement about how advertising works: "Despite the feminists' anger, the second sex will continue to be used [in advertising]. Because [women] are exciting, persuasive, and elicit fantasies of possession."[82] As a model, Xuxa helped perpetuate that role for women. After her television career was launched in 1983, Xuxa's opportunities to influence attitudes multiplied. Just five years later, the director of the Miss Brazil beauty contest reported that the majority of the girls sign up because "they're dreaming of an opportunity to become 'top models' like Xuxa."[83]

The word "dream" is a key element in the vocabulary of the Xuxa phenomenon, and the notion of dreaming is a theme that surfaces on her television show, on her records, and in her movies. One of Xuxa's implied messages is that girls and women don't plan; they dream. A photo from a 1983 *Manchete* article speaks to the promise of those dreams.[84] The picture shows Xuxa dressed in a sparkling gold bathing suit. There are gold pumps on her feet, and a U.S. hundred-dollar bill is tucked into the gold belt around her waist. Her expression and the picture's composition evoke the qualities of independence and pride while alluding to the familiar image of the blond sex symbol. Xuxa is seated on an old-fashioned cash register with her legs spread wide. Money figuratively pours from her gilded crotch as the cash register rings up cruzeiros. Xuxa looks triumphant in the photo; she is the picture of the fulfillment of the dream. In her function as a celebrity icon, Xuxa forms a "symbolic pathway, connecting each aspiring individual to a universal image of fulfillment: to be someone, when 'being no one' is the norm."[85] The degraded quality of the dream the star is pitching and of the gender-specific, racist future it predicts is masked by the powerful promise of riches, freedom, and happiness that Xuxa represents as she smiles back at the camera from her literal throne.

TWO

XUXAVISION

Programmed Euphoria

XUXA WAS A NATIONAL celebrity before she began her television career, but it was television that conferred on her the status of a star. It is in the context of that medium that the mass audience identification with her image has emerged. Beginning with Xuxa's first television program for children, the "Clube da Criança" (Kids' Club), which was broadcast on the Manchete network from 1983 until she moved to the Globo network in 1986, she built on the already established narrative of the fashion model, sexual icon, and girlfriend of Pelé. Xuxa's messages about gender roles and race remained essentially the same, but they were clarified and elaborated upon by new elements that were added to the star's image as well as by the medium itself, its manner of transmitting information, and the expanded audience it brought her.

As it turned out, the transgressive-reactionary figure Xuxa had earlier exploited transferred very successfully to television. One of the ways in which Xuxa's television persona works is by inspiring a cultish devotion. Xuxa-centrism, or the intense focus on her person seen in the shows—especially the later, more extravagant "Xou da Xuxa" on Globo—is one of the more striking characteristics of the phenomenon. At the center of the camera's lens, Xuxa functions as an agent of transcendence, creating a television experience that entertains and moves viewers as it trivializes the feelings they are invited to project on her.

Xuxa's image is built upon cultural anxiety—about gender roles, about race, about Brazil's first world–third world identity—and upon uncertainty about the nation's future, which is symbolized by its children. Xuxa invites viewers not to contemplate those concerns but to relinquish responsibility for them. The pleasurable energy thus released is then channeled toward the consumerism Xuxa fosters among children and adults alike. Her television programs promote consumption as if Xuxa were an unusually insatiable type of idol, as the media texts often call her. Brazil's tribute to its idol is paid in a generation of children virtually reared by the reactionary and commercial messages of TV Globo and the "Xou da Xuxa."

The media texts describe Xuxa's television style as naughty, irreverent, even "revolutionary." Yet an overwhelming ideological conservatism pervades the messages her television programs convey. Xuxa's "revolutionary" style is, in fact, no more than a better-articulated version of what she represented before her television debut. Xuxa's so-called irreverent approach to hosting a children's program and her defiance of the advice of educators and child psychologists stand not for subversion but rather for a kind of permissiveness.

Xuxa's style is consistent with her function of validating conflicting attitudes and values, for example by permitting her public to reconcile the erotic content of her television programs with their orientation toward an audience of children. Xuxa's "spontaneous" and "natural" approach encourages impulsive behavior and masks the fact that the television environment is actually quite limited and controlled. The style issue was widely discussed in the media when Xuxa began hosting the "Clube da Criança" on Manchete in 1983. What was deemed her "revolutionary" approach enabled Xuxa to embody stereotypical femininity, to promote an all-white ideal, to cultivate the entertainment function of television at the expense of television's other potential purposes and to approach children as full-fledged consumers.

The childlike quality that had already been established as an important part of Xuxa's appeal is the element that led to her work with children. Maurício Sherman, a producer at Manchete, thought that her "natural, childlike manner" would make Xuxa a good candidate for host on a children's show the network was developing. Sherman explained, "I saw Xuxa in the hall and I realized that the so-called sex symbol was a child. Men would approach her expecting a woman and they would find a toy. It was hard to confront Xuxa's sexuality without perceiving a certain ingenuousness."[1] Xuxa reportedly responded to the suggestion that she host a children's show by saying, "A kid's program just isn't my style."[2] Her mother is quoted as calling it "a crazy idea."[3] It is, of course, difficult to maintain Xuxa's erotic appeal in a context involving actual children; in the early stages of its development, her television personality came across as rather inconsistent. The dual image that Xuxa projects on television today—as national sex symbol and caretaker of children—is the result of skillful handling by the program's producers.

In the beginning, the emphasis of image management was to distance Xuxa from the children in order to maintain her erotic dimension. The earlier media texts, from the 1983–1986 Manchete network period in particular, reflect the effort to disassociate Xuxa's image from anything that might be construed as maternal. On the Manchete program, attention was continually drawn to manifestations of adult sexuality. In one much-told story, Xuxa turned to a little boy in the studio and, commenting on his cute looks, said, "You're like a bonbon." The child quickly responded, "Then why don't you eat me?"—which in Brazilian Portuguese is slang for "Why don't you have sex with me?"[4] In another story, a boy reportedly told Xuxa he had seen her nude picture in a magazine. When she asked his opinion, he smiled and, "with a leer," answered, "I liked it."[5] Children on the program were said to have asked Xuxa if she slept with Pelé, and boys would try to peek up her miniskirt and kiss her on the mouth instead of giving the traditional pecks on the cheeks. The emphasis on sexual innuendo was a way of reassuring the public that Xuxa's glamour girl–sex symbol role would not be sacrificed to the role of mother figure. The goal of the experiment was to naturalize the joining of the erotic and the domestic, caretaking—but not maternal—expressions of femininity.

Xuxa conspicuously inserted erotic ingredients into the narrative, both on and off the television screen. In one interview she was asked about the large numbers of fathers who brought their children to the taping sessions for the show. In her reply, Xuxa bragged about her sexual rapport with the men in the audience:

> Yes, the fathers bring their kids a lot more than the mothers. One father showed up with his son at one o'clock in the afternoon. I was doing the show wearing some very tight pants. At two o'clock, I changed into a miniskirt, and the guy was right there, in the front row. At three, I switched to some really short shorts, and at that point, the guy went over to Marlene and said, "I need to leave, but every time I get ready to go, she comes back with less clothes on. Tell me she's going to cover up next costume change." And Marlene said, "She's putting on a bathing suit this time because she's going to do exercises." The guy sat down again, and his poor kid complained: "Dad, I have to do my homework; let's go." "Just a little longer, son; now sit down."[6]

A newspaper article from the *Estado de São Paulo*, noting how much of Xuxa's fan mail came from teenagers, added that the only reason adults didn't write was because they were embarrassed, and that "everybody knows they're watching the show." The same piece went on to say that if adults had written in to express their preference, the forthcoming Xuxa doll would have been an inflatable model.[7] Xuxa's role of sexual provocateur on the children's program was easily and successfully marketed from the start. The *Estado de São Paulo* article was published during the brief period between the close of Xuxa's Manchete show and the initiation of the Globo program. The piece was accompanied by a set of graphics that reflected how effectively the star's image had maintained its erotic aspect—the caretaker function hardly fit into the equation, even after she had spent three years hosting a children's program. (Xuxa, in fact, told an interviewer about a month before the "Xou" started that she planned to quit working with children in a year or so.)[8] The *Estado de São Paulo* reprinted two still photographs from *Amor Estranho Amor*: one shows Xuxa in her bear costume, and in the other she is in bed with the young boy, unbuttoning his pajamas. A third photo shows Xuxa in the back of a limousine with Pelé. Finally, there is a caricature of Xuxa in a low-cut blouse, holding one hand over a child's face like a muzzle, pushing him behind her, out of view.

During her early years on television, Xuxa was sometimes portrayed not only as lacking a vocation for work with children but as actively disliking them. There were articles about her hostility toward youngsters. She was said to be rude to children on the set, to yell at them, and even to pinch and hit them. This element of Xuxa's image has endured: *Contigo* magazine reminded readers of Xuxa's reputation in a 1990 issue by publishing a photo of her on the "Xou," grasping the hand of a grimacing young guest. A balloon pointing to Xuxa has her asking her manager, "What do you mean, Marlene? Pinching is out?"[9] Xuxa's brother and two sisters, who are psychologists, were reported to be "horrified" by the way she treated the children on the show.[10]

Neither these critical attacks nor the erotic emphasis disqualified Xuxa as a suitable figure for children's television. On the contrary, they seem to have been orchestrated to serve specific purposes in the imaging process: to distance the star from the maternal role, to assert the idea of Xuxa as a child herself, and to promote and sanction permissiveness and lack of restraint. Years later, Xuxa used the same endorsement of impulsiveness as a form of liberation in her explanation of what her program could contribute to children's television in the United States: "There is no TV show in the U.S. where children can scream or cry or dance or do whatever they want."[11]

Throughout her career in children's television, Xuxa has tried to associate herself with the notions of rebellion and liberation through a kind of naughtiness. A consultant, hired by Manchete to respond to criticism of the way she interacted with children on the show, defended Xuxa by invoking that element of her television personality: "[Xuxa] respects a child's potential, and she has a healthy disrespect for theories and analyses. She is a positive symbol who sets standards of eating, of breathing, good habits. She puts forward the myth that you can be anything you want. And the kids love her uninhibited behavior."[12] This not disinterested, corporate apology for Xuxa's approach validates a permissiveness that, in the context of the television show, is intended not to promote the belief that "you can be anything you want" but rather the idea that "you can *buy* anything you want"—perhaps a more attractive message, since it offers tangible and immediate gratification. The lame list of positive "standards" the star is purported to encourage among children suggests that the true lessons of the show lie elsewhere. The debate continues as to whether Xuxa has "revolutionized years and years of study about child psychology," or whether her attachment to children is merely part of a "well-elaborated marketing strategy," which is no less accepted because of its mercenary intentions.[13]

Another device employed to distance Xuxa from a motherly role was to make her one of the kids. Xuxa is repeatedly placed in the children's sphere by media texts that contrast her with other, more maternal, children's television show hosts. It has been reported that Xuxa did not want children to think of her as an adult, as a *tia* (auntie), or as a teacher, but rather as one of them. She has explained to the press on numerous occasions how she operates on the children's level: "I get down on the floor with them, join the circle. I speak their language."[14] She once insisted, "You don't have to treat kids like they're mentally retarded. I would never say to a child, 'Better not go over there, sweetheart.' I say, 'Get out of there!' "[15] Xuxa argued that children hated the "aren't we just the cutest little thing" approach: "I treat children as my equals. . . . I act like them, I talk like them."[16] Making Xuxa childlike was consistent with maintaining the innocent, vulnerable aspect of her sexual appeal. The juvenile element of her personality also helped to separate Xuxa from the asexual, maternal role and suggested a naughtiness that corresponded to the permissive approach.

The success of the strategy to disassociate Xuxa from the maternal role is evidenced by the many references in the media to the way she alienated mothers. One newspaper reported that, after three years at Manchete, 60 percent of the letters Xuxa received from mothers were complaints about her treatment of children.[17] In one interview, Xuxa rather openly tried to discredit protective maternal feelings in her account of an incident involving the mother of one of the young guests on the television program. In telling the story, Xuxa casts herself as uncomplicated, honest, and natural, in contrast to the overprotective, slightly neurotic mother figure. The account describes an incident that occurred during the taping of a show, when Xuxa asked a small boy his age, and he said he was nine. Having assumed he was about six, Xuxa recalls saying to him, "Wow, you sure are short." The reaction of the boy's mother, overheard by Xuxa's manager and reported to Xuxa, was, "My son is going to be traumatized. He already has a complex about being so small. Now I'm going to have to take him to a psychoanalyst." Xuxa concluded her story by explaining unapologetically, "I say things like that, spontaneously, without thinking about what the words might do to someone."[18] Here, Xuxa assigns herself characteristics associated with childhood, offering an inviting image of freedom and self-indulgence, perhaps especially appealing in this case to male readers who might be predisposed to feel negatively toward the controlling mother in the relationship depicted. Xuxa seems to blur the distinction between adult and child, absolving herself of responsibility for blunders. In another interview, Xuxa dismissed the difference altogether: "According to [my brother and sisters], there are age groups and one has to talk a certain way to kids in each group. I talk to kids like they're my equals, no matter what the age group. They like it, because I seem just like someone their own age."[19]

Some media texts accused Xuxa of lacking the most elementary understanding of how to deal with children. She herself reported that she received many letters from child psychologists stating that "they were completely against my theories. The truth is," Xuxa said, "I don't have any theories."[20] Besides asserting the authority of the amateur over the professional, of improvisation over training, Xuxa's defiance invites a loosening of the definition of childhood. The effect is to mask the vulnerability and malleability of children, endowing them instead with an adult's capacity to be, among other things, discriminating consumers.[21] The creation of consumers is the aim of the Xuxa phenomenon. Her permissive style serves to challenge social and cultural control mechanisms and to assert instead the authority of the marketplace.

In this context, it is useful to examine Xuxa's special word for children, *baixinhos*. The term is sometimes used today in Brazilian Portuguese as a synonym for *crianças* (children). *Baixinho* is literally the diminutive of "short." Xuxa explains how she began using the word when she was young: "My friends were seven, eight, nine years old. I was about eleven, but I was very tall and they were really little. So I started calling them 'baixinhos.' I preferred playing with them. . . . The kids my age were trying to grow up fast, they were afraid of being children, but I thought it was wonderful."[22] In this statement, Xuxa evokes and endorses the freedom from responsibility and the indulgent impulsivity that childhood represents—an infantilized ideal that takes on other meanings, however, in the context of her television shows. There, the term "baixinho" is used not only to invoke those pleasant qualities but also to imply that children are merely small-sized adults, a notion Xuxa has articulated in numerous interviews over the years: "For me, children are grown-ups, only they're not grown up in terms of size, and so I call them 'baixinhos.'"[23] The functions of that definition, much stressed in the media texts about Xuxa—that children are the same as adults, only shorter—are various: to construct the child as a consumer (whose appetite Xuxa's programs seek to satisfy); to call attention away from children's other needs, such as education, which the programs do little to address; and, at the same time, to invoke an infantilized condition for all viewers, young and old.

When Xuxa declared she did not care for the "goody-goody" act as a way of behaving toward children, she appeared to be advocating the opposite—a juvenile ideal of naughtiness. Xuxa's show on Manchete was in some ways a celebration of the urge to be naughty, that is, to give in to impulses. Xuxa herself was the embodiment of surrender. She reconciled the incompatible but warmly embraced wishes that women be blond yet Brazilian and that they be sexually provocative yet devoted above all to caring for children. Xuxa's impact—the effective reinforcement of the attitudes behind those conflicting desires—grew to huge proportions after her image was paired with the Globo network's history and practice of deep penetration of Brazilian culture.

Xuxa's switch from Manchete to Globo was described as a business decision: "The reason I went with Globo was the professional and serious nature of their proposal. What had kept me at Manchete was my strong attachment to [network president] Adolfo Bloch. Now, I've stopped thinking with my heart, and instead I acted professionally."[24] But Xuxa's image handlers were careful to remedy the impression of business acumen given by such a statement with an alternative narrative of the star's relationship with the powerful network bosses. Xuxa's negotiations with José Bonifácio de Oliveira Sobrinho, known as "Boni," vice president of Globo Network Operations, were described by the star to a reporter from the *Folha de São Paulo* as a game of flirtation:

> I didn't know how to approach him [Boni]. I made a list of everything and, at the meeting, I explained what I wanted and he agreed. I told Boni that, at Manchete, Adolfo Bloch

used to sit me down on his lap and do whatever I wanted. He [Boni] laughed and said, "As far as that's concerned, you can sit on my lap anytime you want." Everybody at the meeting thought that was really funny.[25]

These remarks are particularly significant in view of the context. The adversarial nature of the relationship between the *Folha de São Paulo* and Xuxa's team is notable throughout her career. Xuxa's interviews with the newspaper, therefore, generally consist of carefully prepared statements aimed at image enhancement. The account of her approach to boardroom politics was a public affirmation of her willingness to play the sex symbol and the *boazinha*, or "good little girl," pledged to obedience and servility. In the business context, her efforts to maintain an acceptable image by asserting those qualities are constant. Xuxa has consistently tried to conceal her maturity and increasing power in the entertainment industry, and to evoke instead the image of an undemanding, submissive, erotic figure who conducts business by sitting in the laps of television industry executives.

Globo was the first network in Brazil to create market research departments to evaluate consumer trends. It was because research had predicted that the children's show "Balão Mágico" (Magic Balloon) was about to begin a "fatal decline" that Xuxa, whose ratings on Manchete were steadily climbing, was hired as a replacement.[26] The efforts and assets of the fourth-largest commercial television network in the world went into creating the "Xou da Xuxa," which was to blanket Brazil's morning television schedule, broadcasting Monday through Friday from 8:00 A.M. to 12:20 P.M., and on Saturdays starting at 9:00 A.M. The scrupulousness of Xuxa's image handlers was matched by Globo's care in maintaining its trademark *padrão de qualidade* (standard of quality). Xuxa would continue to represent contradictory views and feelings about gender and race, and to channel the public's identification with those values and attitudes into consumer habits, but the structure for projecting her image became much more elaborate. The network deployed its considerable resources in developing strategies to disguise the massive doses of controlled information the "Xou" was designed to administer. The subtitle of one *Jornal do Brasil* article on the show's debut—"Total Freedom"—is a sign of the effectiveness of Globo's techniques for manipulating images and, at the same time, persuading the public that the program represented a natural, unstructured experience.

In conveying the establishment messages Xuxa represents, the power of the Globo network should not be underestimated. Globo's history is one of significant influence on Brazilian culture and politics. Broadcasting since 1965, fifteen years after television was first introduced in Brazil, Globo is the product of an arrangement between the powerful Marinho family, owners of a media empire; the U.S. multimedia group Time-Life; and then-president Castelo Branco, who was willing to overlook an article of the Brazilian Constitution that expressly prohibited the participation of foreign enterprises in the national television industry. From the start, Globo was informed by values imported from the United States. One employee from the early period remembers, "During the first year, we did things the way we learned to do them from the Americans. . . . The inspiration for Globo was a TV station in Indianapolis, WFBM. It was their engineer who put everything together. We didn't know anything."[27]

In 1969, Globo bought out Time-Life's 49 percent of the shares, shedding its attachment to foreign capital, but the Marinho family would continue to cultivate its ties to the government. Globo's radio, television, and newspaper enterprises provided important support for the dictatorship (1964–1985), and later, for establishment candidates favored by the military and by conservative business interests. It has been said that the outcome of Brazil's 1989 presidential race, the first popular, democratic election since 1964, was decided by Globo's influential evening news program, the "Jornal Nacional." One observer, assessing the connections and media support of Fernando Collor de Mello, the winner in that election, concluded that President Collor's administration might as well be called a Globo subsidiary. The same author draws attention to the dimensions of Globo's role in molding other features of Brazilian society: "The fact is that TV Globo was responsible for consolidating the culture industry in Brazil after 1965. By the seventies, Globo television was on a par with TV in the United States. [Globo was] first world TV . . . in the third world."[28]

Globo's influence extends beyond the borders of Brazil. According to one estimate, the network earned fifteen to twenty million dollars in 1987 from exports.[29] By the early 1990s, Globo was producing almost 80 percent of its own programming.[30] The network reported profits in U.S. dollars of $650 million in 1991 (the closest competitor was the SBT network with $140 million). A thirty-second commercial during prime time on Globo sells for $45,000 (as compared with $22,500 on SBT).[31] An advertisement run by Globo in August 1991 boasted that its only competitors worldwide were ABC, NBC, and CBS, and that even "they lose" when it comes to internal production of programs. The ad also claimed that "no commercial network in the whole world controls its market like Globo does. Of every ten television sets turned on [in Brazil], an average of six are tuned to Globo."[32] The network's power in the Brazilian entertainment world has been compared to Metro-Goldwyn-Mayer's influence in the movie-making industry of the 1930s and 1940s.[33]

Globo controls almost one-third of the broadcasting stations in Brazil.[34] One study found that Globo "is preferred by audiences across Brazil and by all social classes."[35] Television reaches 99 percent of Brazil's population through five national networks, two regional networks, and 247 stations.[36] Brazilian television advertising revenues are the sixth largest in the world.[37] In some ways, television is regarded as the most powerful entity in contemporary Brazilian society. Fábio Konder Comparato argues that "television is without a doubt the main vehicle of national communication." The author explains that "it is important to remember that television forges social habits with an efficiency and rapidity absolutely new in history. TV tends to be the main source of social values, more than family, school, the church, political parties, or even the State itself."[38]

Globo has become known as the instrument largely responsible for creating a national culture in a country with many separate regional identities. In keeping with this function of the media giant, Xuxa's Globo show introduced a measure of standardization never before seen in children's programming. In an earlier era, a less formulaic approach characterized local and regional shows. A children's program like "Capitão Furacão" (Captain Hurricane), which aired on Globo from 1965 to 1969, before the network's national expansion, could be picked up only in the greater Rio de Janeiro area and parts of the states of Minas Gerais and Espírito Santo. The host of "Capitão Furacão" would dress up like an old sailor and spin a ship's wheel while telling stories about life at sea. Twenty-three years after the show ended, the actor, Pietro Mário, says, "I didn't treat kids like idiots. I identified with them. I gave them culture and information."[39]

Of course, Xuxa's program provides a great deal of culture and information as well. But since Xuxa's viewers are projected primarily as consumers, the culture and information aimed at them is more selective. The ostensible goal of the "Xou da Xuxa" is to entertain, and the unspoken one is to market Xuxa-related and other children's products. Xuxa's manager, Marlene Mattos, has said that the program is meant "to stimulate children to fantasize."[40] The look the program tries to project on television screens is that of a party. Xuxa's job is to maintain "a climate of euphoria" at all times.[41]

Globo was also responsible for a popular children's program at the other end of the spectrum from Xuxa's trendy, consumer-oriented, party show. The "Sítio do Pica-Pau Amarelo" (The Yellow Woodpecker's Country Place) was produced by Globo and aired from 1976 to 1985. It was based on a series of children's stories written by Brazil's undisputed master of the genre, Monteiro Lobato (1882–1948). The show was called "a daring project to entertain kids and educate them at the same time."[42] Such programs still exist on Brazilian television, including the half-hour daily "Rá Tim Bum" on the public network TV Educativa. But the formula developed for the "Xou", in conjunction with the extraordinary empowerment of its host through an image that taps viewers' deep feelings about themselves and their culture, has proved unbeatable in the ratings contest.

When Xuxa started working for Globo, she became part of the most powerful enterprise in an industry whose influence on the lives of Brazilians was "absolutely new in history," as Comparato puts it. Globo's goal, Kehl writes (which, she says, has been reached) was to "modify the imaginary representation of the nation by creating an ideal of cleanliness, modernity, 'good taste' (or good behavior), and happiness through consumption."[43] Xuxa's "Xou" displays that ideal at every turn through its glossy, cosmopolitan look, and the gender and race configurations that stand for "good taste" and "good behavior."

The "Xou da Xuxa" is a spectacle that obsessively focuses on the star to facilitate her role as an agent of transcendence. Through her, the audience is transported to a state of exaltation. Some children think of Xuxa as a magical being, as did one boy who her heard say on the show that she was going offstage to *"fazer xixi."* The boy wrote a letter asking, "Do you really have to pee too?" He added, "Do you eat real food like us too?"[44] Even if the emotions unleashed by Xuxa are predictably trained in the direction of consumption, the devotion she inspires seems quite genuine. But those feelings are provoked through the use of an elaborate system of image management, starting with the name of the "Xou da Xuxa" itself. Originally intended to be understood as "I am Xuxa's" or "I belong to Xuxa," ("Xou" being a play on *sou*, which means "I am") the name was generally taken to mean "Xuxa's Show" instead—the word *xou* read as the anglicism "show," in Xuxaspell.[45] Both readings point to the Xuxacentrism that dominates every aspect of the program. The spelling game, Xuxa's trademark kisses in their ritual and commercial contexts, and the camera that keeps the star in the center of the television screen, are only a few of the many expressions of the principle of Xuxacentrism.

Xuxa's name is sometimes described as a key to the star's phenomenal success. The tale of the naming of Xuxa herself has been recounted many times for the press: Her brother, Bladimir, or Blade, took a look at his new baby sister, Maria da Graça Meneghel, and said, "Let's call her Xuxa!" or "She's my Xuxa!" Both Xuxa and her manager, Mattos, have explained the name as a gift from God, who, they say, marked Xuxa with two X's, a big one and a little one, so as not to lose sight of her.[46]

The playfulness with which Xuxa's name is used as a publicity device is in keeping with the assertion of her "feminine" character—frivolous, decorative, and adaptable. In Xuxaspell and Xuxaspeak, her tremendous *sucesso* (success) is her tremendous "xuxexo." She is a "xuperstar" and a "xímbolo xexual."[47] The sexual symbolism of Xuxa's image is reinforced by media texts that draw attention to the associations of her name in Portuguese and Spanish. Of the few words in Portuguese containing two X's, one of the most commonly heard is "xoxota," a vulgar term for "vagina." That also happens to be the meaning of the name Xuxa, pronounced "CHOO-cha," in Chile, where the star's expansion into Spanish-speaking America began at the Viña del Mar Thirty-first International Song Festival in February 1990. As one journalist at the festival put it, " 'Xuxa' isn't exactly a word nice girls have in their vocabulary."[48] The same commentator went on to describe Xuxa's response to the linguistic dilemma: "At the beginning of her press conference, which was attended by a record number of nervous journalists reluctant to address her, Xuxa got everyone to stop giggling . . . by having them recite her name out loud, all together." She led another such chorus, according to the newspaper, after stepping onstage for her performance to a crowd of "twenty-five thousand spectators chanting 'a xuxa da Xuxa' (Xuxa's cunt)." The image invoked by this account corresponds to the double meaning of Xuxa's "revolutionary," permissive style. On the one hand, the public chanting of a dirty word constitutes an expression of transgression, a breaking with convention, censorship, and self-censorship. Yet what is released by that process is a reinforcement of convention—in this case viewing women as sex objects, or cunts.

Xuxa quickly discovered that the X's in her name were useful advertising devices. Xuxa's and Globo's publicity teams make extensive use of the letter, having observed, as any reader has, that the X's stand out as the eye skims a page. The X has a variety of connotations, many of which are conveniently universal, or exportable—a quality that is seen as one of Xuxa's fundamental virtues. The X shows the way to a treasure, and directs the aim, as the crosshairs to a target. An X marks the spot, signifying destination, the end of the journey, the place where you are when "You Are Here." Everybody wants to know what is behind the veil of the mysterious Madame X. The one letter of the alphabet everyone can write, the symbolic signature of humankind, is an X. Xuxa's term for children, "baixinhos," already has an X in it. Xuxa is often photographed making an X of her body, stretching and twisting to create variations on the theme for her album covers and publicity photos.

Only a few times has the X game backfired. On one

occasion, a priest from Londrina, in the southern state of Paraná, banned Xuxa's songs from his radio station because he claimed the use of the X in Xuxa's speech taught children bad Portuguese.[49] When her dictionary for children, the *Dicionário da Xuxa*, was published in September 1987, there were complaints that children would be taught to misspell words. The text does not, in fact, take liberties with spelling, but a rumor that the dictionary consisted entirely of Xuxaspell circulated in the city of Recife, in the northeastern state of Pernambuco, and caused sales to plummet there.[50]

Xuxa's name is sometimes shortened affectionately to the first syllable, "Xu," the articulation of which leaves the speaker blowing a kiss—one of the puckered-up, slightly pouty kisses the star has made famous. After her Manchete program began in 1983, Xuxa started adding a kiss to her autographs. She would apply fresh coats of lipstick, over and over again, for her many fans. After one autograph session, Xuxa showed a reporter the inside of her lips and remarked, "Look at this . . . sometimes I even get sores from doing it so much. But it doesn't bother me. On the contrary, it's turning into my trademark."[51] Along with the X's, these kisses are an important element of Xuxa's marketing scheme, and have been used as logos for various products and productions since 1983.

For one of the star's earliest business ventures, involving a California clothing designer, labels were to bear the imprint of a kiss in red lipstick, with the name Xuxa written in cursive letters inside.[52] Another logo shows the name written with the vowels drawn to resemble pairs of lips forming kisses. The double kiss logo is effective for its connotation of intimacy—erotic, romantic, and domestic—and for its association with Brazil's distinctive identity with the standard greeting and farewell ritual of two kisses. The distribution of kisses on the TV show forms part of the elaborate series of star-focused rituals. The expression *"beijinho beijinho"* or "kiss kiss" (*beijinho* is the diminutive of "kiss") became another of Xuxa's trademarks after she began using the phrase as a signature on her television program. By the end of 1987, Xuxa had created a company called "Beijinho Beijinho Promotions," one of several enterprises needed to manage her rapidly expanding empire.[53]

The repetition of self-referential features such as the X's and kisses is part of the construction of a narrative that keeps Xuxa at the very center of the television experience. There are a lot of X's on the "Xou," and a lot of kissing. Xuxa's guest performers and the children who participate in games are each kissed twice. The winners of games are invited to send kisses of their own out to viewers. This activity sometimes lasts longer than the game itself. Xuxa asks each child in turn, "Who do you want to send a kiss to?" and leans down with her microphone so the child can speak into it. The basic formula goes something like, "To my mother, my father, and a special kiss for you." Other relatives, friends, and teachers can be the recipients of children's kisses as well, and sometimes a child sends kisses "to everyone who knows me." The ritual, while it affords an opportunity for the children to perform and occasionally captures an amusing, candid moment, ultimately refers back to Xuxa, who has endowed the kiss with special iconographic significance. During the "Xou," she distributes more kisses—to the guests in the studio audience, to her television viewers at home (or, "on the other side," in her words), to people who sent letters to her, and to those who sent the gifts on display that day. Sometimes Xuxa moves in close to the camera and delivers herself of a kiss right in front of the lens.

The most important kiss event of each show takes place just before the program ends. In a special ceremony, one or two guests, usually children but sometimes adults, receive what is referred to as Xuxa's *marquinha*, or "little mark." This is a kiss bestowed in ritualistic fashion, as a relic to be taken back from the secular pilgrimage to the shrine of Xuxadom. One of the Paquitas hands a lipstick to Xuxa, who applies a thick coat, bends down (at five feet, ten inches and wearing high-heeled boots, Xuxa towers over most of the guests on her show), and presses her lips carefully to the designated left or right cheek. During the closing shots of the show, the camera often lingers on one of the "marked" people. From the routine pecks Xuxa generously distributes throughout the program to the sacramental *marquinhas* bestowed on the chosen few, the delivery of kisses works as a kind of leitmotif on the "Xou." Kissing sets the pace, frames the drama from beginning to end. Xuxa's kisses step outside the familiar Brazilian routine of greeting and parting. Here kissing resonates in two of the principal modes through which Xuxa reaches out to her audience, the childlike and the erotic, a duality that leaves the kiss open to interpretation.

Gilberto Vasconcellos notes that "on Xuxa's program, there is neither shadow nor silence."[54] The sound, lights, and constant motion on the set are distracting and disorienting. These mechanisms help to direct the audience's attention to specific messages by limiting access to others, essentially masking and displacing alternatives. High-volume music, usually a form of disco, plays throughout the program, and there is movement and apparent confusion everywhere. The Paquitas herd children out of the way to clear a spot for a game, kids wave pompoms and banners, and errant "baixinhos" stray in front of cameras or wander under Xuxa's feet. Virtually everyone in the studio is running, swaying, bouncing, or dancing to the booming sound system. The elaborate stage props, forming a semicircle around the set, are adorned with blinking lights and often moving parts as well. Some are designed for children to ride or climb upon, giving the set a playground or amusement park atmosphere. There is a hippopotamus the kids can crawl around on, a bull dressed in a bullfighter's costume, a zebra with a merry-go-round built into its body, and a peacock in whose tail is a small ferris wheel. Model skyscrapers with flashing lights and the Christ the Redeemer figure, a copy of the statue on Corcovado Hill in Rio, establish the symbolic location of the otherwise generic, amusement park setting.

In the middle of the stage set is the "nave da Xuxa," the spaceship on which the star arrives and then departs at the end of the show. There is also a giant bust of Xuxa on the stage. Its eyes gaze into the middle distance with a faraway look. On the floor, for the overhead camera to capture, is a portrait of Xuxa's face superimposed over a large X bordered by twinkling lights. Thus, when Xuxa is on stage, there are always at least three of her. The television viewer's gaze is continually drawn, if not to the star, to one of the representations of her person in a stage prop, a Paquita, a child dressed up for the program in a Xuxa outfit, or one of the many Xuxa dolls advertised on the show and distributed as prizes. Over the years, the "Xou" has become more centered on the star. The roles she used to play—a grandmother character and a horoscope-reading fortune-teller—have been dropped. Many of the activities for the children now revolve around Xuxa. Her face, for example, emerges as the solution to a jigsaw puzzle game played with giant blocks. Xuxa's name is repeated in the lyrics of songs played on the program. Standard segments of the show are devoted to celebrating expressions of love for Xuxa. In one of these, she is crowned and draped with sashes. In another, she examines a table covered with the gifts she has received that day, which the camera slowly scans in close-up as she narrates. In other segments, Xuxa reads letters and banners dedicated to her. A ritual is made of bestowing the lipstick *marquinha*, and of selecting guests from the crowd to have their photographs taken with the star in her dressing room. The stage and the performance refer to Xuxa incessantly.

Xuxa presides over a bright, noisy environment that constitutes a carefully choreographed scene for the television screen. She is the organizing principle, the one who directs all activity, the giver of prizes and granter of wishes, and the only one onstage with a microphone. A typical "Xou" begins at 8:00 A.M. with a brief animated cartoon showing Xuxa journeying to Earth in her spaceship. For small children, this narrative of Xuxa's unearthly origins is real; for older kids and adults, the futuristic fantasy lends the star a gloss of modernity. Xuxa passes other planets before setting a course for Earth and then heading for Rio de Janeiro with its familiar landmarks—a travel sequence that puts Brazil on the map and invokes the cosmopolitanism fostered by TV Globo. Along the journey various pastoral, morning scenes are shown, establishing connections between

Xuxa and nature, between the start of the "Xou" and the beginning of a new day.

When the segment ends, the cartoon spaceship materializes on stage in a cloud of dry-ice "smoke." Xuxa's ship is pink and yellow, and attached to the sides are two pairs of giant red molded plastic lips, puckered up to form kisses. The ship descends (it is actually an elevator), and the door, hinged on the bottom, slowly lowers, forming a small staircase. The crowd below cheers as Xuxa emerges at the top of the steps, smiling, waving, and blowing kisses. She descends and is met at the bottom by two of the elegantly dressed young men called Paquitos, who offer her their arms and escort her into the crowd of children. There follows a series of brief activities such as the delivery of an inspirational message, perhaps about having hope, or being happy, followed by a sing-along, and sometimes the reading of a list of birthday wishes. Xuxa then personally distributes a few food items, such as bananas or other fruit, from two breakfast trays the Paquitos have produced. In a country of hungry children, this last gesture is a powerful one.

All the key features of Xuxa's image are thus alluded to in the first ten minutes of the "Xou." She descends from her spaceship as if it were a fashion show runway, her blondness on display along with her other physical attributes, highlighted by the revealing costumes she never repeats. The ritual of arrival places the star in a glamorous context that conveys the modernity and sophistication of the first world. The caretaker role of the "Queen of the Baixinhos" is affirmed in the greeting Xuxa receives from the children she will baby-sit for the next five hours. The viewer's attention has not left her person for an instant.

At the end of the "Xou," the circle of attention around

the star draws even tighter in an exhibition of both planned and spontaneous adulation. First, she thanks her guests for coming to take part in the show, sometimes from as far away as Portugal, Nigeria, Puerto Rico, and Miami, as well as, of course, from all over Brazil, thus alluding to the grand scale on which her following is measured. Xuxa then turns to the table of presents she has received that day. The display unavoidably suggests an altar spread with offerings, which typically include photographs of children, paintings they have made of Xuxa, candy, flowers, and jewelry. The star regularly reminds the public that she keeps all the gifts she receives, in an effort to play down the impersonality implied by the dimensions of her audience. On one show, Xuxa pledged, "I swear I keep every single thing."[55]

After the gift-viewing ceremony, Xuxa turns to the studio audience where people are holding up homemade signs and banners with messages to her. She reads as many as she has time for, and invites their signers to come forward or to meet her backstage for a kiss or a photograph. Typical signs read, "Xuxa, we adore you," "Xuxa, I love you," "To Princess Xuxa," "You are irreplaceable and eternal," "I want your little mark," "Xuxa, make our dream come true," "Xuxa, my great dream is to have a photo taken with you," "Xuxa, I need you like the sea needs water," and "May you always be the fairy queen."[56] After posing for one or two snapshots and bestowing the ritual *marquinha* like a blessing, Xuxa marches off toward her spaceship.

At the top of the spaceship's stairs stands the child who has been selected for that taping of the show to represent the symbolic "baixinho." Xuxa joins the child to complete the tableau that is the show's final scene before the star disappears from view. Xuxa sometimes elicits wolf whistles from the crowd with a wiggle at the top of the stairs before she addresses the audience with an inspirational message or simply a few words of farewell, such as, "It was wonderful, wonderful to be with you! I love you! Lots of kisses! *Ciao*!"[57] Then, with a final thrown kiss and a wave, the door closes, and the ship begins to rise. The crowd below starts to cry, "Come back! Come back!" as the camera pans the set, pausing on a "marked" guest or another scene before returning to show the spaceship rising, and finally shrinking, as the Corcovado Christ with the two neon Xuxa hearts fills the screen.

The camera's eye is irreverent as it composes the closing frames of the "Xou," placing Christ in a setting that resembles an amusement park and decorating the figure with neon.[58] That same campy informality is found in the large drawing of a smiling Jesus that hangs in Xuxa's living room in her house in Rio. She has said of the picture, "In my house, even He has to smile."[59] Xuxa's mother refers to vaguely divine sources in explaining her daughter's success: "Children don't lie. There's a reason why they adore [Xuxa]. I believe she was chosen for her work as a kind of mission."[60] Beyond the hints of a special relationship with God, Xuxa does function as an agent of transcendence. The reason she often brings tears to the eyes of the children and adults with whom she comes into contact is that her carefully tended image touches key sensibilities in the people of her country. Like Ronald Reagan, another master of communication, Xuxa is both one of the shallowest and one of the deepest measures of the shape of culture.

Among the various activities on the "Xou," some, such as the jigsaw puzzle game where players race to complete a picture of Xuxa's face, are transparently opportunistic in their Xuxacentrism. Another example is a game called "Baixinho Curioso" in which children are invited to interview the star. Typical questions are "When are you going to do a live show in my town?" "Do you bleach your hair?" and, in late 1991, after Xuxa discussed giving up her show and moving to Buenos Aires, "Why are you leaving Brazil?"[61] The last question was asked by a girl about six years old who burst into tears and sobbed throughout the response. The camera moved in to exploit the drama of Xuxa-worship, filling the television screen with a close-up of the child's tear-streaked face as Xuxa comforted her. On another show, the star surrendered the spotlight to one of the Paquitas for the same game. The girl was asked what she wanted to do when her time as a Paquita was over, to which she replied that she hoped it would never end. That response represents a powerful endorsement to attract new legions of aspiring Xuxa clones.[62]

Another "Xou" segment featuring Xuxa is entitled "Nossa Gente Brasileira," which might be translated something like "Hometown Heroes." Ostensibly designed to pay homage to Brazilians who have excelled in some area, the segment focuses on the neutral realm of sports, and the interviews Xuxa conducts with athletes make it clear that the intention is to draw the guests into her orbit, rather than to expand that of the "Xou." Among the athletes featured on the "Nossa Gente Brasileira" segments in late 1991 were members of Brazil's women's basketball team, which had just won a gold medal in the Pan-American Games in Cuba. The media had reported regularly on the team's triumphs, and in particular on the feats of two of the best-known players, Hortência and

Paula (as they were habitually referred to in the press). The two appeared on separate shows in the first week of September. Xuxa used the opportunity presented by their appearances to draw attention to herself, reiterating favorite themes and highlighting certain aspects of her own image with the public.

In her interview with Hortência, Xuxa's questions, read from a set of file cards, inquired about the athlete's happy childhood, spent close to nature, about the number of hours she sleeps, and about the difficulty of combining a career in basketball with married life. These are themes Xuxa frequently dwells on with regard to herself in her own interviews—her intimacy with nature, her nostalgia for the carefree days of youth, her sleeping habits, and the stress of finding time for both a professional and a personal life. Xuxa also asked Hortência whether she currently met with criticism for having posed nude for a magazine spread. A few years earlier, after Hortência had become one of the country's most famous women basketball players, she agreed to appear in *Playboy*, for an undisclosed but reportedly considerable sum of money. Hortência's reply to Xuxa's question—that she had indeed received some negative attention over the episode, but that such criticism was unfair because nude posing in Brazil is acceptable, unlike in the United States and Europe—could have been scripted by Xuxa or her staff. Given the public's knowledge of Xuxa's background, the question was patently self-serving. Lost in the exchange was the celebration of Hortência's athletic achievements. Before the interview was over, Hortência had compared Xuxa's charisma to that of Fidel Castro. Finally, the segment ended to the accompaniment of an announcer shouting, "Brazil! Brazil! Brazil!" implying that points of some kind had been scored. After Xuxa interviewed Hortência's teammate Paula, the Brazilian national anthem was played as the athlete was presented with a lucite model of the letter X mounted on a pink stand, as if it were another trophy to exhibit alongside her medal from the Pan-American Games.[63]

Another "Nossa Gente Brasileira" segment, this time with a male soccer player, developed into a disingenuous minidrama staged to remind viewers of Xuxa's role as national sex symbol and to reaffirm her representation of traditional gender roles. Xuxa began by asking her guest to name the most beautiful women in Brazil, telling him he could pick the face of one, the legs of another, and so on—an exercise that endorsed the concept of feminine beauty as an assemblage of body parts. His answer that Xuxa and another Brazilian model were the most beautiful elicited cheers and hooting from the studio audience. After several more minutes of conspicuous flirtation and questions about love, courtship, and marriage, the two stood up and performed a slow dance. The audience screamed in appreciation while the camera moved in for close-ups of the couple's hands linked and of Xuxa's head resting on the athlete's shoulder.

The purpose of this segment was to reinforce the assertions about femininity that constitute an important feature of Xuxa's image and appeal. Media texts speculating about her romantic involvements provide a constant supply of supporting evidence for those assertions. Since Pelé, Xuxa has been linked with racecar driver Ayrton Senna, magician David Copperfield, television personality Fausto Silva, singers Fagner, Fábio Júnior, and Bebeto, model Enrique Luis Quelle, actors Renato Aragão and Dedé Santana, her Paquitos, her "baixinhos," Argentine President Carlos Menem, and, more recently, John F.

Kennedy, Jr. Most of these texts, like the "Nossa Gente Brasileira" segment with the soccer player, make little pretense of credibility; they often, in fact, include elements that undermine or mock their own assertions. The purpose of such speculation about romance is to maintain the element of sexual desirability and availability in the star's narrative. The media texts linking Xuxa to lesbian lovers including her manager, her personal secretary, her Paquitas, and Brazilian singer Simone, play another role in keeping with her image.[64] In the absence, since Pelé, of a steady or convincing boyfriend (the longest relationship, with Senna, is often referred to by the media as a marketing ploy), the hints of a lesbian lover help to maintain the erotic aspect of Xuxa's image by alluding to her sexual appetite.

On the October 15, 1991, program, the "Xou" staged another version of Xuxa's representation of femininity, this time asserting the condition of the single, childless woman as one of unfulfillment. During a publicity segment for a series of Xuxa dolls, she remarked that they resembled beautiful princesses, but they lacked princes. At that cue, the studio was promptly filled with the amplified sound of a baby crying. Registering recognition, Xuxa lifted her head and uttered a plea, in English, except for the word "Deus" (God): "Oh, Deus, somebody love me; oh, Deus, somebody love me." The episode underscores several key features of the Xuxa television phenomenon—the obsessive focus on the star, the invocation of traditional views of gender (the single, childless woman's incomplete condition), the exaltation of the emotions, and, finally, the allusion to first world superiority and the appeal to a neocolonial mentality through the use of English.[65]

Xuxa's "somebody love me" performance, with its

reference to princes and princesses, also recalls her associations with fairy tale figures such as Sleeping Beauty, Snow White, and Cinderella. This pastiche attaches itself to the star and diverts attention from the potentially damaging truth that Xuxa in the 1990s is a single career woman approaching her thirties with no children. Instead, Xuxa is projected as a vulnerable *menina-mulher*, or "child-woman," longing for a baby (indeed, haunted by disembodied infant voices) and a man. In Xuxa's representation of femininity, she sometimes overtly calls forth the image of the childlike sex symbol or of the sexy child, as, for example, one day on the "Xou" when she held up a photo of an eighteen-month-old girl and remarked how "sexy [she looked] in her diapers."[66] Xuxa herself dressed up like a baby on March 27, 1991, for her twenty-eighth birthday party, which was attended by a number of Globo executives as well as friends and other business acquaintances. Xuxa wore diapers, a bib, and a bonnet, hung an enormous pacifier around her neck, and carried a stuffed animal.[67]

Xuxa's program addresses the gender issue in many ways, and one of the more transparent is the way in which the games are organized. All contests on the show are played by girls against boys, singly or in teams, reflecting "sex-role polarities in which girls and boys have an either/or-type role choice rather than a blending of qualities."[68] Girl and boy winners are awarded gender-coded prizes, the former receiving more "feminine" toys such as dolls. A running score is kept throughout the five-hour show and at the end the winning side, girls or boys, is announced. The separation conveys the message that females and males belong to exclusive groups, and that they are rivals who relate to each other through competition. The insistent division of boys and girls into enemy camps may even suggest that, in fundamental ways, the sexes lack room for mutual understanding.[69]

The routine presentation of girls and boys as opponents affirms the attitudes about gender that are reinforced in many ways by Xuxa's own example. Flirtation and sexual innuendo are constants on the program. Xuxa approvingly points out instances of provocative behavior and dress, for example, on the part of female guests on the program. On one occasion, she teasingly demanded that a blushing, teenaged singer dressed in tight black leather shorts turn around so the audience could see her partially exposed buttocks.[70]

Xuxa's emphasis on fashion and makeup for girls attempts to invest the sight of seven-year-olds wearing lipstick with a natural quality. Her extravagant wardrobe led one commentator to observe that she had created what he called a "fairy tale delirium over apparel."[71] A typical Xuxa costume on the program in 1991 was a clinging black dress barely clearing the buttocks, with fuschia-colored shorts underneath, and thigh-high black boots. The fashion-show aspect of the program, besides contributing to an accelerated narrative of consumption, creates a framework for viewing the female figure as a kind of mannequin or doll. The feminine game of dressing up is played out in a variety of ways on the "Xou," most literally in the segment where children decorate Xuxa with crowns and sashes. The emphasis on fashion also encourages girls and women to associate success with Xuxa's fashion-model looks.

The "Xou" also continually exploits the attraction in the third world of the first world and things associated with it. The cartoons, for example, that make up most of the five hours the "Xou" is on the air (Xuxa's intervals add up to only about forty-five minutes a program), are all from the United States.[72] While they are dubbed into Portuguese, they still have little cultural relevance in Brazil, presenting situations and cultural referents that are all but lost on viewers except as constant reminders of difference. The first world associations are expressed in the program's musical features as well. The majority of the musical guests on the "Xou" are Brazilians, yet Xuxa rarely taps Brazil's musical traditions, catering instead to the public's taste for the generic disco pop sounds associated with the first world. Among Xuxa's Brazilian performers in 1991 was the best-selling children's group "Trem da Alegria," dancing rap style and singing songs including one whose chorus repeated *"tartaruga ninja"* (Ninja Turtle) over and over again. Another native act was a Madonna imitator dressed in the famous underwear-on-the-outside style, who sang "Papa Don't Preach" in English. A repeat guest was manager Marlene Mattos's sister, Angel. Her teen romance songs are accompanied by a polished performance and alluring costumes like the snug black pants, high heels, and black push-up bra under a transparent burgundy blouse that she wore on one program.[73]

The United States has had the greatest influence on the music of the "Xou," from New York acts such as "El General" (originally from Panama, he performs dancehall reggae in Spanish), to the style of Xuxa's own songs —which, except for the Portuguese, could have originated in a Los Angeles recording studio—to the mood-setting selections piped into the studio as background for the show's segments. Whitney Houston's "You Fill Me Up," dance music like the nineties hit "Everybody Dance

Now," or the old Righteous Brothers tune "Unchained Melody," were some of the sounds heard during portions of the program featuring Xuxa reading her fan mail.

Vasconcellos argues that Xuxa's program, while an "autochthonous product," represents "no country and no nationality."[74] References to Xuxa in other media texts as a quintessential Brazilian figure, the "*brasileiríssima* Xuxa," illustrate the contradictions her image embodies.[75] Xuxa's blondness, because it is so unusual in Brazil, is an omnipresent symbol of difference. Every time Xuxa appears on the screen, she validates the desire for whiteness that is harbored by many and legitimized by the articulation of a national philosophy of whitening. Asserting Xuxa's Brazilianness is, in part, a way of reconciling conflictive feelings about race by allowing the exaltation of her whiteness to be, paradoxically, a celebration of nationality at the same time. The promotion of Xuxa's Brazilianness also addresses the question of national identity, in keeping with what Kehl sees as Globo's self-imposed mandate to "modify the imaginary representation of the nation."[76] Xuxa, a product and a symbol of the Globo ideology, stands for the essence of a new Brazilian, supplanting certain notions of identity drawn on traditional cultural ingredients, such as folklore, while retaining others, including gender and race conventions. Vasconcellos concludes that Xuxa is the "lore" of modern Brazilian folklore.[77]

While generic disco and pop music dominates the "Xou," some Brazilian musicians with other sounds and big urban followings make appearances on the program, drawing large viewer audiences to the Globo network. The funk vocalist Sandra de Sá, who dedicated a record album partly to Xuxa, has appeared, as has Beto Barbosa, who made a name for himself exploiting the lambada market. The "Xou" occasionally features Brazil's *música sertaneja,* a type of country music traditionally performed by male duets that is very popular in southern and central rural areas and among recent immigrants to the city. Xuxa's regular, and only, samba guest in the fall of 1991 was Neguinho da Beija Flor, the well-known spokesperson and lead vocalist for the "Beija Flor" samba school.[78]

Neguinho is one of the few blacks seen on the "Xou." His presence on Xuxa's program is virtually the only reference the program makes to the issue of race except through silence and the general absence of blacks. That Neguinho was chosen to play that role is significant. The samba school he represents, Beija Flor, was the first one to reassess the traditional approaches to its Carnaval parade appearances and to work consciously on developing flashy production values and a more marketable image. A talented performer, Neguinho, with his handsome, smiling face and accessible style, is well suited to the commercialized, more heavily produced side of Carnaval and samba music. He has emerged as the ideal front man for marketing black entertainment in the white-dominated media. Between Carnaval seasons, Neguinho performs *pagode,* a style of samba that began developing in the late 1970s and during the 1980s reached huge audiences and sold millions of records.[79] The popularity of *pagode* took off in 1986, the same year the "Xou da Xuxa" went on the air. Through his association with the mass-marketed *pagode* movement and his role in Beija Flor, Neguinho represents the Brazilian trend toward produced culture aimed at broad audiences—a development masterminded by Globo and starring Xuxa. As if to synthesize the messages about race, mass media, and culture the "Xou" represents, Xuxa donned a dark wig for Neguinho's performance on her August 26, 1991 show, and he, in turn, told the audience that the theme for the Beija Flor samba school in the upcoming 1992 Carnaval would be a celebration of television.

The attention Xuxa's image attracts is ultimately channeled toward the lessons of consumerism with which the "Xou" is saturated. Many of the games on the program are transparent advertisements for products such as cereal (cornflakes and chocolate-flavored "Krispis"), pop music hits, television shows, and Coca-Cola. It is hard to see how a child watching the program day after day could miss the connection between buying something and having fun. In the Coca-Cola game, the contestants wear T-shirts printed with the product logo as they race each other to assemble a U.S.–style "picnic" from giant-sized replicas of food items and equipment such as hot dogs, straws, and Coke bottles. The prizes consist of baseball caps, backpacks, and thermal drink holders, all displaying the Coca-Cola logo. Another sponsor of Xuxa's program is the "Estrela" toy company, well known as the Brazilian distributor of Barbie dolls and accessories. A regular "Xou" feature, recorded separately and inserted into the program at different times, shows Xuxa picking a prizewinner from among the many letters she urges children to mail her in order to be eligible to win an "Estrela" toy.

The advertising on the show takes a variety of forms. An example of an indirect advertisement for one of the array of Xuxa products available is a story-telling game in which two children compete by each telling the same fairy tale. Afterward, an actor dressed as a fairy-tale king tells the same story a third time. This is the "official" version, available in Xuxa's book-and-cassette series of children's stories, which is also advertised on the back pages of Xuxa's comic book. These activities, along with the cartoons—such as the Ninja Turtles series that sells Ninja Turtle products—the commercial breaks, and the overt and indirect promotions for Xuxa's and other companies' products, add up to a children's program built around marketing procedures.

One game, called "Yes or No,' sends a more complex version of the message that fun is buying things. This game ties triumph or defeat to the value of goods, and delivers a lesson in the authority of the marketplace. No particular product is promoted; instead, the issue of relative value is raised. The single participant, sitting in a soundproof booth and unable to see what Xuxa and the audience are viewing, is required to agree or not agree to trade one item for another. Without knowing what the items are, the player must respond "yes" or "no" when a light is switched on. Xuxa might ask, for example, "Will you trade your video game for a bicycle?" or "Will you trade your TV for a pacifier?" Afterward, Xuxa releases the player from the booth, awards the prize, and explains what the boy or girl traded away.

This game of chance stimulates in the audience a kind of frenzied appraisal of goods. There is no skill involved, yet the player who ends up with a bag of marbles rather than a video game is disappointed, as is the crowd. "Yes or No" teaches that a video game is more valuable than a bag of marbles and that exercising one's options, even with limited choices and in compelling circumstances, is a way of defining oneself as a winner or a loser. The game also functions as a vicarious shopping spree, turning children's fantasies to notions of consumption, and probably arousing feelings of inadequacy in those viewers with limited resources.

The 1980s saw a "hard sell takeover of kids [*sic*] TV" in the United States, due in part to the deregulatory policies of Ronald Reagan and the mercenary impulses unleashed during that decade.[80] "With the coming of the program-length commercial," as Tom Engelhardt points out, "the barriers between ad and show have been so broken down that often little more than a formal distinction remains." Furthermore, "even if kids can be shown to discount the more obviously false claims and messages of individual ads, what they actually see are ads en masse, a flood of ads that have their own larger messages to offer, their own story to tell about what is desired and not, valued and not, important and not in our society."[81] Xuxa's program similarly provides a context for the language of promotional culture, and also gives children a tremendous amount of information about how to evaluate the world. They learn which soap operas, songs, dances, and fashions are in vogue. The "Xou" teaches lessons about gender roles, race relations, and other social structures. Few elements included on the program could be characterized as having pedagogical value, and Xuxa does not apologize for the fact that her program devotes little time to anything educational. The "Xou" has been accused, in fact, of "uneducating" young people. In the United States, the Children's Television Act, passed by Congress in 1990 in an attempt to restore a degree of control over children's television and to insist that an educational element be a part of programming, is regularly circumvented by broadcasters who redefine "educational" to mean virtually any image of conflict and resolution.

Among the few features of the "Xou" that might be considered educational are a series of short cartoons that appear on the screen just before the show returns from commercial breaks. Lasting a few seconds, the cartoons illustrate homilies such as "Don't give up" or "Don't fight." Engelhardt discusses the same delivery of "prosocial messages" on children's television in the United States, and concludes that the insertion of a few platitudes in an hours-long viewing period is unlikely to influence a child, especially when the rest of the programming undermines those messages.[82] Xuxa's "Xou" does include some songs, and a few games, such as password, that teach counting, the alphabet, or encourage thinking about words. Xuxa promotes sign language by occasionally using it on the "Xou" and sometimes teaching a few phrases to viewers. Mentally retarded children, referred to as *excepcionais* and mostly the victims of Down syndrome, are regularly invited to the program and are sometimes featured as guests, in an effort to recognize their needs.

These gestures, however, viewed against the backdrop of the program's massive doses of consumerism, seem perfunctory and largely cosmetic. Xuxa's expressions of sympathy toward the less privileged are important, however, in the management of Xuxa's image. The use of the impaired—sufferers of Down syndrome, the deaf—as symbols of the needy is convenient because they can be presented as victims of natural processes rather than social, political, or economic conditions. The values that inspire projects such as Xuxa's "Fundação Meneghel," where the star feeds and provides educational and job training to 250 poor children, are generally absent from the "Xou." That absence is, in part, a consequence of the tightly controlled environment of the television program.[83]

The specific content of Xuxa's show on Globo has varied only slightly since the program began on July 30, 1986. By 1990, Xuxa would complain that "all the children's programs are the same."[84] The "Xou" had established a new formula that quickly spawned numerous television imitations. While none of the copies has been as successful as the original, some have done well, particularly the "Clube da Criança," Xuxa's old show on Manchete, which was taken over by another, much younger, blond host named Angélica Ksyvickis. Some speculate that it is the formula and Globo's resources more than Xuxa herself, that keep the "Xou" in the number one position in the hotly contested ratings race in children's television programming. One journalist and television critic, whose insistence that she be cited anonymously reflects the general reluctance to challenge Xuxa's image in Brazil, argued in 1987 that the star herself was easily replaceable: Xuxa's program "is going strong because of the boom in the children's market. Anybody with a more or less pleasant personality, Globo's backing, and 'He-Man' cartoons on the program, could be a Xuxa."[85] That "boom" is really a product of the growth of the mass communications industry in Brazil, in combination with three other elements: Globo's domination of the television market, Xuxa's charismatic personality and powerful image, and the formula for children's programming that she began to develop on Manchete and that emerged in full force with the "Xou."

The new programs are loud, bright, and trendy. They have elaborate stage sets and a "flood of merchandising," and are conducted at a "frantic pace."[86] In keeping with the effort to replace the old-fashioned look with modern features, some traditional children's activities such as storytelling are deemphasized or recontextualized. One observer of television and Brazilian culture writes that "the secret [of the new shows] is the way they mix the old storyteller with the seductiveness and language of television." The traditional storyteller figures, the same commentator adds, "have been replaced by action cartoons, and the games have taken on the dizzying rhythm of today's television."[87] As the rhythm is accelerated, the patterns of childhood are speeded up as well. The new formula is part discotheque, part amusement park, part party—Vasconcellos calls it a "cabaret"—with the latest pop songs and dances and fashions on display. The music and language used on the new shows are aimed at teen tastes and fad culture. Commenting on these programs, the sociologist Maria Celeste Mira says: "Children today love being treated like little adults. They identify more with the daily life of adults than children used to."[88] The kids become, in effect, precisely what Xuxa calls them—not children, but rather "baixinhos," cast as the targets of the commercial pitches on which the new shows, purveyors of consumer culture, thrive.

With the development of the new formula, children's television programming became, naturally, more lucrative. The networks began to invest more time and money in the field, and the industry grew rapidly. In a 1990 interview, Xuxa compared her work with children to that of Steven Spielberg, and acknowledged the role children played in opening new markets:

> If I am where I am today, I owe it all to the children. The records I sell, the material things I have . . . .I know that if I

have reached this level—and I realize I have the biggest piece of the pie—many other people have discovered children too. There are a lot of good people working with kids today. Spielberg is an example. And he has one of the biggest fortunes in the world, simply because he gave some thought to the world of children. They [children] have enormous value, enormous power.[89]

In the fierce competition over ratings, Xuxa's "Xou" has always been the front-runner. Her closest competitor in October 1988, two years and three months after the "Xou" went on the air, was the young, blond Angélica.[90] As one measure of the huge popularity of the "Xou," one article attributes the 30 percent drop from 1986 to 1988 in preschool and first grade morning session enrollment in Brazil's big-city public schools to the children's desire to stay home and watch Xuxa on television.[91] Xuxa is an "electronic baby-sitter" for children, a way to keep up with the latest fashions, music, and dance styles for teens, background noise for housework and lunch breaks, and entertainment for the retired and the elderly.[92] Even members of the elite, from poets to politicians, declare themselves admirers.

Xuxa is, as one article put it, "more than just a craze; she has become part of the childhood of an entire generation of Brazilians."[93] The parade of allusions to Xuxa in Brazilian culture perpetuates the significance with which her person is invested. She is said to receive ten thousand letters a day from young people who project various meanings onto their idol. Some address Xuxa as a muse and send messages such as, "When you see the evening sad, and the night wanting to rain, remember the tears in my eyes, crying because they can't see you."[94] A girl from Bebedouro, São Paulo, writes to Xuxa, "When the present is the past and the future is the present, I will be by your side eternally." A twelve-year-old boy sends the message, "Xuxa, it won't matter if I touch the sky unless you're there with me."[95] A needy teenager appeals to the star for charity, asking for "clothes or some shoes." Xuxa inspires romantic and erotic fantasies in boys and men, such as the nineteen-year-old who writes looking for a "sincere friendship" with the star, or the lovesick sixteen-year-old who asks Xuxa to phone, if she has any free time, on Monday. Another fan demands Xuxa's telephone number as well as a three-foot-high, autographed color poster and her latest record, also autographed—not the previous LP, which he already has.

The main reason the star receives so much mail, however, is that youngsters write in order to be eligible to win prizes. Indeed, the feelings Xuxa herself arouses in children are difficult to separate from those stimulated by their appetite for toys, clothes, and other consumer goods. One article calls Xuxa the "character-symbol" of a formula whose effects are described as if it were an addictive substance: "Using basically the same ingredients, the recipe for kids' programs seems to stimulate children's appetites with increasing intensity."[96] Xuxa encourages children's desires to acquire status, or cultural capital, as represented by the goods and knowledge with which a lifestyle is constructed and made publicly manifest. By the 1990s, it was possible to talk about a "Xuxa generation," a group that grew up in the age of Xuxa, informed by the persistent images of consumption emanating from the "Xou."

In October 1990, *Cláudia* magazine published an article that synthesized the main elements of Xuxa's public persona.[97] The article is preceded by a two-page advertisement co-sponsored by the magazine and Xuxa's clothing boutiques, called "O Bicho Comeu." Youngsters aged two to sixteen are invited to send in drawings showing "how they see Xuxa," to be judged on the basis of "creativity and originality." The winners receive prizes of clothing from the "O Bicho Comeu" shops. The article that follows the contest announcement shares the ad's mingling of the domains of culture and commerce, of entertainment, information, and promotion. The piece is entitled "Queen Xuxa's Castle," and, through photos and narrative, it shows the reader around her house in Rio.

Focusing on the pictures alone, we see Xuxa in seven of the nineteen shots. In three of these she is playing with her pets, including the exotic and much-publicized sloth, which she cuddles. In the other photos, Xuxa is doing exercises in her gym, sitting in a thronelike peacock chair next to a large drawing of herself, and sitting on the floor leaning against the wall with her eyes closed, a dreamy smile on her face, and her legs on display in the trademark boots. A seventh shot shows Xuxa's legs alone, encased in the same pair of elegant, white, above-the-knee boots. This photo is one of five that show her wearing this particular pair of boots, which are elaborately sewn with gathers down the front. Xuxa's boot collection (which, as one article pointed out, "the fetishists love") is featured in another photo showing two shelves with seventeen white, ten black, five red, one pink, and two blue boots.[98] Since they are lined up singly, missing their mates, the picture is presumably not of a shelf in Xuxa's closet, as the house tour context implies, but rather of a display at one of the "O Bicho Comeu" shops. Other photos as well are composed in such a way that house and shop merge into one domain, implying that, by purchasing her products, one might gain some sort of access to the castle-mall over which Queen Xuxa presides.

The *Cláudia* article as a whole alludes to Xuxa's queenliness, from the dimensions of her house (with a special exercise room and a "relic" room where the thousands of gifts she receives are displayed) to the television satellite dish she uses to pick up Mexican television and practice her Spanish, to the photo of her simple breakfast of fresh fruits, served with a vase of cut flowers on the deck by the pool. This kind of luxury is as unreal as a fairy tale to most Brazilians. Along with her regal stature, Xuxa's show-business stardom is alluded to in photos of her trophies and of a wall covered with gold and platinum records. The star's child-woman duality is expressed here as well. Her erotic image is asserted through various sexually charged poses and her childlike character is represented in several other pictures, including one of the stuffed bear she is said never to sleep without.

The *Cláudia* article is followed by a postscript. One more page shows two young girls with long, blond hair modeling Xuxa clothing from "O Bicho Comeu." There are four different photos of the girls wearing miniskirts and boots, doing the lambada or bumping bottoms. A caption reads: "From head to foot, dressed like the queen of the 'baixinhos.' " Some of the items of clothing modeled have words printed on them, such as "kiss" (in English), or "Xuxa." The text on this page begins, "Everything that Xuxa touches turns to gold. Really." At the end is the statement that "Xuxa's empire keeps expanding its borders." These are the facts that define Xuxa during the years of the "Xou." In that period, she grew so large in the public's imagination—as a result of her television show, live performances, movies, records, and the marketing of so many products—that it seems appropriate that Xuxa was pictured next to Ronald Reagan on the cover of the special issue of *Manchete* dedicated to summing up the decade of the eighties.

THREE

MASS MARKETING THE MESSAGES

THE NARRATIVE OF Xuxa's stardom is marked by a deep commitment to consumerism. The star's carefully cultivated image, which draws mass audiences with its embodiment of discordant views and its reassuring stance against change, also generates a loyalty that is readily channeled toward messages of consumption. The array of products Xuxa endorses offers the public a variety of ways to express their allegiance to her and the values for which she stands. With enough money, a child can eat Xuxa food, wear Xuxa clothes, bathe with Xuxa soap, play Xuxa games, records, and videos, read Xuxa comics, and go to sleep between Xuxa sheets. Such items are the substance of the dream the star projects. Through them, the euphoria she generates on the "Xou" materializes as ownership and a sense of belonging. The star has called the "adoration" her fans express a "sickness."[1] Usually, however, Xuxa celebrates the extremes of loyalty she inspires. A constant refrain in Xuxa's media coverage describes her pleasure at learning that children speak her name before saying "mommy" or "daddy." The central image of a song from her sixth record album is that of a child virtually raised by the television personality and fiercely devoted to her.[2]

In a *Jornal do Brasil* interview with Regina Rito, Xuxa describes children's attachment to television programs as inevitable and their attachment to television personalities as an arbitrary function of time and place:

Rito: Children today seem not to like outdoor games very much. They're giving up soccer, marbles and other group activities for a private relationship with you. Don't you think you might be creating a generation of vidiots?
Xuxa: No. After all, television existed long before I was born.
Rito: How do you react to the fact that every morning, all over the country, from north to south, thousands of children don't want to go to school because they prefer you, their electronic babysitter?
Xuxa: If I weren't in that time slot, the children would watch whoever was.[3]

The topic Xuxa avoids by portraying herself as a passive, coincidental product of the times is the deliberate and carefully planned exploitation of circumstance. This strategy is consistent with the philosophy of the Globo network, where characteristically "the profit-making aim is concealed" and instead "television is presented as a community service" and the network as a "cultural institution."[4] The public's strong feelings of allegiance to Xuxa are cultivated in calculated fashion, and they translate into a marketing bonanza that is neither casual nor incidental.

As early as 1988, the word "empire" was introduced by the media to refer to the shape and size of Xuxa's interests in Brazil, which soon expanded throughout the Americas. Like another commemoration of conquest or invasion, Xuxa's team celebrated the first year of the Spanish-language "Xou" in 1992.[5] A variety of enterprises operating under the umbrella Xuxa Artistic Promotions and Productions company run the expanding empire. Xuxa is said to be the sole owner of 99 percent of the business, which does its banking in the Cayman Islands.[6] Xuxa Tourism sells the travel packages that include group tours for children to Florida's Disney World. Xuxa Records markets releases independently of Globo's Som Livre label.[7] O Bicho Comeu is in charge of the clothing boutiques, and Xuxa International takes care of business outside Brazil. A major source of income is the licensing of products under Xuxa's name. Submissions flood in, and from those accepted, Xuxa earns a portion of the profit from sales that, according to one report, averages 12 percent. As of early 1991, by one account, fifty products from thirty different companies were licensed to market products under Xuxa's name.[8] New projects are constantly announced to the media. In 1990, a Rio shopping center devoted exclusively to selling Xuxa merchandise was said to be in the works. The site was to be called a "Xopping," and it was predicted that several million dollars would be spent to adapt the three-story building "to meet the needs of the kiddie consumer." The "Xopping" would resemble a Disney World–style amusement park.[9] Plans to build a "giant Xuxa theme park" in Brazil were reported in the United States in November 1992.[10] A segment about Xuxa on the television show "Entertainment Tonight" showed the star with a model of the theme park and indicated that she had purchased the land and was seeking investors. The program also alluded to Xuxa's recently negotiated contract to produce her show in English for broadcast beginning in 1993.

Xuxa has more than once been chosen "Marketing Personality of the Year," and the achievement is highlighted in the first paragraph of a 1991 press release in English, which boasts about her role in "revolutionizing the entire language of television commercials for children." The document continues: "Xuxa was the first person to speak directly to the children themselves. Before Xuxa, television commercials had been aimed at the mothers rather than their children." [11] Despite the star's evident contributions to the field of marketing, however, her success is attributed to a kind of guileless rapport with children. In keeping with her representation of femininity, the appearance of aggressiveness in the business sphere is downplayed. Xuxa's fortune, similarly, is construed by the media as a natural and even capricious consequence of her status as idol of the young. In an account of how she came to develop a line of products to market to children, Xuxa portrays herself as a servant of the public, responding to, but not creating, demand:

> The idea of presenting products under my name began while I was still with the "Clube da Criança." One day, we were in the hall and a little girl asked me when my doll would come out. I told her there wasn't any Xuxa doll, and she insisted that she wanted [one]. . . . I started thinking, and I talked it over with Marlene. Finally, we passed the idea along to Maurício de Souza who designed the first doll. . . . That's how these products came about, in response to the desires of my "baixinhos." In other cases, naturally, it wasn't like that. For some products we had to do a whole market research analysis, but we always tried to make things that children like to have, or see.[12]

These remarks hint at, but downplay, the industrial and commercial framework within which Xuxa's business enterprises operate. Xuxa emphasizes instead an attitude of simple goodwill. Although, as one journalist points out, Xuxa "imposes no apparent standards of safety or educational value" on the merchandise marketed under her name, she projects the image of a woman devoted primarily to serving the interests of children. That benevolent approach is the façade behind which Xuxa's considerable empire has developed.[13]

Asked whether the "Xou" encouraged children to become consumers, Xuxa replied on one occasion, "No. What I do isn't aggressive, I'm not imposing anything on children; I don't say things like 'you have to buy this.' I explain all the merchandising on my program to them. . . . Besides, all the toys and products I advertise on my program are presented as games, within a context. It's not aggressive."[14] The characteristic childlike innocence stressed in Xuxa's representation of femininity rescues this type of disclaimer from the cynicism with which it might otherwise be regarded. The authority of Xuxa's image is demonstrated in the willingness of the public generally, though not absolutely, to refrain from challenging her on the subject of consumerism. To question her approach seriously would be to undermine values and views in which the public has invested heavily. For the businesses that benefit from the licensing of her name, to raise questions is to put another kind of investment at risk. As Hideo Sawa, who makes Xuxa surfboards, observed, "Any alteration in Xuxa's image has to be carefully considered. . . . If her image doesn't correspond to the product, it's worthless."[15]

Yet some public criticism of Xuxa does appear from

time to time. The most notable instance occurred in late 1991. Brazil's economic decline and the *Forbes* announcement of Xuxa's inclusion on the list of the world's forty highest-paid entertainers placed an unusually sharp focus on the country's disparities of income and opportunity. Letters to *Veja* expressed resentment toward the star. One writer blamed Xuxa for some of Brazil's violence: "Our greatest host must be going through a crisis of conscience for making nineteen million dollars through a consumerist approach the results of which can be seen on the streets with children killing for a pair of tennis shoes or some other pointless thing." Another letter accused Xuxa of "imposing on the 'baixinhos'" a consumerism that is a "kind of vice" that causes "dependence," just like drugs.[16]

This kind of public discussion is rare, however, especially in the mainstream media. Xuxa is generally protected from serious questioning of the commercial approach of the "Xou" by the predisposition of Brazilians to preserve the meaning of her image and the various forms of capital it represents. The reluctance to jeopardize the stability of the symbol can be seen in the way media references to the promotion of consumerism on the "Xou" are often shaped to protect Xuxa. Her ex-colleague, model Luiza Brunet, adopts this approach in an article in *Contigo* magazine that shows her holding her newborn baby and declaring, "I will never let my daughter watch the 'Xou da Xuxa.'" In the text, however, Brunet assures readers that the excessive consumerism of the program is not "the fault of Brazil's most beloved blonde."[17] Brunet goes on to give her opinion of formulaic children's shows in general: "Personally, I think these programs are anti-educational and counterproductive in the sense that they encourage the child to sit passively in front of a television set for hours in a row. They don't stimulate creativity or development."[18] Even these remarks are packaged to diminish their critical impact, contextualized as a spat between two famous beauties. The article also uses class markers (especially the view of leisure) that are likely to distance the message from the working- and middle-class audiences at which the publication *Contigo* is aimed.

Another example of the strategy to protect the integrity of Xuxa's image is seen in a 1987 *Veja* piece. While children are described as being "bombarded" by products from their idol, and their mothers as "tired of Xuxa" because their children demand "these items as if they were necessary to their survival," the article also naturalizes the consumerism by placing the debate in the domestic sphere. The issue is cast as a domestic problem, and a minor one at that. The children's demands are a nuisance, but not important enough to involve fathers.[19] In the new sphere of empowerment Xuxa had opened up—that of children as consumers—women were reduced to an even lower position in the social hierarchy.

It is television, of course, and specifically the Globo network, that has built Xuxa's empire. What one author calls Globo's "virtual monopoly of Brazilian commercial television" means that the network's influence is necessarily measured on a different scale from that of ABC, CBS, or NBC.[20] Borrowing from the English, Brazilians call one of the techniques that Globo uses to exploit its advantage "merchandising." The term is used in Brazil to refer to in-program product placement, the kind of indirect advertising that occurs, for example, when a character on a soap opera casually orders a Coca-Cola in a restaurant scene. Globo claims to be the television pioneer of the technique, which pays for a considerable portion of the production costs of its shows.[21]

On the use of in-program advertising, one article states: "Probably nowhere does it occur more blatantly than on television in Brazil."[22] A marketing executive with Coca-Cola in Brazil explains that his company pays for in-program product placement because "we're looking for a complement to our advertising. . . . Rather than getting an exact message across, you're associating yourself with people and events that are relevant to your target audience."[23] According to Jane Sarques, the arrangement also allows networks to violate the law that limits advertising to fifteen minutes per hour.[24] She notes that Brazilian television has always been characterized by the heavy use of advertising. What is more recent, Sarques argues, is the "intense exploitation of children in the interests not only of immediate consumption, but also of the formation of a consumer mentality starting in childhood."[25]

A marketing expert with a firm in São Paulo says the in-program advertising technique is extremely effective "because the product is placed inside an illusion."[26] The viewer is not supposed to notice that the Coca-Cola downed by the soap opera character in the restaurant scene is a message. That product placements like the Coca-Cola game on the "Xou" are much more intrusive, and are barely disguised as anything other than advertisement, reflects both the power of the fiction Xuxa conjures up and the willingness of her audience to be absorbed in the illusion. The overt in-program advertising on the "Xou" also follows the television habit of acknowledging its own techniques and intentions.[27] The demystified ad is presented as a way of coming clean with viewers, as if that were a form of audience innoculation. This view is, in effect, what Xuxa was trying to convey when she insisted that the advertising on her program is not harmful to children because it is all out in the open.

But people are not immune to a sales pitch simply because they know they are its targets. Small children, who are probably not even aware of such rhetorical strategies, are uniquely vulnerable to illusions such as those that Xuxa commands. Just as cartoon characters are real to little children, and Xuxa is a real fairy godmother to them, the delicious taste of the chocolate milk she says she likes so much must also be real. Moreover, as the director of one research firm in Brazil observed, confirming what numerous studies have found, "Children watch the commercial breaks [on television] as if they were programs."[28] Very young children watching the "Xou da Xuxa" will not distinguish between the program and the commercial breaks, much less recognize the in-program publicity as advertisement.[29] For children, and perhaps for adults with little education or sophistication with regard to television's methods and motives, everything on the screen tends to speak with the same voice of authority. In fact, according to Sérgio Miceli, "the plain and brutal fact" of high rates of illiteracy "constitutes the structural foundation of the colossal penetration of television in Brazilian society."[30]

Viewers with little economic, educational, or cultural capital are particularly vulnerable to television's messages. These include lessons about what to perceive and what not to perceive, which are thus perpetuated by Xuxa and absorbed indiscriminately along with advertisements for cereal, soft drinks, and soap operas. In Sarques's study of the effects that the advertising on children's programs has on young audiences, she found that the gender roles of "a society still strongly marked by masculine domination" was one of the lessons taught by television. Xuxa's representations of race and gender send powerful messages, whose implications are rarely discussed in the Brazilian media. Sarques also noted television's influence on "the power of children in the context of the family to assert themselves as consumers."[31] This is a development for which Xuxa can claim some credit.

In one interview, Xuxa confessed that she found herself sometimes repeating in her sleep the slogans associated with products promoted on the program.[32] Later, showing the list of products to her interviewer, Xuxa laughingly recited each one's slogan, explaining that "they burst out automatically." The interviewer described Xuxa as a "little robot," parroting the slogans for merchandise she endorses on television, such as cookies, bicycles, coloring books, clothes, pens, yogurts, soft drinks, bubble gum, colored pencils, stationery, cameras, backpacks, tennis shoes, toys, posters, and discount travel tickets for children. Xuxa's own products advertised on the "Xou" include soup, records, dolls, a toy Xuxa spaceship, and shoes. These are promoted during the program as well as in standard commercials the network runs. Xuxa's Maggi soup is, she says in the ad, "as good as a kiss from me," and has noodles shaped like the letters in her famous name.

Xuxa's dolls, also promoted on the "Xou," are made in, and for the enhancement of, the star's image. The first, for which Xuxa began negotiating with one toy manufacturer after another in 1984, finally reached stores in May 1987. It was originally conceived as a "Barbie-type doll with Xuxa's features," and received a great deal of attention in the media.[33] The erotic, glamour girl aspect of her image was attached to the doll from the start. The first doll was described as "the only Brazilian doll to be modeled after a human being . . . [Xuxa], the blonde in motion, with her blue eyes and sensual body."[34] Chilean sculptor Sergio Rosales, hired after the first design was rejected, reported it was "an indescribable emotion to portray a personality who is practically idolized by the kids. I tried to capture the essence of the Xuxa phenomenon."[35] Later versions of Xuxa's dolls reveal a variety of attempts to shape the myths that inform the star's image. The first in the "Xuxa Fairy Tale" series was the "Xuxa Rapunzel" doll, which, bearing features of both its namesakes—Xuxa and the storybook character—drew on a traditional source to strengthen the star's association with fantasy, and especially with female fantasy figures. With "Xuxa Signos," a set of dolls that stand for the signs of the zodiac, a connection is established to the realm of destiny and fortune, a notion already suggested in Xuxa's discovery myth. *Veja* devoted a two-page article to describing the design, development, manufacture, and impressive sales figures of the first Xuxa doll. Media coverage of Xuxa's products often stresses their technological innovation and sophistication. Personal attention is also frequently emphasized in stories about the selection and production of Xuxa's merchandise. It is reported that she insists on inspecting each model personally, and she vetoes anything that does not meet her standards. Such accounts draw attention away from the business side of the operations and underline instead the notion of Xuxa's devotion to her "baixinhos."

One "Xou" promotion in 1991 was for a new Xuxa

product, the "Love Xu," a plastic children's sandal. The "Love Xu" was also advertised during regular television programming in a commercial that was striking for the way it projected adult sexuality onto children. The ad featured Xuxa and several little girls around age six or seven. They are shown individually, cuddling the sandal and addressing it in English with phrases such as, "I love you, baby," "Give me a kiss," and "Yes! No! Yes! No!" delivered in tones seemingly drenched with romantic and sexual desire. The ad captures attention by showing the expression of aroused passion emanating from the mouths of children. The commercial also used English to draw on the prestige accorded to things associated with the United States. The product's name, "Love Xu," uses English, plus Xuxaspeak for the English "shoe," also an abbreviated form of the star's name. Xuxa, in her familiar role as child-woman, enhances the erotic fantasy suggested in the ad, joining child to woman in the context of attraction to a desired object.

The commercial implies that the solution to the tension evoked by the little girls' pleading voices is to buy the "Love Xu." In this exclusively female realm, anxiety is relieved by shopping. Xuxa openly recommended shopping as a sensual experience in her promotion of the product on the "Xou" on November 27, 1991. Holding a "Love Xu" next to her face for the cameras, Xuxa turned suddenly and buried her nose in the sandal. After a deep and prolonged sniff, she raised her head, faced the cameras, and confessed in a breathy voice, "It's *so* good!" The scene ended with Xuxa's advice to viewers to go out shopping, if only to smell the "Love Xu." The scene contains connotations of other kinds of sniffing (glue, cocaine) as well as a reminder of the footwear fetish long associated with Xuxa as a result of her admitted fascination with boots. Xuxa confessed in a 1982 interview that she has a "real psychosis about boots."[36] She is seldom seen without a pair on, and they have become one of her signature symbols, along with the X's and the kisses.

The "Love Xu" ad and the sniffing scene, whether regarded as part of the fetishistic footwear discourse or not, invoked an erotic context for selling the new product. The connection between love, sex, and shopping is directed here toward the female consumer who is the target of the majority of Xuxa's ads. Yet the male view is implied in the way this and many other items are marketed. The dolls, for example, are attractive to little girls because they represent Xuxa, and Xuxa is attractive, in part, because daddies like her. In the end, the doll, the daughter, and Xuxa are all daddy's little girls, and these images of femininity are defined and circumscribed by the masculine universe.

Movies "Super Xuxa"

Movies are another vehicle used to market and enhance Xuxa's image. Her first major starring role was in *Super Xuxa contra Baixo Astral* (1988), a feature film written around Xuxa's "personality" (i.e., image) and developed in response to a market analysis showing that Brazil's highest box office earnings at the time were for children's films (the Portuguese term *infanto-juvenil* covers small children through adolescence).[37] The realms of commerce and culture mingled in what was labeled the film's "ambitious and unique" financing scheme, whereby investors were invited to take advantage of President José Sarney's law that allowed income tax deductions for money applied to cultural activities. The rest of the financing was obtained by selling "merchandising" opportunities in the film, including two "diamond"

"Super Xuxa"

shares costing eighty thousand dollars each, a record price in the Brazilian movie industry. These were sold to the Mimo toy company and the Tabacow company, whose stuffed dog toy, Xuxo, functions as a major mechanism of the plot of *Super Xuxa*.

The cost of the movie's production, a little over a million dollars, was covered before a single ticket was sold, and the film generated additional profits from spin-off products including the video, the soundtrack, and likenesses of various stuffed animals that make appearances in the film. That the *Super Xuxa* project was conceived and executed as a commercial venture did not escape the notice of the public. In a long article about the film and Xuxa's "empire" in the *Jornal do Brasil*, the letter *s* is replaced throughout by dollar signs. The article concludes by saying, "Poor Xuxa will receive 30% of all the promotional item$ plu$ 16.5% of the box office. In other word$, if everything work$ out, more than a million dollar$ for a little over a month'$ work. Can anybody think of a better candidate for Trea$ury $ecretary?"[38] If there is sarcasm in these remarks, the article is also a reminder of the success myth promoted by Xuxa's image and reinforced by the movie's plot, with its tale of overcoming odds and obstacles.

In *Super Xuxa*, the villainous Baixo Astral, which translates to something like "downer," is angered at the "alto astral," or "upper" that Xuxa is on. He decides to lure her to his underworld by kidnapping her dog, Xuxo. Xuxa goes through a series of adventures and ordeals, in scenes that make use of a number of special effects, before she manages to defeat Baixo Astral and rescue her dog. The movie plays heavily on the emotions, as Xuxa herself demonstrated, according to one account, by crying at the end of the film at a private preview showing held in downtown Rio at the bank in charge of administering the movie's financing.[39] Among those attending the screening were representatives of some of the companies that had purchased in-program advertisements in the film. They watched as the movie plugged their products "without subtlety," according to the *Jornal do Brasil*: "In less than a minute after the film started rolling, various products were 'sold.' Xuxa rode an Agrale motorcycle, went to a Shell gas station, painted a rainbow with Suvinil paints, and passed a Coca-Cola billboard." Xuxa anticipated some criticism of what *Manchete* called the "heavy scheme of commercialization," and, to defend herself from those who she said "insist on calling me an agent of consumerism," adopted the strategy of the anecdotal defense:

> A lot of people are making a living from my commercial success. A little while ago, I received a letter from a gentleman who thanked me for helping him support his family. He said he prayed for me every night, and told how he made counterfeit [Xuxa] dolls and sold them to street vendors. It made me happy, even though I know, if the idea catches on, I might end up losing my livelihood. But the truth is, I feel happy to be able to contribute to improving someone's life.[40]

By casting herself in the role of benefactress of the entrepreneur and, in keeping with the permissive aspect of her image, as a sort of accomplice in crime, Xuxa draws attention away from more systematic analysis of her tactics.

Super Xuxa was seen by 2.5 million people, the third-largest box office of the year. Xuxa's next feature film, *Lua de Cristal* (Crystal Moon) (1990), turned in ten million dollars, double the gross box office receipts of *Super Xuxa*.

For *Lua de Cristal*, Xuxa Productions and the Dream Vision company were joined by Columbia Pictures, which is described as sharing the risk, co-producing, and distributing the film.[41] Here Xuxa's standard messages about gender, race, culture, and Brazil's future are assembled into a narrative that buzzes with button-pushing devices, emanating from a Xuxacentric formula.

In *Lua de Cristal*, Xuxa plays a small-town teenager who leaves home to follow her dream of becoming a singer. She goes to the big city to stay with her aunt and cousins, who turn out to be vicious creatures. There are a number of allusions to the Cinderella story as the aunt and female cousin put Xuxa to work as a maid in the house. The male cousin sexually harasses her at every opportunity and eventually kidnaps her. But in the meantime, Xuxa has met a prince charming, who works in a U.S.–style pizza parlor. When the kidnapping is botched, ending in Xuxa's apparent drowning, the pizza parlor prince revives her with a kiss. The final scene shows Xuxa, now a singing star, on a stage performing the movie's eponymous theme song. The plot is interrupted by dream sequences in which Xuxa, as a fairy-tale princess, and the pizza parlor character, as a prince on a white horse, enact a romantic narrative that parallels the main story development. In the dream sequences, set in a forest, the couple is joined by the Paquitas and the Paquitos, who dance around in slow motion.

The Xuxacentrism of the film begins with the use of Xuxa's real name, Maria da Graça, for the protagonist. Attention is drawn to the name throughout the film. The first and last words of the opening segment are "Maria da Graça." The audience hears the name seven times in the five-minute scene showing Xuxa's arrival at her aunt's apartment. Yet the star of the movie insists that the protagonist has "nothing to do" with her.[42] (In one interview, Xuxa admitted some connection: "In this film, my character resembles me, but it's a character.")[43] But *Lua de Cristal* is about enhancing Xuxa's image in the interests of marketing the various products, and promoting the attitudes, associated with it. To that end, the film uses this and a variety of other techniques of association to construct an extremely self-referential (or star-referential) narrative. Even the fragments of fairy tales included in the film are part of the Xuxacentric process. Elements of "Cinderella," "Sleeping Beauty," and "Hansel and Gretel" are alluded to quite explicitly, but the film appropriates the original fairy-tale narratives opportunistically, as disconnected and incomplete discourse. These fragments are incorporated into the film as motifs surrounding the star's image, rather than as intact forms. They contribute to the Xuxacentric aims of the film by placing Xuxa in an allegorical dimension that helps to mask some of the contradictions her image embodies.

Race is one of those contradictory aspects, and it is the theme of a brief vignette at the beginning of *Lua de Cristal.* The scene reminds the audience of the racial discourse that informs Xuxa's image, rationalizing an all-white aesthetic by depicting the absence of personal racial prejudice. If the original proof was Xuxa's relationship with Pelé, here Xuxa is shown establishing friendly relations with a group of six black teenagers. She has just arrived in the big city (Rio) and is headed for her aunt's apartment when the teenagers surround her under a highway overpass. She is trapped and alone, and is carrying all her possessions, including, as the audience well knows, the hard-earned money her mother handed her in a tearful farewell scene. Viewers are clearly meant to perceive Xuxa's fear as she turns and scans for an escape route, which she fails to find. She stands very still and looks afraid. The camera holds on the figure of Xuxa, surrounded, inviting the audience to focus attention on a paradigm of racial conflict. Viewers are presented, for a few seconds, with what Dyer calls "the extreme figures in [the] conflation of race and gender stereotypes . . . the black stud/rapist [in this case, more than one] and the white maiden."[44] But the frightening situation, which has been deliberately framed in racial terms, turns out to be a gratuitous display. The tension between Xuxa and the blacks is dispelled when she smiles and breaks into dance. As the confrontation is neutralized, the problems of racism are symbolically resolved, and Xuxa emerges the beneficiary, since she is depicted as the agent of transformation. Just as Xuxa is not assaulted, neither is the comfortable, imaginary construct of Brazil as a "racial democracy."

The strategy to use race in order to allow viewers a vicarious tingle of fear without challenging cherished beliefs about the absence of racism in Brazil, also involves connecting the black characters to the United States. As they surround Xuxa, they are dancing to, and eventually performing, a rap tune playing on the boom box one of them carries. Although they are speaking native Portuguese, the musical form and their expressions and clothing mark them as not Brazilian. They look as if they have stepped off an MTV screen, and the scene is photographed to resemble a music video. By making the menacing blacks ambivalently Brazilian and non-Brazilian, the scene evokes a set of fears but carefully manipulates viewers to keep the race issue within acceptable limits.

The misreading of a foreign mode of expression is offered as one explanation of the possibly racist, and therefore un-Brazilian, fear that Xuxa initially shows. As it turns out, however, the blacks' unsmiling faces, challenging vocal tones, and aggressive use of "the walk," are only expressions of style. The vignette shows black and white, North and South America, coming together in the dance arena. The sense of distance is erased, along with cultural and racial identity, which are replaced by the global values of television tourism.

There is only one other black character with a speaking role in *Lua de Cristal*, a man who appears just as the scene with the rappers is ending. He does not seem typically Brazilian either, in his gold-rimmed sunglasses and designer T-shirt and scarf, although he plays the familiar role of the *crioulo doido*, a comedic figure that forms part of the limited set of black stereotypes seen on Brazilian television. He has a brief encounter with Xuxa, who asks him for directions and rolls her eyes at his silly answers. This black figure, like the rappers, is costumed and cast in a role that keeps him at a safe distance. After these characters disappear about ten minutes into the movie, the only other blacks, or nonwhites, in the film are a couple of ambulance attendants, two grocery store customers, and a store clerk with her back turned to the camera. These people appear in the background, and only for a few seconds. The all-white scenes at the evil aunt's apartment house, at the pizza parlor, at the school where Xuxa takes singing lessons, in the dream sequence forest setting, and on the stage where Xuxa performs her song at the end of the film present reassuring, familiar messages about race. These scenes confirm the meaning of the wink of reassurance one of the rappers gives at the beginning of the highway underpass episode. As he strides past the camera, the teenager turns, lowers his sunglasses, opens his eyes wide, and smiles. It is a brief signal, but enough to let the audience know that the racial confrontation is all in the spirit of fun.

Lua de Cristal also addresses gender in a variety of ways, one of which is by showing sexual harassment as a natural and inevitable consequence of female attractiveness.[45] There are ten scenes in which Xuxa is shown being sexually harassed, verbally and physically, by her cousin and his friends: she is pushed down on her back on a bed while the cousin tries to climb on top of her, chased around her bedroom, and repeatedly grabbed. In one scene, Xuxa's "prince," observing from afar, thinks she and the cousin are embracing, but what he is really watching is an attempted sexual assault from which the star escapes by screaming. Finally the cousin kidnaps Xuxa and ties her to his motorcycle, apparently causing Xuxa to drown when the vehicle veers off a beach highway and crashes into the sea. The movie exploits the theme of sexuality broadly: it taps the motif of sexual awakening encoded in the "Sleeping Beauty" and "Cinderella" fairy tales, builds drama by presenting scenes of sexual menace, and draws attention to Xuxa's erotic image in other ways as well, such as by including a scene of her taking a bath.

The movie also stresses various aspects of conventional femininity. Xuxa's character is, for example, skillful at house cleaning and cooking, but a joke is made of her inability to perform other simple tasks outside the home, such as operating a cash register or an automatic car wash machine (by pushing a button) or preparing a sandwich to serve in a restaurant. The other female roles in the movie reinforce various gender stereotypes as well. The wicked aunt, who exercises some authority as the manager of her apartment building, is depicted as a cackling witch who ends up being carted out of the building attached to a toilet to which she has gotten stuck. (The permissiveness associated with Xuxa's style on the "Xou" surfaces here, as on her records, in the expression of a vulgar, juvenile kind of humor of which the toilet scene is an example. *Lua de Cristal* also features graphic vomiting, public belching, nose picking, and snot eating.) The female cousin, who is about Xuxa's age, orders her around rudely, plots against her, kills her plants, envies her blond hair, and doesn't like children. She is the anti-Xuxa of the movie. The Paquitas' roles are decorative: they drink sodas in the pizza parlor and dance in flowing dresses in the forest. Finally, one other female, a little girl about eight or ten years old, is the movie's symbolic "baixinho." The girl's parents are absent from the film narrative to highlight her relationship with Xuxa.

The press release for *Lua de Cristal* includes a page on the director, Tizuka Yamasaki, who had a reputation as a serious artist and something of a feminist. The press release worked to modify both impressions with comments such as "It is to be hoped that the [movie] releases the award-winning Tizuka Yamasaki once and for all from the stigma of being an art-film director, an intellectual . . . and a feminist."[46] Two pages later, the film's photographer, Edgar Moura, is cited discussing the concerns people had when they learned who was going to direct the new Xuxa film: "[There was] fear that Tizuka was going to make Xuxa a feminist."[47] Later on the same page, readers are assured that the film does not follow the European art-film style of *cinema d'auteur* with which

Yamasaki was associated through earlier films. Instead, it follows the Hollywood style: The movie "is not a Tizuka Yamasaki product. It's the result of team work. A fast-moving, accessible film with strong visual appeal and a commercial approach like in the American cinema." *Lua de Cristal*, like the press release, is a narrative of reassurance. The point of the movie, Xuxa declares, is that "we should never give up our dreams"—a congenial, innocuous message, offered in a context in which dreams are defined within strict parameters and according to unchanging patterns.

Another important way in which Xuxa's image is established in the public imagination is through her records. She has recorded an album of her own each year beginning in 1986, and each has been a best-seller.[48] Among 1987 releases by national artists, Xuxa's LP ranked number one with 3.3 million records sold, far ahead of second-place Roberto Carlos (the Julio Iglesias of Brazil) with only 1.1 million.[49] Today, Xuxa is "the biggest seller of records in Brazil."[50] Media features on the recording industry regularly point out the irony of the Xuxa phenomenon in Brazilian music. *Veja* writes, "Today, in the country that gave birth to the samba, Bossa Nova and Tropicalism, the most successful musical attraction is a singer who doesn't want to be a singer, who admits she can't sing, and is herself shocked at her sales figures in the millions."[51]

Xuxa has achieved musical success as products aimed at the children's market have played an increasing role in the record industry. That trend began in 1982 with the first recording by the Turma do Balão Mágico (Magic Balloon Gang), a children's group associated with the "Balão Mágico" children's TV program, which Xuxa's

"Xou" replaced on the Globo network. The Turma do Balão Mágico was a commercial venture from the start, "invented," as one article states, "in the offices of CBS Records."[52] Another children's musical group with best-selling LPs, the Trem da Alegria (Train of Happiness), started out performing on Xuxa's "Clube da Criança" program on the Manchete network. They too were a business creation; all four members were "recruited by advertising agencies."[53] By 1987, three of the five top-selling Brazilian artists and groups—Xuxa, Trem da Alegria, and Jairzinho e Simony—produced LPs exclusively for the children's market.

The commercialization of children's music had its critics, among them André Midani, president of WEA (Brazil).[54] His 1988 observations on the new recordings made by children refer to the produced, formulaic qualities that characterize Xuxa's albums as well: "These young artists are strictly controlled by their parents and their performances are memorized. If I ever meet a child who composes, plays and sings using his or her own imagination, I'll sign a contract on the spot."[55] The sales figures, however, were hard to ignore. Xuxa's records even competed successfully in the adult market against leading Brazilian groups in *sertaneja* and rock music, as well as against foreign hits. Her 1990 LP had sold more than six times as many copies as Madonna's new record in Brazil by June of that year.[56]

In keeping with the notion that her business ventures are simply responses to the needs of her "baixinhos," Xuxa confessed on the occasion of her first recording in 1984 that the idea of singing on an LP "terrified" her.[57] She says she was able to overcome her reluctance thanks to two men, Paulo Massadas and Michael Sullivan: "They were the ones who convinced me to sing. They taught me that the "baixinhos" don't want a wonderful voice, just someone to sing for them."[58] The song from Xuxa's first recording that received some radio airplay was "E de Chocolate," composed by Massadas and Sullivan. The former a musician with a degree in advertising, and the latter a vocalist who picked his English name for promotional purposes out of a New York City phone book, these two Brazilians have since become known as the country's leading songwriters of commercial hits.[59]

Massadas and Sullivan are labeled masters of mediocrity by the critics, but their ballads, rock tunes, and children's songs are tremendously appealing to mass audiences. A Massadas and Sullivan composition is a virtual guarantee of sales, and recording artists have flocked to the prolific duo. By 1987, one article observed, it was "practically impossible to listen to the radio, buy a Brazilian pop record, or watch music shows on television without running across a Massadas and Sullivan creation."[60] In one week in mid-August 1987, the pair had no less than fifteen songs among those most often played on radio stations around the country. *Veja* estimated that listeners in Rio and São Paulo heard a Massadas and Sullivan tune on the radio every five minutes.[61] The duo continued to work with Xuxa, some of whose annual albums on the Som Livre label (Globo's recording company) are produced, and have as many as five cuts, by Massadas and Sullivan.

Xuxa's recording history is uniform in its critical failure and spectacular mass appeal.[62] The pattern began to emerge with her early recordings, but its reliability was established with the annual Som Livre LPs. The first in that series was released shortly after Xuxa began hosting her program on Globo. The newspaper *O Globo* was not exaggerating when it reported, "With 2.5 million copies sold in only three months, the LP 'Xou da Xuxa' has broken all sales records in the Brazilian phonograph industry."[63] The president of Som Livre, João Araújo, is quoted explaining the album's success this way: "In the first place, Xuxa discovered the right way to communicate with kids. Then, she has talent in picking a good repertory, and the record was very well produced. All this, plus Xuxa's enormous popularity all over Brazil, resulted in the unprecedented sales figures." One reason for Xuxa's felicitous selection of repertory is the informal market testing performed during recording sessions of the television show: "The tape is played during breaks and I watch to see if the 'baixinhos' wave their pompoms or move their little feet."[64] If the kids don't respond, the tune is dropped. Still, Xuxa said she didn't understand the LP's success, although she thought it was "fantastic." She told the story of one child who said he bought four copies of the album. When Xuxa asked why, he answered it was because the store didn't have any more.[65]

The "Xou da Xuxa" LPs are heavily manipulated products of a sophisticated marketing team. They function as vehicles of reinforcement, reproducing the messages of the television program. The Xuxa-centeredness of the albums, the cover and lyrics sheet designs that draw attention to the innocent-erotic, child-woman duality of the star's image, the international pop sound with its first world associations, the element of vulgarity that corresponds to Xuxa's permissive style, and the fundamental appeal to the emotions all point to commercial principles operating behind an artistic entertainment front. In keeping with the appeal to emotions, the lyrics of one song by Massadas and Sullivan from the third "Xou da Xuxa" album (1988) literally urge listeners not to speak but rather to feel, and not to think but rather to dream.[66]

Of all the "Xou da Xuxa" albums, the first one has what is probably the raciest cover, consisting of a photo of Xuxa wearing a semitransparent blouse through which one naked breast is visible. The effort to attract the adult male gaze is particularly notable here, but it is a constant in the "Xou da Xuxa" album jackets. On the first LP, the star is posed bending down with her arms and legs arranged to form trademark X's. The logo appears on the back cover of the LP as well, where Xuxa's name is written over and over as a decorative border across the top and bottom of the square. In the middle, between the rows of *Xuxa*s, is a broad X outlined in red and filled in with a variety of snapshots of the star on the set of the "Xou." The scenes are colorful and busy, crowded with kids, costumed characters, and set props, to give the impression of excitement and fun. Xuxa is in the center of each of the thirteen shots, displaying the star focus of the "Xou" experience, as well as the fashion-show aspect and the adult sexuality to which her costumes make reference. (In three of the photos, for example, she is shown wearing gold boots and a gold-and-white miniskirt split high up the left hip.)

The front and back record cover designs are clearly meant to have adult appeal. The lyrics sheet inside, on which Xuxa is depicted in various drawings illustrating the songs, is aimed at children. The star is shown, for example, riding on the back of a large bee, comforting a weeping dog, flying in a Peter Pan costume, dressed as cartoon superheroine She-Ra sitting in the palm of the huge hand of He-Man, and, twice, riding in her spaceship. The combination of the juvenile (represented in the drawings, the lyrics, and the children's choruses that sing on almost every cut) and the adult (as in the various photos of Xuxa, including the peek-a-boo cover pose) reinforces the child-woman duality cultivated as a part of Xuxa's appeal.

The listener's attention is continually directed to Xuxa on the first "Xou da Xuxa" LP. Besides her vocal performances, two tunes have her name in the title, "Turma da Xuxa" (Xuxa's Gang) and "Amiguinha Xuxa" (Little Friend Xuxa).[67] The narrative voice is specifically identified with Xuxa in six of the ten songs on the album. Xuxa discusses her horse in "Meu Cavalo Frankenstein" (My Horse Frankenstein) and her dog in "Meu Cãozinho Xuxo" (My Little Dog Xuxo).[68] (Xuxo was a stuffed animal toy then available in stores, giving the song a specific marketing function as well; in 1988, the dog was featured in the movie *Super Xuxa contra Baixo Astral.*) Xuxa is everybody's friend in one song and the leader of the gang in another.[69] A song about Peter Pan is a clear reference to Xuxa, whose desire to play the role in a theater production had been widely reported in the media.[70] In another tune, "She-Ra," Xuxa attends a party with a group of cartoon superheroes. In "Garoto Problema" (Problem Kid), she acts as a therapist to a mixed-up boy.[71]

There are only three cuts in which Xuxa does not surface either in the title, as a narrator, or as a subject. One is the Stevie Wonder tune "Miragem Viagem" ("Black Orchid"). The second is a song about eating bread that creates a nostalgic vision of Brazil by evoking the sights and smells of an old-fashioned bakery.[72] The third Xuxa-less tune is "Doce Mel" (Sweet Honey), which typifies one category of song frequently found on later albums.[73]

These feel-good tunes rely on simple melodic hooks and innocuous lyrics. They use an enumerative strategy to join disconnected words and ideas—such as, in this case, "child," "good," being with others, playing, and freedom—in a sanitary, celebratory context.

One song on Xuxa's first "Xou" album, "Turma da Xuxa," had the special aim of trying to establish her identity as separate from the other children's *turmas*, or gangs. Itself a neutral term meaning a gang, a group, a work crew, or a section at school, the word *turma* has also been appropriated for commercial purposes. The Turma do Balão Mágico, mentioned earlier, used the device to market its records, stimulating identification with their "turma" in the same way brand loyalties are developed around a label. Another well-known "gang" is a set of comic book characters called the Turma da Mônica, created by artist Maurício de Souza (who later helped design the first Xuxa doll). His popular "turma" characters adorn everything from T-shirts to notebooks to posters to pencils. In 1987, only Disney marketed more items for children in Brazil.[74] The Turma da Mônica comic books dominated the market for a decade. By 1991, however, Xuxa's comics had taken the lead.

The "Turma da Xuxa" song differentiates Xuxa's brand of gang from others, just as her style on the "Xou" distinguishes her among children's show hosts. The lyrics to "Turma da Xuxa" use an aggressive, naughty humor that corresponds to the star's permissive approach. The lyrics are not "nice," just as Xuxa is not a conventionally "nice" host on the program. The refrain, which is sung by a chorus of children and repeats the song's title to reinforce the purpose of the exercise, is interrupted by verses that name and characterize members of the "gang." There are two boys with smelly feet, a girl who smells bad because she hasn't taken a bath in a month, a girl who wets her bed, an oafish kid with an oversized rear end, a boy who tries to kiss a girl and misses her mouth, a boy who jumps over a wall and loses his shorts, a girl who jumps over a fence and loses her underpants, a boy who is so fat he can't see his feet, a girl who talks too much and has onion breath, and a boy who fell in the toilet. Each of these characters is illustrated by a drawing on the lyrics sheet. One shows a little girl waking up in the morning. There is a pool of urine under her bed, and a dog with its leg lifted is making another pool next to hers. Another drawing shows a boy with his pants pulled down to reveal his bottom. Two other kids are pointing and laughing, taunting him with the cry "Big Butt! Big Butt! Big Butt!"

The ten jokes rely heavily on bad smells and bare buttocks, and are of the type universally snickered about on playgrounds. It is this naughty laughter that defines Xuxa's "gang." The group is united behind the frank, permissive, irreverent attitude of its leader, who appears to challenge such elements of social control as etiquette and discretion. These are normally enforced by parents and teachers, who are replaced here by the more engaging, seemingly subversive Xuxa. Her message is not about the undermining of convention, however, but only the surrender to impulse. Xuxa's apparent endorsement of disobedience masks the messages of obedience that her narrative insistently promotes.

The second "Xou da Xuxa" LP (1987) was produced by the Massadas and Sullivan team, who also supplied three of the fourteen songs.[75] *Playboy* magazine ran a brief review of the album under a photo of Xuxa in a provocative pose reproduced from the LP's back cover. She is shown turned to the side, leaning over, with one leg exposed up to her waist. Her head is raised as she blows a kiss at the camera. The *Playboy* review, captioned "A foxy Xuxa, for both fathers and sons," focuses on the erotic elements of the star's image as conveyed by the LP cover:

> For fathers, buying Xuxa's records has at least one advantage: while your kid entertains himself with her silly songs, you can amuse yourself with the cover. On the second "Xou da Xuxa," she appears in boots, naked thighs, a microblouse that seems to have been sewn on to her skin, and nothing around her waist but an enormous bow of pink and yellow tulle, as if she were a giant bonbon wrapped up like a present and ready to eat. The image on the cover is juvenile, but not entirely so. . . . The content of the record isn't just childish. It's enough to drive you nuts. But why pay attention to that, when you can make yourself and your son happy at the same time. And, if the boy's smart, *he'll* be interested in the cover too.[76]

Xuxa's annual album covers, like the swim suit issues of *Sports Illustrated* in the United States, serve as iconographic reminders of an ideal of femininity. The erotic aspect of the "Xou da Xuxa" album covers is treated playfully in the media. In a review of the second LP, the *Jornal do Brasil*, for example, made a pun with the verb "transar" (which can mean "to deal with," but more commonly is understood as "to have sex"), pointing out that another photo on the back cover shows Xuxa "in transparent veils," but that the star "guarantees that the kids deal with her nudity without difficulty, 'because it's natural.' "[77] The LPs play an important role in the projection of Xuxa's meticulously tended image. The fascination and loyalty she inspires sell records. Xuxa performed the second LP's repertory day after day on the "Xou," and the commercial sounds the critics and many parents complained about represented the first world values and symbolic intimacy with the star that were just what the children were after. João Araújo explained the record's success as a product of the feelings Xuxa generates in her public: "The 'baixinhos' are very loyal to Xuxa. Some kids even buy another LP to replace the one they've worn out from playing it so much. It's a product that doesn't require a special marketing strategy to sell."[78]

The third "Xou" LP established without a doubt that Xuxa was the champion in record sales. She had soundly defeated her closest competitor, Roberto Carlos, to whom there are a number of allusions on the new disc (in one cut Xuxa even appropriates his sixties slogan, "Nossa turma / E uma brasa" (Our gang / Is really hot), for her own use as a "gang" identification device.[79]) *Veja* pronounced Xuxa's new LP formulaic, like the others, and lamented the decline of musical quality in children's recordings.[80] But, *Veja* admitted, what counts is that "the kids adore" the album. One of the songs, "Ilariê," later became the "anthem" of children all over Portuguese and Spanish-speaking America.[81] It is a cheerful song of welcome designed to warm up a crowd with calls to join the fun and games with Xuxa's "gang." The third LP also exhibits the characteristic Xuxacentrism. Her name appears in the titles of two songs and in the lyrics of five, and Xuxa is the narrator of almost all the cuts. One of them makes a game of repeating the syllables of her name separately.[82] The permissive element surfaces in a song that ends with the shout "*bunda*" (butt), and then, in the last line, "*bicha*," which is slang for homosexual.[83]

Five of the third album's thirteen songs are by Massadas and Sullivan. These make references to things children like, such as chocolate, playing, and make believe, and to things everybody likes. One song associates the colors of the rainbow with a variety of appealing concepts such as "happiness," "friendship," "hope," "love," and "emotions." The aim of the song is to elicit generally pleasant feelings among listeners and to enhance the star's image by alluding to one of her symbolic properties, the rainbow, which Xuxa has explained is the translation of her famous name in Korean, Chinese, and "for Orientals."[84] Another Massadas and Sullivan tune narrates a fantasy of riding a horse up into the clouds toward "freedom" and a peaceful, happy, beautiful place where people are equal.[85] These lyrics, in which the horse is white and "peace" is white, may serve as a reminder of the view of race that the "Xou" asserts daily with its all-white cast and white images of success.

The Massadas and Sullivan songs often adopt the first-person narrative form. In the tune "Bombom" (Bonbon), Xuxa sings the word "I" eight times, and uses the first-person verb form without the pronoun five more times. The "I" invokes "you" directly five times, and, using the imperative verb form, fourteen more. This construction furthers the aim of strengthening the bonds between the listener and Xuxa. Other lyrics on the third album perform the same function, urging the child to join her gang, to fly, play, and dance with her, and to see Xuxa as the supplier of rainbows and sweets.

In keeping with the pursuit of an ever more intimate bond between Xuxa and her public, the back of the lyrics sheet of the third album has a "personal" message from the star. The note appears beneath a poster-size photo showing Xuxa's face and her bare arms and shoulders, with a bouquet of flowers strategically placed over her implicitly naked breasts. Written in cursive letters to give a personal effect, the message reads: " 'Baixinho,' thank you for your affection and respect. You changed me into a special person. Bonbon-flavored bursting kisses, Xuxa." The signature is superimposed on a pair of lips outlined in lipstick, just like the real pair in the photo above. The bonbons and bursting kisses are references to songs on the album. The poster displays a compelling array of symbols that represent various features of the Xuxa universe.

For her fourth "Xou da Xuxa" album (1989), the naked-shoulders look has moved to the cover. Here, the star is shown taking a beauty bath in a pool, the surface of which is sprinkled with flower petals. Xuxa's slightly puzzled expression as she faces the camera is an invitation to look. The viewer is cast as the stranger, or friend, who has caught her in her bath. The album was produced by Massadas and Sullivan, and five of the fourteen cuts are theirs as well. Three songs with didactic aims are presented alongside the routine expressions of Xuxacentrism and other typical "Xou da Xuxa" messages. In one song, called "Alerta," Xuxa uses her celebrity status to warn kids to stay away from drugs. Another tune practices basic arithmetic, and one more instructs kids how to tell time. (The latter is not an entirely disinterested exercise, since the song teaches time-telling by explaining where the big and little hands are when the "Xou" comes on television.)[86]

A particularly memorable cut on the fourth album is a Massadas and Sullivan composition called "Recado pra Xuxa" (Message for Xuxa), a type of homage to the star. The song is sung by a child and backed up by a chorus of Paquitas to stress the authenticity of the message. The lyrics begin and end with the singer declaring in simple language that she likes Xuxa both "in the movies" and "on TV." Having placed the subject in that "natural" context, the singer goes on to construct a metaphorical portrait of the star: Xuxa is a child, a little girl, a symbol of hope, a fairy godmother, a dream world, light, freedom, and an infinite journey. The hyperbole is familiar: Xuxa often reads banners and letters containing similar expressions of adulation and devotion on the "Xou." But the source of the message—a cut on Xuxa's own album—lends it another meaning, inscribing it in a context where its function as self-promotion is unmistakable.

On the covers of the 1990 and 1991 "Xou da Xuxa" albums, the bright pink, yellow, and red colors of earlier LPs are replaced by a more sophisticated, subdued look. Here, the record jackets are blue and gold (the blue hues supplied by the sky and Xuxa's eyes, the gold by the sun and her hair). On the 1990 LP, the blue scheme is reinforced by Xuxa's fashionable denim jacket, and the gold is echoed in the shiny jewelry she wears: a bracelet made of two chains of thick gold links and earrings made of many long strands of tiny gold links. On the 1990 cover, Xuxa is lying on her stomach, on the beach, and is lifting her head to smile at a camera shooting level with her face. Xuxa's arms are resting in front of her, and a sprinkling of sand is visible on the heavy gold chains that encircle one wrist.

The picture conveys a carefree, playful attitude, as if Xuxa had just flung herself down after a romp on the beach. That she has worn her substantial jewelry on the outing implies a kind of casualness toward wealth that is enviable if not inconceivable to most Brazilians. The denim jacket seems to make a similarly casual statement about wealth by understating the wearer's status. But if, in the United States, the use of denim in such a context represents the chic appropriation of a working-class symbol, it is an import to Brazil, where it stands for first world superiority and privilege. The jacket and the jewelry are strategic elements of a composition designed to flaunt carefully chosen symbols of privilege. The photo represents a powerful portrait of desirability that is intended to appeal to the Brazilian mass audience who buys the millions of Xuxa records. To own the LP is to participate in some way in the glamorous world it evokes, to be linked by that vision of gold links to Xuxa and what she represents—her "gang," her party, her lifestyle.

On the back cover, the same scene is altered to express vulnerability and uncertainty. Xuxa's smile and relaxed, prone position on the front are replaced here by an apprehensive pose. She is standing, looking over her shoulder at the camera, and has not bothered to brush the hair from her face, as if whatever it is she is looking at requires her full attention. The grains of sand on her jacket lend the front and back compositions a chronology. It is as if the star's playful romp has been interrupted, and she startled, perhaps by the viewer. The back cover depicts tension, vulnerability, and a carelessness that extends from the jewelry to the body. One gold earring drips down the back of the denim jacket as if it were a strand of very expensive hair. The fantasy the picture suggests derives from the understanding that anyone looking like Xuxa, alone on the beach, wearing that kind of jewelry, is asking for trouble.

The front and back covers of the sixth album (1991) are again blue and gold. Here the square space is completely dominated by Xuxa's face. The only clues to a setting are small spots of unidentified blue around the edges. Xuxa is alone and nowhere, or everywhere, a cover girl inventing herself in the context of the fashion close-up. The look in both front and back photographs is clean and natural, and Xuxa appears to be glowing with health. She wears a wide-brimmed straw hat, its golden strands finely woven into a texture that combines simplicity with complexity and suggests old-fashioned craftsmanship. Xuxa's child-woman duality is present here in the contrasting expressions on the front and back of the jacket. On the front, she is serious and seductive. On the back, she wears a big grin, her head is tipped back, one arm is raised, and her long neck emerges from a pair of smooth, golden, bare shoulders.

The only jewelry in these two compositions is a broad hoop earring of thin gold wire that adorns Xuxa's left ear on the back cover photo. The hoop makes an arc that mirrors the golden circle of straw around Xuxa's head, producing a harmonious aesthetic effect that also suggests, in its roundness, the notion of a whole or wholesomeness. A kind of secular halo is perhaps implied, hovering above the head of Brazil's consecrated symbol of goodness, who is pronounced *verdadeira* ("true" or "real") in the album's official press release.

The lyrics of the sixth "Xou da Xuxa" LP carry a number of allusions to the idea of Xuxa as indispensable to a happy childhood, a happy family, and a happy Brazil. As Xuxa's embodiment of the caretaker aspect of femininity is extended, she acquires a larger, symbolic dimension as a substitute—like television—for the missing family. A number of lyrics deal with feelings of inadequacy and estrangement, posing situations of personal and family distress, and introducing Xuxa as a figure of solution.

"Não Basta" (It's Not Enough), for example, is about a father's failure to establish a relationship with his son.[87] The song's theme is discussed in the album's press release: "It's not enough to give your child a toy when what he needs is affection, understanding, dialogue. [Kids] have problems that gifts can't solve."[88] "Hoje E Dia de Folia" (Let's Party Today) is a happy song, but the singer invokes a child's feelings of loneliness, which the tune is meant to banish.[89] In "Meu Cachorrinho Pimpo" (My little dog Pimpo), a relationship with a dog keeps the narrator from feeling alone.[90]

Loneliness and alienation are presented in these songs in contrast to the feelings Xuxa inspires. A father may fail his son, a person may turn to a dog for affection and attention, but Xuxa is always there to supply love and understanding. A similar message is given in an ad for a new Xuxa product, the *Conte Outra Vez* (Tell It Again) storybook series with accompanying cassette tapes that appeared about the same time as the LP. The ad copy urges parents to purchase the item for their "baixinho," so that "one day he'll be able to say he had a childhood."[91] The ad implies that parents alone are inadequate to provide for their children, but that Xuxa can supply what is missing.

The idea of Xuxa as a substitute for a mother and father is celebrated in one cut from the sixth "Xou da Xuxa" album, "Fã No. 1" (Fan No. 1), by Massadas and Sullivan. Here, Xuxa sings about a little boy she calls her number one fan. She boasts that his devotion to her is superior to his devotion to his parents. The boy hasn't yet learned to say mommy and daddy, but he says her name. At his birthday party, instead of giving his mother and father the first pieces of cake, he wants to give Xuxa

* would this be true? % of population born out of wedlock or orphans

the whole thing. Xuxa is devoted to him as well, and, as evidence, explains that she didn't mind when he went to sleep in her lap one day and urinated on her. The lyrics explain that the boy's affection for Xuxa is important because it enables her to dream.

In this and other songs, and in the movie *Lua de Cristal* where "Maria da Graça" achieves her dream thanks to a little girl, children are envisioned apart from their parents and in intimate contact with Xuxa instead. Through these allusions to the drama of Brazil's future, as represented by its children, Xuxa taps a field of deep emotions. To propose the notion of Xuxa as a substitute for the family is to exploit distressing and ambivalent feelings that are caused in part by single and poor parents' fears of their own inadequacy to provide for their offspring, but even more by the problems of neglect and violence toward Brazil's neediest and abandoned children.

Covered daily in the media, the issue of violence toward children in Brazil is especially traumatic because it calls up mixed feelings: if, on the one hand, it is difficult for Brazilians to accept the idea of hungry, homeless, abandoned, tortured, and murdered children, on the other hand, because of the violence practiced *by* children, they are often more feared than pitied. Since the majority of poor, abandoned, and street kids are nonwhite, racism figures in the ambivalent feelings toward them. The specter of a ragged figure asking for money haunts Brazilians, because in the dark, or even in the daylight, it is hard to distinguish between misery and a threat. These children are the targets of Brazil's infamous exterminators, murder-for-hire groups composed mostly of former and off-duty police officers or security guards. More than seven thousand children were murdered by exterminators between 1987 and 1991.[92] Lists of the names of the killers and their areas of operation have been published in the newspapers. A few of the men are listed as dead or in prison, but most are free.

In 1991, a government committee convened to examine the problem issued a report of its seven-month investigation. The committee named some of the sponsors of the extermination groups, including the Merchants Association of Duque de Caxias, a city in the flatlands outside Rio de Janeiro, and the president of an organization of general managers of large retail stores in Rio. The latter is quoted as saying, "Each *pivete* [street kid] killed is a contribution to society." Three shopping centers in the northeastern city of Salvador, Bahia, were accused of the "torture and intimidation" of children and adolescents. Nationwide, the report said, 82 percent of the murdered children are black (by the Brazilian definition of black; by U.S. standards, the percentage would be higher).[93]

In late November, 1991, the media covered a story about an attack by an extermination group on an informal "family" of six street kids, ages nine to sixteen. Xuxa was reported to have offered to provide financial assistance to the survivor of the "massacre," a fifteen-year-old girl who was shot but was spared because she played dead. Amnesty International and others were trying to protect her from death threats presumably issued by those she had identified as the killers. One article reported that Xuxa was investigating sending the girl abroad because it was doubtful that her safety could be guaranteed in Brazil.[94] The survivor had witnessed and experienced other violence as well: she had seen her father murder her mother, and the neighbor to whom she then fled had forced her into prostitution in exchange for food. After the massacre, another neighbor said, "If I had been through what she had, I wouldn't have held my breath and pretended to be dead. I would have asked them to kill me."[95]

In these circumstances, Xuxa's promise to the girl, couched in the terms used daily on the "Xou" to award prizes of dolls and kisses, seemed incongruous: "I'm going to make [your] dream come true," she is said to have told the survivor.[96] According to another report, "Xuxa invited the girl to live in her house and suggested becoming her legal guardian. The girl thanked Xuxa, but refused, saying what she really wanted was real parents."[97] The episode questioned the viability of the star's role as "Queen of the 'Baixinhos,'" fairy godmother of Brazil, the symbolic provider and protector of children. The girl's response to Xuxa was especially striking because, as Nancy Scheper-Hughes has noted in her book, *Death Without Weeping: The Violence of Everyday Life in Brazil,* the very poor tend to "try to make alliances with the strong, the beautiful, and the powerful" as a way of insuring a better chance of survival, or creating the hope of one. Thus voters from the slums, for example, will support "the local, regional, and national candidates who are most likely to win, and they will avoid association with likely losers, even if the 'weaker' candidate has expressed solidarity with their class."[98] That the survivor of the massacre should reject Xuxa's offer of protection represents an unusual break from the pattern.

Xuxa's intervention in the massacre episode also threatened to expose the way the integrity of her image depends upon keeping dolls and records and clothes in the forefront, and social realities at a distance. When the distance collapses, the image becomes unstable, as exemplified by a cartoon treatment from the period. Entitled "Xuxa Helps Poor Children," it refers to the star's charitable foundation, the Fundação Xuxa Meneghel.[99] The cartoon shows one child saying to another, more poorly dressed one, "You know who you're talking to? I'm one of the 250 street kids supported by Xuxa!" The other child responds, "Shit, I'm one of the 6,999,750 who sleep on the street."[100]

In late 1991, the star began discussing the possibility of addressing social problems on the show. But the dilemma, as her manager pointed out, was that "Xuxa's image is associated with entertainment." Mattos elaborated: "I don't know how to add the more serious side without taking away from the happy approach that characterizes the current program."[101] The difficulty in finding a way to reconcile the two Brazils in the program's narrative was evident on November 12 when the "Xou" returned from a commercial break. Instead of showing the set with its bright colors and joyful, dancing crowd presided over by the fairy godmother of Brazil, the screen was filled with a child's drawing. The picture showed an adult male figure shooting an adult female figure with a gun held close to her head. Below the drawing, in a childish hand, was written "Homem atirando na mulher" (Man shooting his wife). After a few seconds, the drawing disappeared and, without comment, the TV screen returned to the euphoria of the "Xou."

Xuxa's "happy approach" represents a model of deliverance from the future that most Brazilians face, because, in fact, as Sarques points out, the needs of the majority of Brazilian children "can only be fulfilled at the level of dreams and fantasy."[102] Xuxa's mandate is to serve up a sample of what dreaming can do. Through Xuxa's static image, she markets the messages of the status quo, nourishing its dreams of privilege and holding out the promise of "peace, love, and happiness," as a song on the sixth LP puts it, for both "baixinhos" and grown-up "*altinhos*."[103] If Brazil, in a sense, is sanctified by the "Xou da Xuxa," it is also sanitized and estranged by that narrative of consumption and its unencumbered demand for loyalty.

Xuxa, age nineteen, Rio de Janeiro, 1982 (photo courtesy of AP/Wide World Photos)

Xuxa and soccer champion Pelé, 1982 (photo by Gilson Barreto/Abril Imagens)

Xuxa on the set of the "Xou da Xuxa," 1991 (photo by Ari Lago/Abril Imagens)

Xuxa with some of her merchandise, 1987 (photo by Flávio Rodrigues/ Abril Imagens)

A live performance by Xuxa in the Palmeiras Club soccer stadium, São Paulo, 1989 (photo by Roberto Loffel/Abril Imagens)

Shoe store window advertisement for the "Love Xu," Xuxa's sandal for children, Rio de Janeiro, 1991 (photo by Amelia Simpson)

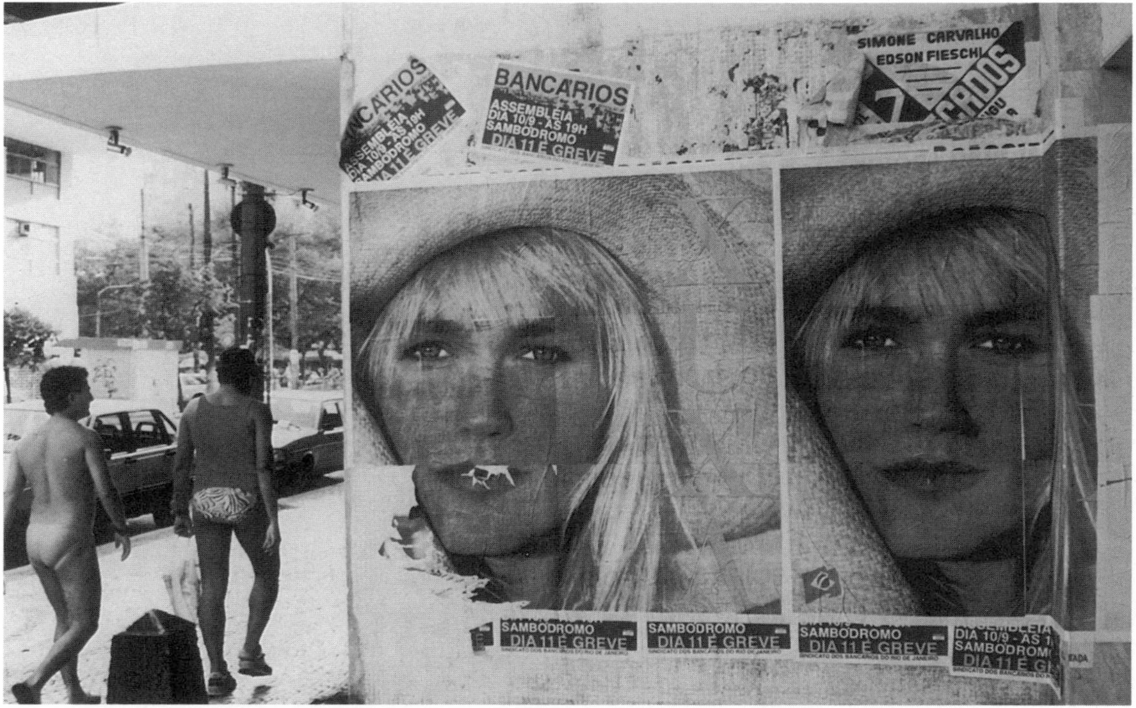

Wall of posters advertising Xuxa's sixth record album, Rio de Janeiro, 1991 (photo by Amelia Simpson)

A magazine kiosk in Rio de Janeiro showing Xuxa on the covers of the September 25, 1991, issues of Brazil's leading news magazines (photo by Amelia Simpson)

Xuxa and her dog, Gringa, 1986 (photo by Paulo Marcos/Abril Imagens)

FOUR

XHAPING THE FUTURE

THE VIGILANCE WITH which Xuxa's image is tended and the unusual consensus with which its meanings are negotiated by the public, have led to the creation of a media giant that *Veja* magazine calls "bigger than Globo."[1] One measure of the impact of Xuxa on Brazilian society is the proliferation of live replicas of the star. It is a sign of the authority she wields in the cultural and economic marketplace that an increasing number of clonelike manifestations have emerged over the years. Some are encouraged by Xuxa, such as the many children called "Xuxetes" or "mini-Xuxas" who dress and try to act like their idol. Others, such as the Paquitas, are her invention, while someone like Angélica, who has her own clones in turn, uses the star as an example.[2] These imitations reaffirm the white ideal Xuxa projects, underscore the generic nature of her representation of female beauty, and are reflections of the mass-produced view of culture the star markets.

The replicas also function as forms of expansion.

Through her surrogate Paquitas, her look-alike fans, clones such as Angélica, and the occasional impersonator, Xuxa's sphere of influence is enlarged.[3] The reach of her financial empire is extended, too, as each replica reminds the public of the original. In the case of the Paquitas, Xuxa shares directly in the profits from their business ventures. Given the undisputed fact of television as "hegemonic in the field of the production, distribution, and consumption of cultural goods in Brazil," the reproduction of Xuxa's image in her television clones must be understood as more than a publicity gimmick.[4] The various imitation Xuxas constitute an endorsement of a specific map of culture. They also work to naturalize and perpetuate an established hierarchy of social domination. With the tremendous popularity of blond, child-woman Angélica—ten years younger than Xuxa and promoted as her likely replacement—the future seems to be already mapped out.

Xuxa imitators began to emerge soon after the star initiated her career in television. All over Brazil little girls started dressing like Xuxa and copying their idol's behavior. The first of Xuxa's chain of clothing shops, O Bicho Comeu, opened in 1985, and soon had lines of youngsters waiting outside to purchase "replicas, in miniature, of all the clothes" the star wears on the "Xou."[5] Before long, "legions of mini-Xuxas [were] parading around in colorful miniskirts in the style used by their television heroine."[6] Little girls sought "total identification."[7] They were described as aspiring to be "xerox copies of their mythical idol," whose "poses and facial expressions" they "millimetrically copied."[8] Xuxa promoted the imitative mode in many ways, including making statements such as "I just adore . . . children dressed like me."[9]

Along with the prestige attached to the goods, of course, are other implications including significant ones about gender. The O Bicho Comeu spring/summer 1988 collection, for girls ages one to fourteen, was described as "sexy and explosive." The basic "uniform" consisted of "a miniblouse, miniskirt, boots, and lots of costume jewelry."[10] "It's great," Xuxa reportedly said, "because that way the girls won't have cellulite or stretch marks.... Besides, skirts are much more suitable for little girls than pants."[11] The skirts Xuxa refers to are described in an article as "very short and as tight as possible," and the same article shows a three- and five-year-old as examples of typical "Xuxetes."

The little girls dressed up like Xuxa reproduce the child-woman duality that informs the star's image, drawing viewers to a sphere of daring sanctioned by her authority. Xuxa defends the child-woman synthesis as a sign of modernity, an adaptation to the times. To reject what her critics call the eroticization of children, Xuxa implies, is old-fashioned, even though the values asserted through the association of mature sexuality with the ingenuousness and vulnerability of a child, and, conversely, the sexualization of children, are deeply traditional. The Paquitas' representation of a type of young girl Brazilians refer to as *ninfetas* (nymphets) is certainly hostile to progressive views. Xuxa has developed responses to interview questions on the topic, which the foreign press, in particular, seldom neglects to explore. A *Los Angeles Times* interview from April 1992 provides a typical exchange. Asked about the eroticism on the "Xou," Xuxa replied, "I am not sexual with the children. I am sensual and loving and I don't believe it is wrong to dress beautifully."[12] She went on to suggest that the criticism in the United States of the erotic aspect of her show is a product of a cultural imbalance: "Americans have lots of perfection but very little emotion. A perfect mechanism loses its spirit. I think Americans could use some more emotion." Another tactic Xuxa has adopted to try to naturalize the eroticism on the "Xou" is to draw on Brazil's international image as a popular destination on the sexual tourism circuit. In an interview on "Entertainment Tonight," Xuxa explained that, if the "Xou" seemed "sensual," that couldn't be helped, since that's the way Brazilian women are.[13]

The issue of Xuxa's representation of sexuality is often framed in terms of cultural, rather than gender, stereotypes. The principal obstacle to her entrance into the U.S. market, apart from her lack of a strong command of English, is generally seen as the prudish attitudes of the "conservative *wasp* population," as *Manchete* magazine put it.[14] Framing the issue of sexual expression in children's television programming as a debate between U.S. puritans and uninhibited Brazilians diverts attention from such questions as those raised by Brazilian psychologist Marta Suplicy. Suplicy reports that her assessment of the growing impact of television on children was generally positive until she began noticing another aspect of television—the "eroticization of children" as a result of the influence of Xuxa's image: "You see children three, four, five, ten years old, dressed up like Xuxa, displaying themselves physically as very sexually attractive adults, which does not correspond to what they are. The child isn't an adult and hasn't developed an adult's sexuality."[15] Xuxa responded to Suplicy's published remarks by saying that "sexuality [had] changed since their mothers' day," implying the psychologist is old-fashioned.[16]

Contardo Calligaris, an observer with some cultural distance from the star is less tentative than Suplicy in articulating his reading of the Xuxa phenomenon. An Italian resident of Brazil and president of the Psychoanalytical Association of Porto Alegre, Calligaris writes:

> At all social levels I notice girls from three to ten years old dressed and painted like improbable sex symbols.
>
> After a while I discover the origin of this juvenile masquerade: Xuxa's program.
>
> The idea is ingenious and unique: design a program for children . . . hosted by a woman who manifestly appears to stimulate masculine desire in adult discourse.
>
> The point is not to entertain or please the children. The point is that Xuxa pleases men. And that leaves kids with no choice. For the girls: how not to identify with her, dress like her, dance and sing like her, if she is the object of the father's desire? Xuxa responds to the basic question every girl asks: how to be a woman? . . . And [for] boys, liking Xuxa is a . . . way of being like dad.[17]

Naomi Wolf, author of *The Beauty Myth*, regards the earlier age at which girls are initiated in the codes of the beauty myth as a dangerous development. She cites evidence that younger and younger girls, exposed to adult representations and their implied appraisals of femininity, express dissatisfaction with their bodies.[18] It is a question not only of exposure but of pressure on children to consume and conform. Xuxa's image penetrates every corner of Brazil, her marketing strategies are sophisticated, and her products for little girls—from dolls to clothes to cosmetics—represent effective lessons in society's expectations.

As Wolf sees it, the problem with "these little girls, born around the time of Ronald Reagan's first election" (precisely the first wave of the Xuxa generation in Brazil) is that "they lack childhoods."[19] What begins as mimicry—a six-year-old putting on lipstick and a miniskirt—becomes a way of viewing and of being viewed involving deprivation (dieting if she is too fat), competition (to establish a hierarchy within the limited zone of expression available to females) and, most of all, simply distraction from thinking and behaving outside that sphere. Being too disfigured, by race or poverty, for example, to be considered for candidacy may be dispiriting, or devastating (or, of course, liberating).[20] Virtually the only public debate in Brazil on the issue of girls dressing up like Xuxa concerns the expense of acceding to the children's demands for costly clothes and accessories. Discussion revolves around the question of access rather than the nature of the narrative itself. The television text, with its messages about what constitutes female desirability, obscures alternatives by convincingly asserting those confining fictions.

The expression of adult sexuality on children's television began to be treated as a trend in Brazil during the late 1980s. "Everything's turning sensual," *Manchete* announced. "The kids are baptized with a volley of sexual marketing. . . . Today's Little Red Riding Hood knows just what the wolf wants."[21] Xuxa is regarded as the principal inspiration for the new style: "Success [*xuxexo*] is kiss kiss [*beijinho beijinho*] with Xuxa's seduction [*xedução*]." *Manchete* illustrates Xuxa's role in the development of the trend, citing a song by ten-year-old child star, Juninho Bill, from the children's musical group Trem da Alegria. In the tune, he "makes a sensual and lewd declaration to the muse of the 'baixinhos' [Xuxa]: 'You're the reason I take so long in the bathroom.'" The trend is continued in the person of Xuxa's leading clone, who was then just emerging as a television phenomenon: "Children's program ratings are soaring with the daring costumes of kiddie-host Angélica, fourteen, on Manchete's "Clube da Criança."

The same article cites some of Xuxa's critics, including a sociologist who argues, "Without a defined sexuality, a child can turn *xuxiform* [as in "uniform"], condemned to the repetitive patterns . . . of existential *sex-shopping*." A psychologist comments, "There's nothing wrong with Xuxa herself. The problem is she's the only feminine figure available to emulate." There is little doubt Xuxa's television image is the one most widely and effectively disseminated among children, especially if her clones are taken into account. Another European observer, German filmmaker Werner Herzog, singled out the "Xou da Xuxa" as an index of sexuality in Brazilian culture. Visiting the country in 1992, he remarked: "[Xuxa's] program enhanced my understanding of what it means to be Latin. The Latin man wants to unite vulgar sex and a certain infantilism."[22]

Articles on "nymphets" and "Lolitas" invariably mention Xuxa, and often the Paquitas and Angélica as well, as reference points in the development of what one article, entitled "Ninfetomania," labeled "a wave of juvenile eroticism in the country."[23] Indeed, *Veja* magazine's retrospective issue at the end of 1991, highlighting one hundred worldwide events and people of the year, devoted an entry to a controversy over the publication in Brazil of a book of photographs of girls between the ages of ten and seventeen who appear "in very abbreviated or no clothing."[24] *Veja* describes *Anjos Proibidos* (Forbidden Angels) as the latest product of the nation's "nymphetmania," aimed at "voyeurs" who already "had at their disposal Xuxa's Paquitas and . . . Angélica on TV."

A *Manchete* piece entitled "The New Nymphets" defined these figures as "object[s] of *soft* erotic attention . . . prepubscent Evas who are seen on the little screen, the big screen, magazine covers, and billboards, sending a message of seduction mixed with provocative ingenuousness."[25] The text is illustrated with photos of girls from ages twelve to sixteen, some modeling underwear or partially dressed. Most of the so-called "nymphets" are photographed with conventional up-from-under sultry expressions of the type used in media representations of femininity to convey notions of availability and sexual readiness. Thirteen-year-old Angélica is shown with her top open to reveal part of a naked breast. Wearing lipstick and makeup, with her long blond hair hanging loosely to one side, she looks up at the camera with a mischievous smile.[26] These displays of the erotic qualities of young girls, published in mainstream, middle-class, family magazines such as *Manchete*, present the nymphet as an acceptable, and indeed desirable, model of femininity, endowing it, moreover, with prestige and status.

The Paquitas, who range from age thirteen to eighteen and are often referred to in the press as "Lolitas" or "nymphets," represent one of the most important ways in which the significance of Xuxa's image is extended into the culture and into the future.[27] According to one account, "the biggest dream of the majority of Brazilian girls between the ages of ten and fifteen is to become a Paquita."[28] (There is evidence that this is now the case all over Spanish-speaking America as well.) Xuxa is quoted in a publicity document: "All the little girls want to be Paquitas. Because they want to be near me, to help me. . . .

They're my continuation."[29] The Paquitas have tasks to perform on the "Xou": they help Xuxa by choosing children to participate in games, controlling the kids onstage, and handing the star notes to read during the program. But *Veja* contends that it would be "hypocrisy" to "attribute the success of the Paquitas solely to their ability to deal with children on television."[30] Instead, the magazine describes the Paquitas as the principal manifestation of the nymphet cult, "with their plump legs on display and their butts permanently turned to face the television audience."

Not surprisingly, Xuxa denies that there are any sexual connotations attached to the Paquitas. The issue was raised by Regina Rito in an interview published in the *Jornal do Brasil*:

> *Rito*: Xuxa, do your . . . Paquitas stimulate sexual precocity in your TV viewers? Have you thought about that?
>
> *Xuxa*: I think it's so ridiculous that someone would look at a Paquita with something else in mind. . . . If I were nearby and I thought that kind of situation were developing, I think I'd sock him. Above all, people have to realize the Paquitas are eleven, twelve years old. . . . If they're sensual, it's because they were born that way. Sexuality is in the heads of perverts. That's a sickness. Anybody who sees a Paquita and gets aroused in that way is a sex maniac.[31]

Xuxa exaggerates the youth of the Paquitas when she says they are eleven and twelve. At the time of the interview, September 1991, of the group of eight Paquitas, two were thirteen, one was fourteen, three were fifteen, one was sixteen, and one was eighteen. In any case, without the collaboration of the public, such a statement would be an invitation to ridicule.

The Paquitas, like the star in whose image they are made, are protected by the audience's desire to view femininity in the innocent-erotic configuration the young girls are groomed to represent. When it was learned that the original Paquita, Andréa Veiga, was to be featured as a *Playboy* magazine centerfold not long after quitting the "Xou," there was no noticeable public reaction; Xuxa's teen helpers are viewed as sex symbol apprentices, and highly valued ones at that.[32] Veiga declared in a recent interview, "There's nothing better than being a Paquita," and "Being a Paquita today means a girl's big chance to make her dreams come true."[33] The ex-Paquita also admitted that her nude posing was part of a "strategy to launch her acting career," and remarked that "after the *Playboy* photos, doors opened. I received various offers [for acting work] and things got easier."[34] Every page of the magazine spread entitled "Andréa Veiga: The Most Sensual Paquita from the 'Xou da Xuxa'" that carries text or a caption refers to her role as a Paquita, to Xuxa, or to childhood.[35]

The Paquitas' images are conveyed to the public through a variety of media texts, including the girls' "Xou" performances, their movie and live appearances, their LPs, coverage in the press, and even an MTV spot about them broadcast in 1991. These sources supply "all the little girls" who aspire to be Paquitas with the information they need about standards of beauty and conduct. Here, a child discovers that the eight most coveted jobs for girls in the country (now there are nine, but the last Paquita was hired only for appearances in Argentina and Spain) go to those who look like Xuxa. The first requirement, therefore, is to be white.

The promotion of a white aesthetic on the "Xou,"

as was noted earlier, is almost never challenged in the Brazilian media. In a random sample of forty feature articles and major interviews with Xuxa in Brazilian newspapers and magazines from 1982 to 1992, the question of racism was raised twice.[36] The issue has been insistently pursued, however, in the foreign press. James Brooke focused on racism in a 1990 article on Xuxa in the *New York Times*. He reported on the abundance of blondes in prominent modeling and television positions in Brazil, including Xuxa, the Paquitas, and Angélica, whose "promotional photographs invariably stress her enormous head of blond hair."[37] Brooke noted the irony in the fact that, on the occasion of a live performance in Salvador, Bahia, known as the capital of black Brazil, "ten children were hurt in a mad scramble to get closer to Xuxa."[38]

Tova Chapoval, in a Reuters article on Xuxa published in the United States, observed that "Brazilian children idolize the blond beauties they see on TV" and reported that Xuxa's manager Mattos "indignantly rejects criticism, noting that southern Brazil has many 'Aryan' types among its immigrants." Mattos asked the rhetorical question "Can Xuxa help it if she was born with blond hair and blue eyes?"[39] Jeb Blount raised the race issue in a feature article on Xuxa in the *Los Angeles Times*, quoting remarks by the star: "Some people say that I shouldn't do a show because I am blond. . . . But Brazil is a country of mixed races. You can be blond, brunette, mulatto; you can be anything."[40]

An account of one of the rare instances when Xuxa was questioned in Brazil about her all-white (and, for the most part, all-blond) cast was published in a newspaper in Brasilia in 1989. She was asked why none of the

Paquitas was black, and there is no mistaking the racist assumption in Xuxa's reply: "Oh! I've already explained; the tests [auditions for positions as Paquitas] are very difficult."[41] She continued, "I think blondes have more drive. Besides, we're all blond, but we're all Brazilian!" Probably in response to increasing attention from the foreign media, a more diplomatic strategy was developed for Xuxa to deal with the press on the issue of racism. Brooke's aforementioned article illustrates the later approach. He cites Xuxa who explained that her "all-blond cast responds to the 'children's choice' ": "Children like Snow White, Cinderella, Barbie. . . . When they see me close to them, it's as if the mythical person has become reality."

The issue of racism was raised again on a Spanish-language interview program, the "Show de Cristina," broadcast in the United States on the Univisión network on May 14, 1992. The awkwardness with which Xuxa and the four Paquitas present responded to host Cristina's question "Do you have to be blond to be a Paquita?" underlines their discomfort with the subject of racism. Xuxa first replied to the question by saying that the four Paquitas she had brought with her for the program were all blond, but others weren't. After prompting from one of the Paquitas, who said there used to be one nonblonde, and another Paquita who interrupted to say there used to be two, one of whom had black hair, Xuxa revised her original statement. The first Paquita, Xuxa explained, was not blond, nor was another girl named Tatiana, who was called Paquitita on the "Xou."

Both the girls Xuxa mentions are indisputably white and are *louras* (blondes) in the Brazilian use of the term. The first Paquita, Andréa Veiga, has undeniably blond hair in the shot of her in her Paquita outfit that *Playboy* published along with her twelve-page nude spread, in which her hair is a light brown. Tatiana Maranhão, nicknamed Paquitita, is listed as one of the group on the 1989 "Paquitas" LP, which displays photos of seven very blond girls on the jacket and on the lyrics sheet inside. The "Show de Cristina" exchange may have been the product of Xuxa's assumption that the Hispanic audience in the United States would expect white images of beauty and success to dominate television screens, as they do throughout the rest of Spanish-speaking America.[42]

Xuxa's program in Spanish, the "Show de Xuxa," is "incredibly popular" in the United States, according to the research director for one Univisión station that airs the show. A February 1992 analysis of Spanish-speaking households in the United States showed that "Xuxa commanded an 80 percent share of Latino viewers . . . between the ages of two and eleven."[43] According to the same source, all that is keeping Xuxa from "spreading her kisses to children throughout the United States is the English language." An account published in the *Jornal do Brasil* raised the issue of Xuxa's reception in the United States, pointing out that two organizations there had issued statements protesting the association of children with someone contaminated by involvement with soft pornography that included a child (a reference to Xuxa's role in the movie *Amor Estranho Amor*).[44] However, the discussion is more appropriately framed not in these narrow terms but as a serious consideration of the power of television images of gender and race to perpetuate conditions of inequality.

At the end of the exchange on the "Show de Cristina" about the requirements for being a Paquita, the girls agreed with the host that it was just "a coincidence" that they were all blondes. The four Paquitas also, however, admitted that in order to be selected for the group it is necessary to look like Xuxa. When asked why, one Paquita replied, "Because she's so pretty." Another explained, "Everyone wants to be like her." The Paquitas represent not only a specific norm of attractiveness but also the idea of generic female beauty. The cover photo for the Paquitas' 1991 LP reinforces the cloning effect: shot on a beach, the picture shows the eight Paquitas lined up shoulder to shoulder, each with a right leg forward as if they were marching in step toward the camera. The girls are all approximately the same height, they all wear their blond hair in the same style (long, with bangs), and they are dressed in thigh-length black T-shirts, identical except for a large white letter. Together the group spells out "Paquitas."

The girls are presented as a kind of chorus line, their individuality undercut by the word they spell, which names them only in the context of the group. Inside, on the lyrics sheet, each girl is identified by her Paquita name, rather than her real name, compounding the surrender of identity. They are shown in individual photos wearing the same T-shirts, underlining the idea that each Paquita is a letter, just as Xuxa is associated with a letter (X)—although the star's stands alone, while the sub-Xuxas' letters alone signify nothing.

The photo on the back of the 1991 album shows the Paquitas in the same lineup as on the front cover, but they are standing a few feet back, in the surf. The girls' mouths are open as they laughingly try to hold on to one another. The implications of this pose involve the idea of control over the body: to maintain that control is to keep the word and its privileged meaning intact. The *s* has been separated a little, pushed out of the line by a wave, leaving a text that can be read in the singular ("Paquita"), to create a new narrative of the girl alone (*separada* or *sozinha*, which means "alone"), or, to be alone with the girl. The story line is completed by a group of male surfers, masters of the waves, who float in the distance, just above the Paquitas' heads, waiting for a ride.

Through a variety of techniques the teenaged Paquitas are invoked as sub-Xuxas—derivative, but nonetheless providing crucial support for the narrative that defines the feminine ideal. The Paquitas are carefully groomed in the star's signature image of the child-woman. The girls' new identities as Paquitas are severely circumscribed by discipline, most of which is aimed at controlling the body. Xuxa's manager, Mattos, strictly monitors the girls' weight and eating habits in order to keep them ready for display in the identical outfits that highlight the thighs and buttocks. The first item on Mattos's list of the requirements for a Paquita is not having "excess fat." The requirements of maintaining good grades and choosing a profession for the post-Paquita future are added as perfunctory appendages. The girls function inside a strictly controlled sphere of preparation for the display roles they are hired to fulfill. One Paquita, Bianca Rinaldi, explained that after the auditions, "when they called my name, it was as if I disappeared from the world."[45]

Xuxa explains that her role is to keep an eye on the Paquitas' hair, diet, exercise, manicures, and clothes.[46] Xuxa is also reportedly the source of the stage names the girls are given when they join the group, almost all of which feature a trademark X—Pituxita, Catuxa, Xiquita, Pituxa, Paquitita, Miúxa, Catuxita, Xiquitita. Sometimes a new girl will replace another Paquita and adopt her name; thus Paquitita was Tatiana Maranhão in 1989 and Flávia Fernandes in 1991, and Xiquita was Andréa Faria in 1989 and Roberta Cipriani two years later. Maranhão and Faria were reportedly both suspended from the group for putting on excess weight. Such accounts attach to eating the aura of danger, and alert girls and women to the importance of control over the body, internalizing the mechanisms by which the beauty myth is enforced. Faria was reportedly caught eating ice cream after a performance in Belém, in violation of Mattos' dietary orders.[47] The choice, as Mattos put it, according to Faria, was between "being a Paquita or being Andréa."[48] Maranhão, age thirteen, was taken off the show for gaining weight and suffered an "attack of nerves" as a result. She confessed, "If it weren't for her [Mattos], we'd be nothing."[49] Mattos explains, "If a mother wants a fat, famous daughter, she'll have to go somewhere else."[50]

The rigidity with which weight standards are enforced for the Paquitas reflects the situation among first world, Western women, where, to use Wolf's expression, dieting has become "the essence of contemporary femininity."[51] There is a perverse premise in the girls' display of "hunger as good" on television screens watched by thousands of people for whom it is a daily struggle to eat in sufficient quantity and quality so as not to fall ill. The controlled bodies of the Paquitas, themselves acknowledged imitations of another controlled body, reproduce the connection between food and status that works at all levels of the social hierarchy, informing rich and poor women alike about their relative value in society.[52]

In the Paquitas' 1989 and 1991 LPs, released on the Xuxa Discos label, the group functions in its role as a surrogate delivery system for the star's image and its messages. The albums call attention to Xuxa at every turn, from the photographs of her lookalikes on the covers and on the lyrics sheets—which are designed to double as wall posters—to the songs, which incorporate words such as "Xou," "fada madrinha" (fairy godmother), "o bicho comeu" (the name of the clothing shops), and Xuxa's name itself. Xuxa is listed on the LP's credits; both albums prominently advertise the phone number for Xuxa Productions to hire the Paquitas for shows; and each black vinyl disc revolves around a center decorated with a white, signature X and the words "Xuxa Discos" over a rainbow-colored background.

Like Xuxa's own LPs, the Paquitas' discs are produced by Massadas and Sullivan, who also author some of the songs. The music and themes are similar to those found on Xuxa's records, except for the greater emphasis on teen love (one song is even titled "Amor Adolescente" [Teen Love]).[53] The Xuxacentrism is evident in such tunes as "Alegres Paquitas" (Happy Paquitas) and "Fada Madrinha (E Tão Bom)" (The Fairy Godmother [Is So Good]), which allude to Xuxa (the latter celebrates how "good" it is to be with Xuxa "on television").[54] Some songs simply invoke pleasant ideas such as "happiness," "energy," "feeling emotion," and "being together."[55]

A pseudo-rap tune from the second LP makes an appeal to the prestige of first world cultural models. MTV aired a video, shot on the set of the "Xou," of the Paquitas performing this song.[56] The lyrics integrate a merchandising device (repetition of the phrase, "o bicho comeu," for which Xuxa's clothing shops are named) into the format of the trendy genre. The Paquita narrator adopts an aggressive, challenging tone in asserting her right to participate in the funk and rap music cultures, and portrays herself giving a "war cry" of "freedom" with the "multitudes." The Paquita's improbable claims, her incongruous appropriation of rap as a form of self-expression, and the unlikelihood of a young, blond, middle-class girl attending one of Brazil's giant funk dances, which function as important outlets for the expression of black pride, did not escape the notice of the MTV commentator, who rolled his eyes incredulously when the clip was over and wearily announced, "Well, now we know these things happen."[57]

One of the Massadas and Sullivan tunes from the 1989 LP is about Andréa Faria, the Paquita who left the "Xou" in 1990. The song's name is Faria's other nickname on the show, "Sorvetão," which alludes to her taste for ice cream, the trait that led to disputes with Mattos over the Paquita's weight. Faria narrates some of the verses, while others describe her putting on and losing weight and give an inventory of her favorite foods. To make Faria's eating habits the theme of a song heard by girls all over Brazil validates the idea of diet as a problematic feature of femininity. The tune also reminds listeners of the child-woman, or "nymphet," ideal the Paquita is supposed to embody. Faria likes "dolls," but "melts" when she sees a "cute guy." At the end, the lyrics envision the Paquita as a "dream," an ideal "mixture" of a "child" and a "woman."

One of the most powerful current manifestations of the blond child-woman on Brazilian television is "half child, half woman" Angélica Ksyvickis, the most successful of the numerous imitations Xuxa has spawned.[58] Born in 1973, ten years after Xuxa, Angélica started modeling as a child and was invited to host her first television show at age thirteen. She replaced the older star on

Manchete's "Clube da Criança," and in 1988 also began hosting "Milk Shake," a variety program that showcases musical acts and is aimed at a teenaged and older audience.[59] An article on the "Clube" described Angélica as "sensual in her dress, makeup, and approach . . . one of the many children hired to seduce the 'baixinhos.' With body and soul."[60]

Sometimes referred to as a "Lolita" as well, Angélica is one of Brazil's exemplary nymphets.[61] The image she projects in the media relies heavily upon innocent-erotic suggestion. At thirteen, she posed with a partially exposed breast in an article on "The New Nymphets." At fourteen, she was described behaving like a little girl one moment, and the next, "displaying her figure, stretched out on a bed . . . the child canceled out by the seductive power of the woman." At fifteen, Angélica appeared on a magazine cover wearing a black bra under an open, transparent blouse.[62] These exhibitions of nymphetism were all published in *Manchete* magazine, a part of the corporate entity that employs Angélica. Other media texts from less compromised sources also confirm, and with very few exceptions, celebrate, the nymphet image. This evidence of the widespread willingness to exploit the appeal of the "Lolita" figure reflects the institutionalized network of compromise and complicity that defines the terms of femininity for the society at large.

Veja's photographs of Angélica in a 1989 article about her illustrate the child-woman image the then–sixteen year old projected.[63] The four-page piece shows Angélica in three photos. The first two are of identical size and are placed in the same position on consecutive pages. In the first shot, taken in her bedroom, Angélica is presented as a privileged, but normal, teenager. She is posed sitting on her bed, fully dressed, surrounded by the stuffed animal and ruffled pillow clichés of female adolescence. There is no erotic insinuation in the shot. The second photo, taken on the set of her television show "Milk Shake," shows Angélica wearing exaggerated makeup and performing in a black leather bra-and-pants outfit accessorized with boots, gloves, chains, and a riding crop. The presentation of the pictures in the prestigious medium of Brazil's leading news magazine has the effect of legitimizing the double identity evoked by the contrasting private and public images. The third, smaller photo reproduces the cover of Angélica's 1989 LP. She is shown lying on her stomach, looking up at the camera. One forearm is raised to prop up her head. The viewer looks down at Angélica, who is visible from the breasts up. Her torso emerges from a background of smoky, red light that is suggestive of a semantic field contrasting with that her "angelic" name implies. (A song on the album underscores this connection with a line labeling her a "little devil" with the "face of an angel.")[64] Angélica wears a low-cut top that reveals a bit of cleavage. One hand is lifting her long blond hair off her forehead. Wavy tendrils whose color is echoed in the only writing on the album cover—her name in gold script—drift down over her bare shoulders, arms, and bosom. The pose is reminiscent of the promotional photos of sex workers. The lifted hair, the direct look with slightly pouty lips, the low-cut top inviting the viewer to explore, and the loose tresses are clichés of erotic publicity photography. The red light recalls the familiar Western symbol advertising women as sexual commodities. The fact that Angélica's name is hard to read reinforces the suggestion of the anonymous, generic sex symbol. The attempt to attract the adult male gaze, which is typical of Xuxa's LPs, is reproduced here in the product of her leading imitator.[65]

A *Manchete* article from 1988 was illustrated with a picture of Angélica at the beach, posed on her knees in the sand.[66] Two boys carrying a surfboard (conspicuously displaying its brand label) walk by in the background. The caption announces, "This is soon to be an almost everyday sight," since Angélica had decided to move from São Paulo to Rio. Like the Paquitas album cover that features the girls at the beach, the photo of Angélica conveys the notion of availability. It seems to say, look for this item—Angélica, or a similar representation of the generic, ideal female—at your neighborhood beach, just as an advertisement directs the consumer to a particular commodity at the local grocery store or shopping mall.

According to the director of Angélica's two Manchete programs, "her 'vamp' side is exclusively a marketing device because she's still a child."[67] Angélica's success depends to a great degree on her ability to project the nymphet duality and thus represent a valuable commodity in the image marketplace. When the fifteen-year-old Angélica granted an interview to *Playboy* magazine, the event marked an important step in the construction of a narrative of profit by exploiting her sexuality. Although Angélica's fully clothed photograph accompanied the interview, the magazine's reputation invited another interpretation, which she encouraged with her remarks about receiving letters from "twenty-five, thirty, forty-year-old men, asking me to go out, to get engaged, even to marry." Angélica made other disingenuous comments about men "threatening to commit suicide" if she did not respond to their epistolary advances.[68] Angélica's narrative perpetuates Xuxa's representation of femininity, and the younger star's successful career shows just how handsomely the child-woman configuration can pay off.

While using various strategies to achieve a sexually provocative image, Xuxa's most successful imitator also carefully stresses the qualities of modesty, obedience, and compliance that are crucial to the representation of nonthreatening femininity. Angélica counterbalances the nymphet side of her person by projecting the image of an obedient daughter in a traditional family. *Manchete* magazine's not disinterested articles regularly remind readers of Angélica's family background. Her mother is described as "a typical, provincial woman [who] tries to maintain traditional customs."[69] Angélica's Polish father is the head of the family. He decides what his daughter eats, chaperones her everywhere in the "conviction that his daughter cannot be left alone," and in remarks comparing his two daughters, implicitly recommends the domestic lifestyle as the ideal for women: "[Angélica's older sister, Márcia] is also very talented, but she prefers to dedicate herself to being a housewife. Nothing could separate her from her child. I think she's correct. She lives only for her family. She made a successful publicity film, but all she cares about now is her home. This makes us very happy."[70] On the same page it is noted that Angélica "does not challenge her father." On the contrary, she "tries to maintain a traditional lifestyle and habits." "All that stuff about adolescent rebellion," she says, "just isn't for me."[71]

Angélica's announced intentions to go to the altar a virgin, widely publicized in television and gossip magazines as well as in the mainstream press, are another manifestation of the assertion of traditional femininity: "I'm a romantic, traditional, straight kind of person. I'm a virgin because I want to be. I made that choice. I look forward to getting married and going on a honeymoon with all that atmosphere."[72] These affirmations of traditional gender roles, significantly, link that ideology to the success myth the young star exemplifies. Angélica's demonstrations of willingness to submit to male authority, both as an obedient daughter and through the erotic figure of the nymphet, work to reconcile and reinforce the contradictory values and attitudes of the status quo with regard to femininity. The close control exercised over Angélica's image is analogous to the ideological view of control as the dominant approach to the female in society.

Angélica's narrative of femininity also affirms the primacy of looks in the valuation of women and girls. The idea that beauty establishes a competitive hierarchy is also present—for example, in Angélica's discovery myth, which features her twice winning the "Prettiest Girl in Brazil" beauty contest (in 1979 and 1980). Reinforcing the idea that a girl's physical appearance is the appropriate focus for a successful life, *Manchete* observes that, although Angélica is willing to discuss such topics as politics, AIDS, and the problem of drug abuse, she prefers to talk about fashion.[73] Angélica demonstrates the virtue of compliance when she apologetically explains that she refuses to accede to the many requests she receives to pose nude only because she is "embarrassed."[74] The idea of men's magazines pursuing children's television program hosts for nude photo spreads remains unchallenged. Angélica may also have found, in her refusal to pose nude, a useful tactic to distinguish herself from Xuxa. The same strategy is probably behind Angélica's assertions about her movie career. In a probable veiled reference to Xuxa's role in *Amor Estranho Amor*, Angélica explains her own approach to films: "For now, I'm only going to accept roles that correspond to my image. If the movie is appropriate for children, I'll do it."[75]

Angélica and her model, however, are vastly more alike than they are different. With regard to money, for example, both try to avoid the appearance of intruding in the masculine realm of business and finance by proclaiming ignorance of their own financial affairs. More than just the protective reflex of the wealthy, both Xuxa's and Angélica's disavowals represent public declarations of relinquishing control in a traditionally masculine sphere. When asked how much money she makes, Angélica told the *Folha de São Paulo*, "I don't know. My father takes care of all that."[76] *Manchete* reports that Angélica is "innocent [and] doesn't get involved with the commercial side of things."[77] Because she began her television career as a child, Angélica's narrative in some ways goes further than Xuxa's to depict the controlled, submissive female. Angélica's fifteenth birthday party, for example, included a waltz that she danced first with her father, and then with a representative of her employer, in a formal display of allegiance.[78] The accounts of the birthday party idealized a hierarchical configuration by their recognition of Angélica's public celebration of tradition. In a symbolic act of solidarity, fifteen girls dressed in "rigorously identical" gowns attended the fifteen-year-old Angélica.

Some of the guests at Angélica's birthday party bleached their hair for the occasion, turning themselves into blondes, "to imitate the guest of honor."[79] Angélica's reiteration of the blond norm of attractiveness that Xuxa so forcefully promotes is another significant feature of the younger star's appeal. For *Manchete* readers, Angélica is "the girl with hair dipped in gold and skin as white as snow."[80] Elsewhere, she is a "broad smile, a perfect body, blonde with blue-green eyes, not just an angel, but a goddess now."[81]

In these and many other cases, blondness, the projected ideal of beauty, is attached to the notion of happiness and success. Angélica's helpers, the Angélicos and the Angeliquetes, are not all blond, but it is hard to find a trace of Africa in their features. Of Brazil's television hosts of major children's programs in the decade beginning with Xuxa's first show on Manchete—including, besides Xuxa, Lucinha Lins, Angélica, Mariane, and Mara Maravilha—all are white, and all but Maravilha are blond.[82] When ex-Paquita Andréa Veiga began hosting a show, she was described as "one more little blonde . . . coming out of the Xuxa mold."[83] In another article, becoming a Paquita—the dream of "all young girls"—is equated with joining a "blond paradise."[84]

Brazilian television is a stage on which the virtues of being white, and the invisibility or misfortune of blackness, are dramatized. Racism on television is denounced in the media, as, for example, when *Veja* magazine reported in 1992 that black youngsters are deliberately barred from participating on the children's program "Dó-Ré-Mi com Vovó Mafalda" on the SBT network, whose owner was fielded as a presidential candidate in 1989.[85] Instances of discrimination that come to the public's attention, however, are more often treated as transgressions in Brazil's mythical racial democracy than as opportunities for change.

Another *Veja* article from the same period discusses racist stereotypes of women on Brazil's famous prime-time soap operas. The magazine cites anthropologist Maria Andréa Loyola, who says: "We find in the soap operas many different types of white females: single women, mothers with families, good, bad, rich, poor, businesswomen, housewives. . . . But among brown and black women, the types are very limited. They are maids, prostitutes, factory workers—and they can only improve their status through marriage, by exploiting their physical attributes, or by becoming entertainers."[86]

The promotion of the white ideal on Xuxa's program and through her surrogates and imitators is consistent with the general pattern on Brazilian television, which the soap operas exemplify with their racist casting policies. Race operates as a hierarchy within the already restricted sphere assigned to women. As filmmaker Arnaldo Jabor points out, television reinforces an old picture: "Television imprints the concept immortalized by the Portuguese colonizer: white women are for marrying, mulattas are for bed, and blacks are only good for putting to work. . . . Blondes [as distinguished from dark-haired whites] are untouchable since they're imports."[87]

Muniz Sodré also makes the connection between television, sex roles, and race: "On TV, the signs are very clear. Dark-skinned women have sex, white ones have love. Dark women are defined from the belly button down, and white ones from the belly button up."[88] The emergence in the soaps of actress Sonia Braga, who is sometimes said to legitimize a less pale ideal of beauty, is little more than "the exaltation of a dark type that men desire for their own entertainment."[89] The "tyranny" of the blonde is nothing new, but the potential for dissemination, naturalization, and perpetuation of the white aesthetic has multiplied with the growth of the media in Brazil.[90] Television means that "children may have blondes and only blondes as models of beauty and perfection."[91]

Jabor interprets Xuxa's projection of the white ideal as a bizarre episode in Brazilian culture: "Xuxa emerged from the lap of a black man into the world of the media. And a strange birth it was for Pelé to perform. A "pure" blonde, practically an actress in a Nazi film . . . emerging from the bed of the "black-god" . . . [Xuxa] proceeded to build an empire of blonde purity, a Third Reich of eunuch 'baixinhos.' "[92]

Although Xuxa prompts Jabor to invoke Nazi notions of racial purity, Gilberto Gil, one of Brazil's leading black recording artists, was moved to compose an homage to her for his 1992 release.[93] "Neve na Bahia" (Snow in Bahia) uses a series of metaphors to construct a portrait of Xuxa as a figure of mystery, a *bruxa* (witch) who arouses the narrator, stirring up a "hurricane" in his "sea." The subject is associated with the question of color through a series of contrasting pairs of descriptive terms ("moor"/"blonde," "Bahia"/"snow," "Sudanese"/"German"). Another set of pairs associates Xuxa with other opposite or dissimilar elements ("fire"/"water," "sweet"/"sour," "naive"/"astute").

The strategy of enumerating contrasting ideas and qualities renders a semantic field characterized by separation and difference. The lyrics reflect the way Xuxa's image constitutes a fabricated weave, a texture of disparate elements that the star's alchemy, or, in Gil's composition, her "alchemist's gold," transforms into the pleasure of consumption. Here, the narrator, his appetite aroused, literally consumes the object of his desire by taking a bite out of her cheek, which is like an apple in its "eternal obviousness." The urge to consume the body of the other evokes the figure of eros.

In the many incidental references to Xuxa that form part of her narrative, she is associated primarily with the erotic. In a random sampling of over thirty media texts that make stray references to Xuxa, the sex symbol role emerges by far the most often: an X-rated comic book incorporates a Xuxa character; *Playboy* runs photo essays on Xuxa's sister-in-law, her cousin, and a lookalike, prominently featuring their connections to the star; a brief clip asks whether soul singer Tim Maia would pay a million dollars to sleep with Xuxa.[94] The star's celebrity status surfaces as the second-most frequent association (as, for example, she is compared with Madonna or M. C. Hammer).[95] In third and fourth place are allusions to her logos (including appropriations of Xuxaspell and the trademark kiss), and finally, in last place, are references to "baixinhos."[96]

Xuxa has been handsomely paid for her services, and the income of her number one clone Angélica, from television and live performances, movies, records, dolls, comic books, cosmetics, and other products, is further proof of the reward potential of the display of conventional femininity, of the white aesthetic, and of a television version of culture as a kind of modernity without memory.[97] On the Xuxa and Angélica programs, the past is measured in television season increments, and progress is ticked off by the introduction of a new LP or doll, a new game segment or fashion statement. The formula is so mindless and so profitable that it is difficult to ignore and even harder to abandon. Angélica tells one interviewer, "Me give up television? Never!"[98] The president of Mexico's influential Televisa network tells Xuxa, "If you change the program, I'll kill you." [99] Xuxa's television formula for fun and profits is perpetuated by figures such as Angélica, who, like her model, "dreams of a career abroad," and, to that end, has reportedly been studying Spanish and English.[100] Xuxa expressed her own plans for the future in her April 1992 *Los Angeles Times* interview: "I've been a success in the third world, and now I want to get to know the first world." [101]

The possibility of Xuxa and Angélica expanding their domains throughout the Americas, Europe, and beyond (already more than just a possibility in Xuxa's case) brings to mind legions of generic female clones—all, necessarily, young. One of the central features of Xuxa's authoritative representation of ideal femininity is the primacy of youthfulness. The cult of youth is a consequence of viewing beauty as conformity to an ideal and of overvaluing looks in general. The youth cult is also an instrument of control, to attenuate the power implied by the experience and knowledge that come with age. Xuxa and Angélica repeatedly voice the internalized lessons of the beauty myth with regard to aging. The younger star expressed her feelings: "I don't want to grow up, and I don't want to get old." [102] Xuxa told an interviewer, "If I could be an eternal Peter Pan, I would." [103] In another interview, with Márcia Pereira, the connection between beauty, aging, and value is clear:

Pereira: Are you afraid of getting old?
Xuxa: Yes. I'm terrified . . .
Pereira: Why?
Xuxa: Because nobody forgives an idol for aging. Look at Brigitte Bardot . . . even I catch myself saying: "Goodness,

she used to be so beautiful!" I know they're going to say the same thing about me.

Pereira: Do you plan on having plastic surgery in order to stay young?

Xuxa: Absolutely. "Tio" Pitanguy [Brazil's most celebrated cosmetic surgeon] is going to be seeing me regularly in his clinic.[104]

The sense of being trapped conveyed by these comments is echoed in Muniz Sodré and Francisco Antonio Doria's analysis of Xuxa as a Snow White surrounded by her "baixinho"-dwarfs. They are imprisoned together in the glass coffin that is the television set. The authors argue that

> what Snow Xuxa really suggests is a kind of sensuality, the sensuality of visuality, of the narcissistic personality. A being in a world without time: Xuxa is always young and beautiful, and the children who surround her on the television screen are always the same age. Here, sensuality is the privilege of those who live outside time, beyond the flow of things. In this paradigm, the passing of time, . . . birth and decadence, are not permitted. It is the simulation of the atemporal; the suggestion that sensuality is the privilege of young women, permanently young, incorruptibly young, machines far beyond the satisfaction of desire. . . .
>
> The Snow White of the Brothers Grimm still belongs to Freud or his theory. Snow Xuxa and her television clones belong to a plasticized, pasteurized realm. They are prostheses for beyond desire.[105]

In the timeless sphere that the current and future "fairy godmothers" and "queens of the 'baixinhos'" occupy, history has no place. The television formula Xuxa's "Xou" represents is designed to repeat itself endlessly: it stands for culture on a loop, and the appeal of such timelessness is strong. The formula masks choices and alternatives by providing a paralyzing kind of pleasure that gathers the family around the coffin of culture to view a parody of progress and an imitation of modernity. The figures that move about on the screen are dolls in the house of children's television. In Gil's "Neve na Bahia," Xuxa is "disguised as a doll," and in one of Angélica's songs, she assumes "the form of a doll." [106] The children's television dollhouse is a place of consumption that mirrors another kind of house of dolls, the brothel. In neither case do the inhabitants age well. Xuxa is continually replaced by her clones, while her own image remains the same, indelibly inscribed in the national imagination: "more real than reality," as one observer put it.[107]

In the last decade of the twentieth century, Xuxa has become a consecrated icon of Brazilian culture. If all the television sets in Brazil vanished tomorrow, her image would remain a staple for generations to come. Not to know who Xuxa is signifies the most desolate form of marginalization. Amaro João da Silva is one of the very few Brazilians who do not recognize Xuxa's name. He was singled out for an interview by *Veja* because of his extreme ignorance and tiny stature. One of a destitute population in the Northeast who are stunted by a process of slow starvation (one observer describes the region as "a veritable concentration camp for more than thirty million people"), Silva is a Brazilian-made mutant in more ways than one.[108] At the other end of the spectrum is the twenty-four-year-old official dwarf of the "Xou," who lies still on the stage while the Paquitas dance around him in a circle, each resting a foot on his child-sized body.[109] The Paquitas, dwarfed, in turn, by the star herself, kneel and bow their heads on a darkened stage, genuflecting before the spaceship from which a goddess is about to emerge. The star's mastery of the media has produced a dream of phenomenal promise. The myths of beauty, racial democracy, modernity, progress, and success join to create the myth of Xuxa. In one sense she stands at the door to an inaccessible room, extending an invitation to join in a profoundly alienating experience. In another way, Xuxa brings all Brazilians together in an enormously attractive, virtually irresistible dream of eternal youth and beauty, of unending joy, of riches beyond measure.

FIVE

KIDS AND KIDNAPPERS

THE LEAD STORY ON THE evening news in Brazil on Wednesday, August 7, 1991, was that Xuxa and one of her look-alikes, seventeen-year-old Paquita Letícia Spiller, had apparently been the targets of a bizarre kidnapping attempt. Two young men had bought a car, customized it for battle, and allegedly tried to snatch the two women from the TV Globo studio where the "Xou da Xuxa" was being taped. Although kidnapping was so common at the time that a new case might not even have made the top of the newscast, this particular plot took on special meaning as a compelling symbol of social disintegration. The episode became emblematic of a national mood of cynicism and distrust about the future. The events also triggered what one article called Xuxa's "existential crisis."[1] For a brief period, the star's mask slipped, and it was possible to catch a glimpse of a real person who, for the first time, publicly expressed anger and unhappiness in the face of the country's increasing violence and uncertainty.

Xuxa's breakdown (one editorial observed that she was "subverting her own script") meant a breach of the consensus that endows her image with its authority.[2] The star's own questioning of her ability or willingness to sustain the euphoric illusion of Brazil she projects on television threatened to expose the contradictions inherent in the values and attitudes her image embodies. The sudden and striking glimpse of the distance between the symbolic and the real fulfillment of needs undermined the foundations of Xuxa's mass appeal by casting doubt on the principles to which her followers subscribe—the supremacy of consumerism as the defining characteristic of modernity, and the adequacy of the dominant ideology for promoting access to the modern Brazil thus postulated. The cracks in the star's image prompted one journalist to observe that "it was as if there were two Xuxas: a happy one who does the television program, and a sad one watching it."[3] Another reporter suggested that the episode "sharpened the contradiction," for someone like Xuxa, who was "making a living off happiness in a country going through sad times."[4] Xuxa herself "sobbed," in one interview, and complained, "I'm not a character. The country's situation affects me like anybody else, and I ask myself: I should have hope? Hope for what?"[5]

The circumstances of the alleged kidnapping were dramatic. It was a Wednesday afternoon, and Xuxa was inside the Fenix Theater, TV Globo's studio in the upscale Botanical Gardens neighborhood of Rio de Janeiro. The star had arrived, as usual, around one o'clock and would be there until about midnight, taping three shows to go on the air the following week. A group of approximately a hundred children and adults were waiting outside on the sidewalk. They would be guests on the day's first taping of the "Xou." At a little after one o'clock, a yellow Chevette with São Paulo license plates pulled up and parked about fifty meters from the entrance to the Fenix on Lineu de Paula Machado Street. Nearby is one of the guard boxes that are scattered around Rio's wealthier neighborhoods to inhibit crime. These are staffed by members of the military police, the most visible of Brazil's police forces. In the guard box was Officer Alves. He may have been suspicious of the Chevette and its two occupants. At any rate, he observed that the car had stopped in a no-parking zone. Alves walked over to the Chevette to explain that the car would have to be moved. The occupant in the front passenger seat raised a .38-caliber revolver and shot Alves. A second member of the military police, Officer Aílton, went to aid Alves. Aílton was shot and died on the spot. The Chevette took off, followed by an armored vehicle that happened to be in the neighborhood performing a routine delivery.[6]

The Fenix security guards escorted the people waiting in line into the Fenix Theater and rushed to the aid of the fallen police officers. Meanwhile, four men in the armored vehicle exchanged shots with one of the occupants of the Chevette. The gunfire and the high-speed chase continued for about ten minutes through the Botanical Gardens as the two vehicles were joined by others of the military police. Pedestrians in the crowded neighborhood scattered as motorists drove their cars up onto the sidewalk in an effort to get out of the path of the bullets and clear the road. The armored vehicle managed to bump the rear end of the Chevette several times, but the chase did not end until the car turned into a one-way street, headed the wrong way, and collided with a Fiat Oggi.

Unaccountably, the fate of the driver of the Fiat was not reported in the newspapers. The driver of the Chevette, Douglas Loricchio, eighteen years old, was shot in the head and, depending on the news source, died immediately following the collision or soon after arriving at the hospital. His brother, Alberto, twenty-one or twenty-three years old, depending on the news report, had a bullet in the left leg and cuts in the neck and thorax. By some accounts, his wrists were also cut when he was thrown through the windshield upon impact with the Fiat. Rio's most prestigious newspaper, the *Jornal do Brasil*, reported on August 9 that Alberto arrived at the Miguel Couto hospital with deep cuts in his wrists. On the same page, the paper stated that the director of the hospital had denied the rumor that Alberto had tried to commit suicide and maintained that the patient had "not suffered any type of lesion on his wrists."

From the beginning, there was a certain amount of confusion in the reporting of the case. Questions arose immediately—whether Alberto tried to commit suicide, what Alberto said on the way to the hospital, whether he could talk at all with his throat wounds. Even today, serious doubts linger about the conduct of investigators in the case. There are suspicions that evidence was tampered with or suppressed and that various cover-ups occurred, including one involving a witness silenced by murder committed by, or with the complicity of, the police. The strong element of backstage intrigue may have been inevitable since the case involved Xuxa, although even her involvement is only supposition, resting primarily on the fragile evidence of one brief exchange between a police officer and a wounded suspect.

On the way to the hospital, Alberto Loricchio is

said to have made a statement to Lieutenant Oliveira of the second Battalion of Military Police in Botafogo, a neighborhood bordering the Botanical Gardens to the east. Officer Oliveira reported that Alberto said he "was going to take Letícia and 'Ruça' to São Paulo because he's in love with them."[7] Later news articles have Oliveira describing Alberto's statement as follows: "We're going to grab the two of them. I love Letícia and I'm going to take 'Ruça.' Both of them are being sexually exploited."[8] "Ruça" (pronounced WHO-suh) was immediately assumed to mean "Xuxa." According to one news article, "Ruça" is a nickname for Xuxa used backstage on the set of the show.[9] It was not hard to imagine, as well, that "Ruça" may have been the closest a man in shock, and with injuries to his throat, could come to saying "Xuxa."

Immediately, the media began moving to defend the star's violated image by transforming the Loricchio brothers into something more than just villains. *Veja* announced that what the Loricchios had done was the kind of "crazy thing that Brazilians thought only happened in developed countries."[10] The magazine tried to establish a view of the brothers as psycho killers, a breed often depicted in Brazil as unique to the United States. The brothers were portrayed in the media as different from typical Brazilian kidnappers, who tend to have criminal records and be connected to police corruption or to one or another of the big gangs that traffic in drugs and weapons.

Some of the sensitivity over the Loricchios derived from the fact that certain features of their own story seemed to connect in significant ways with the apparent targets of their alleged plot. For instance, it appeared that the Loricchios may have been influenced by television to commit the crime. The press reported the television connection, but avoided exploring its uncomfortable implications, especially as they might pertain to Xuxa, to Brazil, and to Brazilian television. But there was indeed evidence that the Loricchio brothers had turned bad because they had been watching too much television. In fact, their neighbors said that was what Douglas and Alberto spent most of their time doing. Moreover, when the brothers went to Rio on August 4, 1991, presumably to commit the crime, they may have been enacting a television-inspired fantasy.

One of the Loricchios registered at an inexpensive hotel in Leme, a beachfront neighborhood next to Copacabana, under the name Humberto Lococco. Roger Lococco is the name of a character in the TV series "Mafia Man," shown Saturday afternoons on Globo, the network that carries Xuxa's show as well. In one episode of "Mafia Man," Lococco's mission is to infiltrate the criminal organization and kill one of its members. For that purpose, he rigs a car with machine guns and grenade launchers built into the chassis. The Loricchio brothers, too, had remodeled their vehicle. They moved the gas tank to the middle of the trunk and encased it in a thick wooden box. Under the rear bumper, on the left side of the car, the brothers installed four iron pipes thirty-two inches long. These were designed to direct the aim of four shotguns. Two more pipes for shotguns were placed under the hood and hidden by the front grille. Under the glove compartment, the brothers installed a panel with six buttons. Each button was attached to four 1.5-volt batteries and controlled one of the shotguns. The brothers also prepared holsters to hold homemade bombs. The bombs would explode when a switch worn on the left shoulder was flipped.

The director of the Carlos Eboli Criminalistics Institute, examining the Chevette later, would say it was like something out of a James Bond movie.[11] The press would refer to it as a "Batmobile."[12] These references to Hollywood and U.S. television kept the Loricchios at a distance, reinforcing the view that what they had done was something alien and un-Brazilian. The whole story was made to seem like a warped Hollywood production. The media protected Xuxa's image by establishing the Loricchios' story in the parlance of formulaic crime drama, a familiar but non-native genre. As if to underscore the conventions of the genre for a slow-witted audience, the police produced a map of Rio they had reportedly found in the Chevette. The direction of several one-way streets was marked by hand, and a circle had been drawn around the Fenix Theater.

Another Brazilian sensitivity registered in the coverage of the kidnapping episode concerned Alberto's alleged comment that Xuxa and Letícia were being "sexually exploited." The press was scrupulous in avoiding one particular interpretation of the remark—namely, as a straightforward observation, an honest assessment of the way sexuality is used on Xuxa's television program. No one doubts that the sexual posturing and innuendo by Xuxa and the Paquitas constitute one of the principal reasons for the show's success. It is no secret that Xuxa's popularity among "her" children, the "baixinhos," is matched by the interest she inspires among the "*altinhos*" (adult men), who openly enjoy her flirtatious style, her enticing apparel, and her frankly suggestive signature bestowing of kisses. Likewise, no one is unaware that the Paquitas are selected for their physical attractions and dressed to display them. If Alberto's alleged remark is read as an authentic insight about Xuxa's show, however, it signifies an unmasking of, and thus a challenge to, one aspect of the star's representation of femininity, an essential ingredient of the star alchemy. As the kidnapping episode developed, it took on increasing importance precisely because it revealed such vulnerabilities beyond those involving Xuxa's physical security. The authority of Xuxa's image was undermined by the mere suggestion of raising questions about something as sacred as the erotic content of the "Xou."

The Loricchio brothers episode threatened to expose a number of nerves in Brazilian society. Besides raising the possibility that the "Xou" was sexually exploitive, the idea that "television is bad for you" surfaced, suggesting, in turn, that maybe Xuxa as a television phenomenon was unhealthy. The suspects' twenty-seven-year-old brother, Domingos Loricchio Filho (Junior), may have been referring to this idea when, in defense of his family, he declared, "There wasn't any cult, and nobody was going around worshiping idols, not at our house."[13] The media's coverage of the Loricchios continued to betray a predisposition to avoid tarnishing the star's image. A newspaper account of the burial of Douglas, who died in or immediately following the car crash, illustrates one way the media isolated the Loricchios. The press made an outcast of the brother, who was buried in Rio by his older brother, Domingos Junior, at eleven o'clock on the morning of August 9. According to the *Jornal do Brasil,* Domingos Junior was alone in the cemetery viewing chapel, except for a few people who dropped in out of curiosity to see "the man who was going to snatch Xuxa" and twenty-one journalists who the elder brother wished would leave him alone. After a few minutes, Domingos Junior told a cemetery employee, "Let's get this over with." As the pushcart carrying the coffin reached drawer number 247, reporters observed, Domingos Junior began to show signs of distress. They attributed his emotion to the absence of friends and family, and to the conditions at that end of the cemetery, which was described as "full of cockroaches and mosquitoes and giving off an unbearable stench."[14] The description dramatizes the burial as an act of extirpation, the banishing of a wayward son to a place fittingly dirty and diseased. There is a whiff of sulfur, too, in the journalist's sketch of the end of the cemetery, as if to demonize the pariah, and allow the Xuxa versus Douglas configuration to surface as a paradigm of good against evil. Xuxa herself later contributed to this impression by calling the brothers "monsters."[15]

Not surprisingly, Domingos Junior accused the press of exploiting events to promote sales. Along with Ely Bittencourt, who had been appointed to run the investigation, Domingos Junior insisted that reports of a kidnapping attempt were still only speculation. Bittencourt considered the weaponry equally consistent with a plan to commit armed robbery.[16] There were also leads suggesting that someone else may have been involved in the crime. The police were trying to identify the occupants of another car, a white Voyage, which witnesses saw waiting near the Fenix Theater to cover the Loricchios' escape.[17] There were reports about a *flanelinha*, one of the many poor Brazilians who make a living watching people's cars, who was working in the area when the incident occurred. He is said to have testified that a gray Voyage with two men in it provided cover for the Loricchios.[18]

But the media focus remained on the brothers. Reporters began calling on experts and amateurs alike to analyze the presumed personality disorders of the Loricchios in the ongoing attempt to place them outside the sphere of coherent social discourse. One child psychiatrist called the brothers "extremely violent," possibly with a "mother fixation," but not schizophrenic.[19] Forensic psychiatrist Guido Palomba did diagnose schizophrenia and suggested that Alberto may have had "erotic-maniacal deliriums" and been "psychologically enslaved by passion."[20] Even Bittencourt called the brothers psychopaths. He compared their behavior to that of John Hinckley, Jr., noting that Hinckley had tried to kill Ronald Reagan in order to impress actress Jodie Foster, and wondered aloud, "I'll be interested to know if they [Douglas and Alberto] had a similar obsession with Xuxa."[21] One report suggested that "the sensual appeal of the Paquita Letícia led the two boys to plan the kidnapping," the goal of which was simply "sex." As if to compensate for the more prosaic explanation, however, this account labeled the brothers' supposed plot a plan to carry out "the crime of the century."[22]

The casting out of the Loricchios was completed with the silencing of the surviving brother, Alberto. Domingos Junior explained that he had visited Alberto in the hospital two days after the alleged crime took place. The older brother described Alberto's reaction when told that there was talk about a kidnapping. The suspect, who still couldn't speak, had used gestures to deny the accusation vehemently. The father, Domingos Senior, also defied the dominant narrative. He said he had seen the Chevette the Sunday before the crime and the car had seemed normal to him. He said only an idiot would try to grab Xuxa, who had an "army" to protect her, and his sons weren't stupid. He added that he considered the weapons found in the car only "toys." Domingos Senior also insisted that a doctor with the Institute of Legal Medicine had assured him that Alberto couldn't have confessed to attempted kidnap in the ambulance on the way to the hospital because his son's injuries had rendered him incapable of speaking.[23]

The public was naturally anxious to hear what Alberto had to say. He had been moved early in the morning on Friday, August 9, from the Miguel Couto Municipal Hospital in Leblon, a beach neighborhood, to the hospital in the Frei Caneca prison complex in Estácio, near downtown Rio.[24] His condition was said to be improving. Domingos Junior was assured that his brother would be sufficiently recovered to be released from the hospital within a few days. The plan was for Alberto to give a deposition, in writing, on the morning of August 12. But Alberto never got to tell his story. On the day the deposition was to take place, the press was informed that he had suffered cardiac arrest and died at 4:30 A.M.

Domingos Junior, along with many Brazilians, thought he smelled a rat. "I'm convinced something's going on here," he told the press. "My brother had a lot of important things to say about what happened."[25] After burying his second son, Alberto's father called the case "nebulous."[26] Before the month was out, the investigation had dropped from view. One final burst of attention came on August 21 when the Secretary of Justice of the city of Rio de Janeiro and vice-governor of the state of Rio de Janeiro, Nilo Batista, took Ely Bittencourt off the case for "failing to inform his superiors immediately of the gravity of the situation."[27] Batista gave a statement to the press: "This whole thing is very serious. It strikes me there's a lot more behind what's been learned and made public so far. We intend to continue to pay the utmost attention to this investigation."[28]

The story of the crime, nevertheless, faded as quickly from view as the Loricchios had from their brief moment in the spotlight. The brothers had been reduced to social outcasts, one given an unholy burial in the press, and the other buried by a press that was unable or unwilling to pursue a case that could end up inscribed in the tradition of the *queima de arquivo*, the burning of the archive, by which witnesses are eliminated and information mysteriously goes missing. Alberto's untimely death was convenient in that it eliminated the possibility of his turning out to be a sympathetic character. Had he come to be seen as a victim, deserving of pity or protection, he might have cast some doubt on the crime narrative as it had played so far, and thus opened the incident to a more disturbing and complex reading. Denounced and divorced from the social body, the Loricchios were no longer a threat. The first phase of the kidnapping episode had been transformed by the media into a story that bloomed in the imagination like a fairy tale, calling forth simple and satisfying emotions: the desire to protect good and to punish evil.[29]

When Alberto died and the Loricchios' story flickered off the screen, full attention turned toward Xuxa. That the second phase of the kidnapping episode left her exposed to a certain amount of criticism and even, at times, to ridicule, is indicative of the symbolic value attached to the star. The threat to Xuxa was viewed as a threat to Brazil, a serious blow to the way Brazilians regarded themselves and their collective future. When Xuxa talked about moving to Argentina, where she was already spending half of every week taping her show in Buenos Aires for broadcasts on Spanish-speaking networks in Latin America and the United States, some viewed it as a kind of betrayal. What was really betrayed, though, was not Brazil, but the idea of Brazil that Xuxa projects and is expected to protect. That idea was undermined suddenly by a heretofore silent person who emerged from behind the star mask.

Xuxa let off steam in an interview with *Manchete* magazine in which she said, among other things, that "most people don't have any respect" for her. She complained that "in Brazil, being blond means you're either dumb or a prostitute." She went on to say,

> I've worked hard to get where I am today. People are saying I only became aware of the situation in Brazil now that I have thirty-five thousand dollars in my bank account. I've got a lot more than thirty-five thousand. The newspaper *O Globo*, which belongs to the network where I work, thought it was too much of a coincidence that I started talking about quitting the show just when it was time to renew my contract. They seem to think I need their money. I don't even know how much money I make there.[30]

Xuxa's composure broke down in anger at Globo, at people she felt were not treating her as a professional, at her father whom she accused of betraying her mother, and at others who charged the star with "eroticizing" children (to which she responded on one occasion that Wonderwoman wears a low-cut blouse and has bigger breasts, and no one criticizes *her*). When asked if she was in love, Xuxa answered testily: "Does it look like it? I've given up looking for my Prince Charming. I just want a man who respects me and treats me kindly. I'm even telling people they can start calling me *'tia.'*" Meaning "aunt" or "auntie," *tia* is a term children are encouraged to use to address adult family friends, and one that Xuxa has resisted because it has connotations that are at odds with her innocent-erotic, child-woman image. The alleged kidnapping attempt seemed to trigger various concerns, not the least of which was the fact that Xuxa was twenty-eight and, as she put it, "terrified of getting old."[31] The child-woman balance that draws audiences so effectively, through the identification of innocence with sexual maturity, might be hard to maintain after thirty, or forty, or fifty.

Xuxa's complaints threatened to disclose the structure of the narrative itself and reveal its devices, in particular the appeal to the male gaze through a demeaning representation of femininity. The star came close to naming the image she seeks to project when she described the dumb blonde taken for a prostitute. Xuxa did not remain exposed for long, however. Various strategies were quickly instituted to reconstitute the sign. One was an attempt to frame the critical discourse unleashed by the kidnapping episode and Xuxa's outbursts as a pro- or anti-Xuxa debate. The aim was to divert attention from challenging questions of a more systematic nature by directing the discussion instead toward the personal and anecdotal.

One of the ways Xuxa tried to assert control over the crisis was by crying a lot. She began shedding tears regularly on her show, during live performances, and in interviews with the press, in order to personalize and "feminize" the situation and show that it was her crisis, not Brazil's. Xuxa told one interviewer that she had stopped singing in the shower as a result of the kidnapping attempt. She said she was also having trouble sleeping, and confessed to calling fans at three o'clock in the morning to "drink love" on the telephone.[32] One of Xuxa's widely reported comments seemed to have considerable resonance among Brazilians. She said that she felt like the "court fool," singing and dancing and trying to make people happy while the country fell apart. Her costume on the September 25 show appeared to be a deliberate attempt to draw attention to the remark: her blouse was trimmed with a low, round collar from which different-colored spikes with balls on the ends dangled in jesterlike fashion. The sartorial note was a reminder to the public of the role the star plays as an agent of transcendence, sustaining the illusion of a fun, glamorous, happy Brazil. Xuxa emphasized the alchemic qualities of her performance again when she insisted that ransom and rescue be avoided if she were ever kidnapped, because she would have lost that "shine in her eye."[33]

Xuxa's tearful phase was recorded by *Manchete* magazine, which published one of the more striking photos of Xuxa taken during that time, a melodramatic, somewhat campy portrait of a weeping "Queen of the 'Baixinhos.' "[34] The full-color shot, filling two pages, shows Xuxa bathed in red stage lights, dressed in an elaborate black-and-gold costume for a live performance. The camera looks up at the star, whose eyes are closed and whose crowned head is bowed in sorrow. Her lips are pressed together, her chin is wrinkled with emotion, and tear tracks glisten on her cheeks. The viewer's upward gaze, and Xuxa's tear-blinded eyes facing down, seem to build an allegorical dimension, suggesting hopes raised only to be dashed, or hearts lifted and burdens too great. Xuxa's face emerges human and pure from the artifice that surrounds her. The image conveyed is a kind of martyrdom. She seems to be held captive under the red light of violence, and in the black and gold of dread and greed.

The *Manchete* article includes three other, smaller photos as well. Together with the big one, the series adds up to what can only be read as a set of carefully manipulated images intended for the star's promotion. Shot at a live show in São Paulo, the photos place Xuxa in the center of four different situations designed to elicit the maximum emotive response from viewers. The four pictures compose a narrative that illustrates, in addition to the crisis alluded to in the first photo, the standard elements used in manufacturing the star's image. Here, these are exploited as a means of reasserting the authority and integrity of the sign.

The first photo, already described, is designed to elicit the viewer's sympathy, with its presentation of an iconic Xuxa, grieving, vulnerable, and alone. In the second photo, the star is wearing the same black-and-gold costume, but more of it is shown, so that her representation of the sexually provocative ingredient of ideal femininity is underscored. The camera angle, again from below, highlights Xuxa's thighs, which emerge from the tops of her trademark above-the-knee boots, to which are attached black garter belts with gold buckles. The photograph guides the eye up the leg, to peek under a conspicuously brief skirt at Xuxa's undershorts before jumping up to the secondary focus of the shot. Here, Xuxa is turned to the side, planting a kiss on the cheek of her weeping mother. Each has an arm around the other. The mother is dressed in informal (but first-world chic) blue jeans and a black top with a pink Xuxa logo on the front. Xuxa holds a microphone, while her mother uses her free hand to wipe away tears. The photo is an appeal to sentimentality, a celebration of female emotion, eroticized to invite the male viewer's gaze.

The third photo in the *Manchete* series shows Xuxa with a mentally retarded boy whom most Brazilians would recognize as the one who regularly appears on the "Xou." Both are wearing long, white robes, and Xuxa also has a white hood gracefully draped over her head and shoulders. She has a pious expression on her face as she speaks into a microphone, her other hand caressing the boy's head. The boy, who reaches only to her shoulders, is seen in profile, his left arm reaching across Xuxa, the hand resting gently on her waist. As he gazes up at Xuxa tenderly, the tableau calls up visions of saints and angels, perhaps even of the Madonna and child. With its costuming and carefully staged pose, the photo is an unmistakable allusion to Xuxa's representation of the pure, chaste, and domestic aspect of the feminine ideal. Here, she is the ultimate caretaker, a Virgin Mary with a "special" child. Xuxa's innocent-erotic duality is also invoked as anticipation is encouraged: it is just possible to see that, under the white robe, Xuxa is ready for her next costume change, into the shiny, black leather outfit that she wears in the fourth photo, printed alongside the third.

The fourth and last shot in the series shows Xuxa wearing the sexiest outfit in the least sexy context. Her hair is loose, she is smiling warmly in her tight, glistening, black costume, and she is holding up a prop for the audience to see. This consists of a white X, her symbol, which is intended in this instance to resemble a shooting star. Extending from the star (with its additional mnemonic function) to indicate that it is shooting is a white strip on which is written "A NEW PLANET." The audience is thus reminded to associate Xuxa with the fashionable environmental movement. Taken together, the four photographs represent a strategically edited series of appeals to some of the basic emotional sensitivities of Xuxa's public: sex, family, religion, children, and in a popular and trendier vein, ecology.

The *Manchete* article as a whole is revealing of the serious nature of the crisis that resulted from the kidnapping incident. Ambivalent about Xuxa ever since she abandoned the Manchete television network for Globo in 1986, the magazine was unusually provocative in this instance. The photo series, which reinforces the star's image and the conventions of her narrative, was published along with a text in which Xuxa expressed considerable discontent with her status. These contrasting and mutually undermining discourses may represent in part a ploy to take advantage of Xuxa's distress and coax her away from Globo, with whom her contract was about to expire. But the unusual juxtaposition also revealed real cracks in the system that allows Brazil to grant Xuxa its loyalty.

Despite the efforts to control Xuxa's crisis, it came to be viewed as emblematic of the national situation. Xuxa's unhappiness meant the breakdown of a way of understanding Brazil, and became the hook for a story that had been hanging in the air for a long time. The media began to turn one of Xuxa's own allegorical constructions against her, asserting that Brazil was on a "baixo-astral," a "downer"—borrowing a concept that already formed part of the Xuxa narrative, the "Baixo Astral" being the Darth Vader–like villain from her 1988 film *Super Xuxa contra Baixo Astral*. Now, the evil "Baixo

Astral" had the upper hand. Some voices in the media were raising difficult questions about Brazil, about Xuxa, and about her public distress. Journalist Gilberto Dimenstein, for example, wrote an article entitled "The Baixo Astral Conquers Xuxa," admonishing Brazilians for expressing surprise at Xuxa's crisis. He asked how anybody could be shocked in a nation where it had recently been scientifically proven that in some regions malnutrition had created a population that, on the average, showed an IQ of twenty-two points below normal, an 8 percent reduction in skull size, and a stature close to that of dwarfs.[35]

When Xuxa's mask slipped, her magic briefly failed, and she was seen not as a queen or a fairy godmother but as the embodiment of Brazil's crisis of faith in itself. Instead of encouraging feelings of playful, erotic freedom from responsibility, the figure of Xuxa stimulated people to think about the need for a sense of responsibility toward each other and toward society. Most Brazilians remembered a time when city streets were safe. Now, after the kidnapping episode, the streets seemed more dangerous than ever, and Xuxa's efforts to distract from that reality seemed not only to be failing but perhaps to be inappropriate as well. There were reports that Xuxa slept no more than two nights in the same place in fear for her safety.[36] Brazilians heard about Xuxa lowering the window of her limousine on the way to work in Rio and having a gold chain torn from her neck by what she called "two poor children."[37] Suddenly, instead of showing Brazilians the cloistered, sanitized version of childhood seen on the "Xou," Xuxa reminded people of the violence practiced by and against children. The Loricchios, two brothers who had come of age in the Xuxa generation, her own ex-"baixinhos," had apparently turned against her.

Added to this disturbing pattern of critical attention was the suggestion by some of the press that Xuxa was cynically exploiting the kidnapping incident for her own advantage. Some thought it was not exactly chance that Xuxa's crisis coincided with her negotiations with Globo for renewal of her television contract. Several articles appeared denouncing Xuxa's crisis as merely a "marketing ploy," a "strategy to raise the stakes" in her talks with Globo.[38] The open suggestions that Xuxa's public tears were simply a promotional gimmick indicated how seriously the integrity of her image was compromised by the events of late 1991.

Xuxa's threat to quit her show and leave Brazil became the subject of a national debate, widely covered in the media. The country's leading polling institute, Ibope, announced that 95 percent of the children and adults in São Paulo and Rio de Janeiro interviewed felt that Xuxa's presence in Brazil was "important" or "very important" to them; 93 percent stated they believed Xuxa "contributes to the happiness of Brazilian children"; 36 percent admitted that without Xuxa, "life would be very sad"; and 20 percent said life without her "wouldn't be any fun."[39] One company, the Brazilian airline VASP, incorporated the debate into its advertising copy. VASP bought a three-quarter-page ad in the *Jornal do Brasil* that read, "Xuxa, for you there aren't any one-way tickets. Only round trips." Below, in smaller letters, the ad continued, "Xuxa, we know things aren't easy here. But even so, and even though VASP has a daily flight to Buenos Aires, we hope you'll board only if you're booked to return."

The nation's leading newspapers, including the *Jornal do Brasil* and the *Folha de São Paulo*, addressed the topic of whether Xuxa should stay or leave. Feature stories were devoted to the subject in Brazil's major news magazines, *Veja* and *Istoé*, whose covers bore her image. The latter reported her saying, "It's very difficult to live here [in Brazil] because of all the violence. Nobody can relax, especially not us, the rich."[40] That kind of seemingly callous or naive remark invited some rather realistic appraisals. President Collor's spokesperson, Cláudio Humberto, issued a statement saying, "Xuxa radiates happiness, love, hope. . . . To say you can't find happiness anymore in Brazil is unpatriotic."[41] Romeu Tuma, chief of the Federal Police (the equivalent of the FBI in the United States), admitted that the country in general was feeling "unhappy" but added that Xuxa had an "obligation to put up with everything, like any Brazilian, and even more so," because she had a "very important role to play in teaching moral and civic virtues to future generations."[42] Representative Aloízio Mercadante of the Workers' Party said, "If Xuxa . . . is dissatisfied and wants to leave, imagine the thirty million workers who make minimum wage."[43] The poet Waly Salomão said Xuxa reminded him of "the ingenuous Marilyn Monroe in *Bus Stop*. It's hard to believe Xuxa only just now discovered the crisis. When she finally steps out of her glass bubble, I hope she doesn't crack up like Marilyn."[44] A sarcastic bumper sticker appeared bearing the message "Xuxa, stay at home. It's safer."

A comic strip from the October 2 issue of the news magazine *Visão* sums up many of the feelings Brazilians had about Xuxa, and about the country, toward the end of 1991. The strip begins by showing Xuxa leaving Brazil on an airplane. Next is a drawing of a group of children brandishing knives and trying to kill a clown who is shooting at them with a gun. The caption reads, "Kids! You can't control them anymore!!" In the following frame, a citizen demands his money from President Collor, who had frozen private bank accounts in March 1990 in order to slow inflation. When Collor tells the man his money is now available, the citizen says, "I don't want it anymore!!" and throws the cruzado bills in the president's face. A bubble pointed at Collor's head reads, "Something is broken in the delicate balance of the national psyche!" (Manipulation of the frozen money later surfaced in the investigation of corruption that led to President Collor's impeachment in late 1992.) The next frame shows a black man with a length of barbed wire beating a white man tied to a post. The caption is "Old enmities surface . . . historical debts are paid in kind." Finally, there is a drawing of three men drinking beer and laughing as one of them stretches out his leg and trips a man passing by on crutches. The caption here reads, "Jokes and humor are still our trademark, but their true nature is revealed!" Below these sketches of a society in open defiance of authority, and unrestrained in its expression of hostility, appears Xuxa. She is on the telephone with someone who pleads, "Xuxa, come back, for the love of God! The country is out of control!" She answers, "If it's that bad, okay, tell everybody I'm coming back." In the last frame, Xuxa steps out of the airplane and is met by a pie in the face and cries of "Go away! Get out!" The last caption reads, "But it was too late!"[45]

The pie in Xuxa's face is a subversive notion, implying the demystification of the star and the unmasking of the myths that endow her with authority. The kidnapping episode seemed to place Xuxa's image in danger not so much of fading as of being exposed and rejected. The attempted kidnapping took place during the same season in which *Forbes* magazine reported Xuxa's eight-figure income; the juxtaposition sharpened the perception of a narrative increasingly off course and out of touch with reality. The disjunction between the real Brazil and the one Xuxa stands for—patterned on disembodied television models of culture and global media production values, and informed by attitudes about gender and race more and more difficult to reconcile with genuine social needs—became more tangible. Xuxa's role as an agent of transcendence seemed to have reached the limits of its viability.

In one very poor community in the Northeast of Brazil, little girls do not play with dolls.[46] Dolls represent babies and, since a great many babies die, they are not chosen as figures of play. Instead, the children play Xuxa. But in the 1990s, Xuxa's meaning seems to be in the process of shifting away from the benign symbol with which even the most destitute children dream of success, happiness, and security. One story that circulated toward the end of 1991 was that the star had made a pact with the devil. A magazine ran a picture of her upside down.[47] The *Folha de São Paulo* reported that the phrase "the devil is magnificent" had been heard on one of Xuxa's records played backwards.[48] A girl who listened was said to have dropped dead on the spot.[49] Another rumor seemed to signal a further transformation. From northeastern Brazil came the story that a Xuxa doll had wept blood.

In the cartoonist's view, Xuxa is neither a saint nor the devil, but just another target of the nation's frustration. Some of the cynicism the cartoonist observes in Brazil in the nineties is the result of the erosion of faith in the ability of the nation to deliver on the promise of a better future. Television, because of its increasing intrusion into and control over Brazilian culture shares the responsibility for that cynicism. In keeping with that mood, the "Queen of the 'Baixinhos'" conducted tearful television celebrations of her figurative "return" while accelerating her plans to leave the country. Within a year, Xuxa had cut back her hours on Brazilian television and was reportedly hard at work studying English.

NOTES

INTRODUCTION

1. Aydano André Motta, "O país perdeu a graça," *Istoé Senhor*, 25 Sept. 1991, 22.

2. *Folha de São Paulo*, 22 Nov. 1991, sec. 1, p. 10.

3. Fábio Konder Comparato, "E possível democratizar a televisão?" in *Rede imaginária: Televisão e democracia*, ed. Adauto Novaes (São Paulo: Companhia das Letras, 1991), 302.

4. Carlos José Marques, "A empresária saltitante," *Istoé Senhor*, 5 July 1989, 66.

5. Márcia Peltier, "Boneca solitária," *Interview*, June 1991, 23.

6. Richard Dyer, *Stars* (London: British Film Institute, 1982), 7–8.

7. Julia Preston, "Brazil's Tot-to-Teen Idol," *Washington Post*, 2 Dec. 1991, sec. 2, p. 4.

8. Julio César Ribeiro, public relations expert and president of the Talent Agency, quoted in "A loirinha chegou lá," *Veja*, 25 Sept. 1991, 104.

9. Richard Dyer, *Heavenly Bodies: Film Stars and Society* (New York: St. Martin's Press, 1986), 2–3. Dyer also discusses media texts as the source of the signification of stars in *Stars*. Throughout the present book, references to and citations of statements by Xuxa in the various media texts consulted pertain exclu-

sively to the star's image, an imaginary, cultural construction. The present analysis does not presume the accuracy of such reported information, nor does it make any claim of biographical authenticity.

10. Richard Goldstein, "We So Horny: Sado Studs and Super Sluts: America's New Sex 'Tude," *Village Voice*, 16 Oct. 1990, 36, quoted in Rosemary J. Coombe, "The Celebrity Image and Cultural Identity: Publicity Rights and the Subaltern Politics of Gender," *Discourse* 14.3 (Summer 1992): 63.

11. Dyer, *Heavenly Bodies*, 44.

12. Nico Vink, *The Telenovela and Emancipation: A Study on TV and Social Change in Brazil* (Amsterdam: Royal Tropical Institute, 1988), 58.

13. *Folha de São Paulo*, 22 Nov. 1991, sec. 1, p. 10; *Veja*, 20 Nov. 1991, 49; World Bank, cited in *Jornal do Brasil*, 12 Oct. 1991, sec. 1, p. 4.

14. The Brazilian sociologist Sérgio Miceli discusses the question of the paradidactic function of television in "O papel político dos meios de comunicação de massa no Brasil," IDESP (1989): 28. The expression "plugged-in classes" is used in an article about U.S. popular culture and its global reach by Todd Gitlin ("World Leaders: Mickey et al.," *New York Times*, 3 May 1992, sec. 2, pp. 1, 30).

15. It is hardly a coincidence that both Barbie and Xuxa were first introduced to the public in the context of the erotic display industry. The original 1959 Barbie design was purchased from a German manufacturer who modeled the doll after a real life "playgirl" and sold her to adult men in bars and tobacco shops. Cy Schneider, *Children's Television: The Art, the Business, and How It Works* (Lincolnwood [Chicago], Ill.: NTC Business Books, 1987), 26.

16. Schneider, *Children's Television*, 28.

17. Schneider, *Children's Television*, 24. There are many indications of Barbie's huge impact on industry and culture. Her costume sales reportedly make Mattel the "largest manufacturer of women's wear in the world" (Schneider, *Children's*

Television, 36). Over 600 million dolls have been sold in Barbie's more than three decades of existence (Steve Lohr, "And See to It That Ken Composts," *New York Times,* 8 May 1992, sec. 4, p. 4). In 1992, "The American girl own[ed] an average of seven Barbies" (Eben Shapiro, " 'Totally Hot, Totally Cool,' Long-Haired Barbie Is a Hit," *New York Times,* 22 June 1992, sec. 4, p. 9). One TV spot for the doll, the "Barbie Fan Club" commercial, reportedly elicited a larger response than any ad in the first twenty-five years of television in the United States. The fan club itself became the second-largest girls' organization in the world after the Girl Scouts (Schneider, *Children's Television,* 31). During one particularly successful TV ad campaign, Barbie recorded an average of ten thousand letters received per week (Schneider, *Children's Television,* 31). Xuxa reported the same amount of fan mail per week—ten thousand letters—during her first season with Globo ("Rainha das crianças," *Veja,* 19 Nov. 1986, 135).

18. Rosemary Betterton, ed., *Looking On: Images of Femininity in the Visual Arts and Media* (London: Pandora, 1987), contains a number of valuable essays including Betterton's introduction, which brings up important issues of representation. Rosalind Coward's chapter " 'Sexual Liberation' and the Family" discusses, among other issues, the question of advertising and the " 'sexualisation' of areas [of the body] previously not defined as sexual" (54).

19. Susan Faludi, *Backlash: The Undeclared War Against American Women* (New York: Crown, 1991), xxiii. There are many other examples of resistance to Barbie's symbolic femininity. In late 1992, for example, the American Association of University Women complained about a talking version of the doll that seemed to undermine the notion that girls could be capable mathematicians. An "alternative" doll called "Happy to Be Me" appeared in 1991 and challenged Barbie's unrealistic measurements with proportions designed to help girls develop positive body images. Denise Duhamel mentions a series of challenges to the Barbie doll image in her article "Barbie and

Self-Esteem," in *The City of DIS* 2 (1992): 16–17. Duhamel refers to works by Marge Piercy and Sandra Cisneros; to Todd Haynes's film *Superstar: The Life of Karen Carpenter*, in which the singer, who died of bulimia, is played by a Barbie doll; and to the 1991 one-man show *Artificial Reality*, in which Jeffrey Essman "portrayed a washed-up alcoholic Barbie" and "stood on tiptoe the entire skit" to reproduce the doll's posture, which is a consequence of the fact that Barbie's feet are molded into the high-heel shoe position. Duhamel observes that "literary commentary on Barbie has reached such proportion as to warrant a forthcoming anthology—*Mondo Barbie*, edited by Rich Peabody and Linda Ebersole." The emerging work examining Barbie clearly envisions the doll as a cultural icon whose impact has significant implications with regard to the social construction of femininity.

CHAPTER ONE

1. Barry King, "The Social Significance of Stardom," unpublished manuscript, 1974. This summary of King's argument appears in Richard Dyer, *Stars* (London: British Film Institute, 1982), 8.

2. *Veja*, 23 July 1986, 63.

3. Promotional handout, "Un fenómeno llamado 'Xuxa,' " 2.

4. Promotional handout, "Materia tirada de revista Chilena," distributed in 1991, 4.

5. *Playboy* (Brazil), Aug. 1987, 70.

6. Promotional handout, "Profile of Maria da Graça Meneghel," 1990, 4.

7. Promotional handout, "Materia tirada."

8. Nico Vink, in *The Telenovela and Emancipation: A Study on TV and Social Change in Brazil* (Amsterdam: Royal Tropical Institute, 1988), considers working-class views of the rich on page 73, and on page 79 discusses the expression "hei de ven-

cer" (a variation on Xuxa's oft-repeated "Sou uma vencedora") and its connotations for working-class Brazilians.

9. Interview of Xuxa with Ricardo Lombardi, "Xuxa pede a Boni para fazer programa mais sério," *O Estado de São Paulo*, 1 Oct. 1991, sec. 2, p. 10.

10. *Playboy*, Aug. 1987, 123.

11. *Istoé*, July 2, 1986, 75.

12. Christine Ajuz, "Vão ter que me aturar," *Istoé*, 2 July 1986.

13. Interview on the "Show de Cristina," shown on Univisión in the United States, 14 May 1992.

14. *Manchete*, 4 Dec. 1982, 54.

15. *Manchete*, 4 Dec. 1982, 54.

16. *Amiga*, 9 Aug. 1991, 17.

17. *Cláudia*, Feb. 1982, 87.

18. *Veja*, 11 Mar. 1981.

19. *Manchete*, 16 May 1981; *Cláudia*, Feb. 1982, 86.

20. *Cláudia*, Feb. 1982, 86.

21. "Pelé Xuxa: Amor, Estranho Amor," *Manchete*, 4 Dec. 1982, 54.

22. *Para Ti* (Buenos Aires), 26 Aug. 1991.

23. *Manchete*, 19 June 1982, 34.

24. *Veja*, 20 Jan. 1982, 52.

25. *Cláudia*, Feb. 1982, 86.

26. *Cláudia*, Feb. 1982, 88.

27. *Manchete*, 21 Aug. 1982, 131.

28. Erotic interest in women in Brazil generally focuses first on the *bumbuns*, much the way, in the United States, the breasts tend to be highlighted. Every now and then, possibly because of the sexual ambivalence of the buttocks, an effort is made in Brazil to promote the breasts. *Manchete* heralded the "New Boom of the Breasts," for example, on the cover of its 3 September 1988 issue. The opening shots of a 1989 soap opera tried to shift attention by featuring model Isadora Ribeiro's breasts. A subsequent *Manchete* article (9 Sept. 1989), entitled "Voyage to the Breasts of Isadora," garnered some at-

tention. But none of these efforts has seriously damaged the "prestige" of the *bumbum*, as Tom Jobim puts it in *Manchete*, 9 Sept. 1989, 22.

29. *Manchete*, 19 June 1982, 33.

30. The *Folha de São Paulo*, 2 May 1982, says Khoury interrupted "petting and kissing her" for a few moments to compare Xuxa, as well, to "a little animal" and "a child."

31. *Mulherio*, July/Aug. 1982, 20. The article from the *Folha de São Paulo* referred to is by Gisella Bisordi and is from the 2 May 1982 edition.

32. The comments here follow the Brazilian media's habit of referring to Roberta Close as a transvestite, although that may be an inaccurate representation of Close's feelings about sexual identity at that time. In 1989 Close had surgery to become a transsexual.

33. *Manchete*, n.d.

34. Quoted in Marta Suplicy, *Reflexões sobre o Cotidiano* (Rio de Janeiro: Espaço e Tempo, 1986), 235.

35. Maria Rita Kehl, *Mulherio*, Nov.–April 1983, 20. The possibility that the gay male adoption of Xuxa's celebrity image signals a subversive recoding of gender identities, and discloses other impulses including a desire for legitimacy on the part of a marginal group, is a subject that warrants further investigation.

36. *Veja*, 20 Jan. 1982, 52.

37. *Cláudia*, Feb. 1982, 86.

38. *Veja*, 20 Jan. 1982, 53.

39. *Folha de São Paulo*, 2 May 1982.

40. Richard Dyer, *Heavenly Bodies: Film Stars and Society* (New York: St. Martin's Press, 1986), 38–39.

41. Dyer, *Heavenly Bodies*, 32, 35.

42. Dyer, *Heavenly Bodies*, 61.

43. Robin Tolmach Lakoff and Raquel L. Scherr, *Face Value: The Politics of Beauty* (Boston: Routledge and Kegan Paul, 1984), 91.

44. *Veja*, 20 Jan. 1982, 52.

45. *Jornal do Brasil*, 18 May 1991, sec. 2, p. 2.

46. *Amiga*, 24 May 1991, 4.

47. *Manchete,* Special Supplement, 30 April 1983, 4.

48. Lakoff and Scherr, *Face Value,* 35–36.

49. The inset citation is from T. Lynn Smith, *Brazil: People and Institutions* (Baton Rouge: Louisiana State University Press, 1964), 66, quoted by Carlos A. Hasenbalg in *Race Relations in Modern Brazil* (New Mexico: Latin American Institute, n.d.), 8. Hasenbalg's work, a curriculum guide, is a useful source of information on race relations in Brazil and includes a basic bibliography of studies in English and Portuguese. Among other books on the subject of likely interest to North Americans are David J. Hellwig, ed., *African-American Reflections on Brazil's Racial Paradise* (Philadelphia: Temple University Press, 1992), which explores the changing views of North American blacks toward race relations in Brazil; Pierre-Michel Fontaine, ed., *Race, Class, and Power in Brazil* (Los Angeles: Center for Afro-American Studies, University of California, 1991); and recent studies on race and Brazil by George Reid Andrews and Howard Winant.

50. Stuart Hall, "The Whites of Their Eyes: Racist Ideologies and the Media," in *The Media Reader,* ed. Manuel Alvarado and John O. Thompson (London: BFI, 1990). Hall defines "inferential" racism as "those apparently naturalised representations of events and situations relating to race, whether 'factual' or 'fictional,' which have racist premisses and propositions inscribed in them as a set of *unquestioned assumptions*. These enable racist statements to be formulated without ever bringing into awareness the racist predicates on which the statements are grounded" (13). Italics in the citations from Hall are all original.

51. William R. Long, "Brazil: No Equality for Blacks Yet," *Los Angeles Times,* 9 Apr. 1988.

52. *Manchete,* 12 May 1984, 47.

53. *Manchete,* 12 May 1984, 47.

54. Hasenbalg, *Race Relations,* 8.

55. In January 1986 the press was still referring to Xuxa as "Pelé's girlfriend," but during that year, the romance cooled. An allusion to a racist slur in a story Xuxa tells about the period

may be intended to wound her ex-lover. According to Xuxa's story, she took her pet parrot, which she had taught to say "Pelé Pelé," up on the roof of her apartment building in Rio one day. The parrot saw three vultures flying by overhead and began screaming "Pelé Pelé." Xuxa says she tried to shush the bird, because what it was doing was "nasty" ("*sacanagem*"). "Vulture"—*urubu* in Portuguese—is a derogatory term for black people, as Xuxa was obviously aware when she told the story, which was published in " 'Xou da Xuxa' estréia só depois da Copa," *Folha de São Paulo*, 19 May 1986.

56. *Contigo*, 3 Aug. 1990, 31.

57. *Manchete*, 20 Oct. 1984, 117.

58. *Veja*, 11 Mar. 1987, 86.

59. Quoted in Alfredo Ribeiro and Virgínia Leite, "Bloco dos ressentidos," *Veja*, 22 Apr. 1992, 87.

60. *Manchete*, 3 Sept. 1983, 30–31.

61. Dyer, *Heavenly Bodies*, 44.

62. Hasenbalg, *Race Relations*, 6.

63. Carlos Hasenbalg and Nelson do Valle Silva, "As imagens do negro na publicidade," in *Estrutura social, mobilidade e raça* (São Paulo: Edições Vértice, 1988), 185–188, 200.

64. "Calvário da cor," *Veja*, 30 March 1988, 92.

65. "Concurso de Racismo," *Jornal do Brasil*, 8 Oct. 1988, sec. 1, p. 4.

66. See, among other articles, Luciene Balbino, "Preconceito racial desfila no mundo da moda: Modelos negras revelam que não é fácil trabalhar no Brasil e que ainda existem muitas barreiras profissionais por causa da cor," *Folha da Tarde*, 1 Nov. 1990.

67. Sueli A. Carneiro, " 'Me ensinaram a ser mais branca do que negra . . . ,' " *Mulherio*, Sept.–Oct. 1984, 14.

68. Hasenbalg and Silva, "As imagens," 200.

69. Christine Ajuz, "Vão ter que me aturar," *Istoé*, 2 July 1986.

70. "Beleza é fundamental, sim," Maria Rita Kehl, *Mulherio*, Jan.–Feb. 1982, 14.

71. Naomi Wolf, *The Beauty Myth: How Images of Beauty Are Used Against Women* (New York: William Morrow, 1991), 12.

72. *Veja*, 12 Feb. 1986, 43, 40.

73. Wolf, *The Beauty Myth*, 19.

74. Interview with Rose Marie Muraro, *Playboy*, July 1981, 26, 42.

75. Fábio Konder Comparato, "E Possível Democratizar a Televisão?" in *Rede Imaginária: Televisão e Democracia*, ed. Adauto Novaes (São Paulo: Companhia das Letras, 1991), 302. Comparato bases his statement on a 1987 UNESCO study.

76. Sérgio Miceli, "O papel político dos meios de comunicação de massa no Brasil" (São Paulo: USP-IDESP, 1989), 3.

77. Regina Festa and Luiz Fernando Santoro, "A Terceira Idade da TV: O Local e o Internacional," in *Rede Imaginária*, 180–181.

78. Vink, *The Telenovela*, 49.

79. *Manchete*, 15 Jan. 1983, 38.

80. *Manchete*, 7 June 1986, 71.

81. In *The Telenovela*, 45, Vink observes: "It is striking that television provided space for such themes as feminism, contrary to the press, which makes this movement ridiculous. A series like "Malu" and many of the telenovelas have shown very active, thinking women. Ruth Cardoso ("Sociedade civil e meios de comunicação democrático, [Porto Alegre: Mercado Aberto, 1985]) views this openness of television as a consequence of the fact that the political opposition did not take up this topic, so the state did not feel threatened. Because of its modernity, feminism became an attractive theme for the networks, aiming at a female audience." Xuxa's television program, the "Xou da Xuxa," contrasts to the soap operas to which Vink refers in its general tendency toward closure, a defensive posture that attempts to restrict any but the preferred reading of the television text, which is, in this case, antifeminist.

82. Rafael Sampaio, "Publicidade: A mulher é a alma e o corpo do negócio," *Manchete*, 16 July 1983, 71, 78.

83. *Manchete*, 23 Apr. 1988, 110. Another example of the

dream motif associated with Xuxa involves one of her earliest television appearances, consisting of a brief scene in the soap opera "Elas por Elas," which aired in 1982. Here, she played a model in the dream of a character who wanted to be a professional model.

84. *Manchete*, 19 Apr. 1983, 30–31.

85. Stewart Ewen, *All Consuming Images: The Politics of Style in Contemporary Culture* (New York: Basic, 1988), 95–96, quoted in Rosemary J. Coombe, "The Celebrity Image and Cultural Identity: Publicity Rights and the Subaltern Politics of Gender," *Discourse* 14.3 (Summer 1992): 66.

CHAPTER TWO

1. Belisa Ribeiro, "Só falta beijinho, beijinho na vida de Xuxa," *Playboy*, Aug. 1987, 125.

2. *Veja*, 19 Nov. 1986, 135.

3. *Veja*, 19 Nov. 1986, 135.

4. This story appears in various articles including one in *Afinal*, 17 June 1986, 77.

5. Joaquim Ferreira dos Santos, "Xuxa: A Alegria das Crianças (e dos Adultos Também)," *Jornal do Brasil*, 1984.

6. Interview with Christine Ajuz, *Istoé*, 2 July 1986.

7. Telmo Martino, "Xuxa: Um xou de xuxexo," *O Estado de São Paulo*, 8 June 1986, 7.

8. Interview with Christine Ajuz, *Istoé*, 2 July 1986.

9. *Contigo*, Dec. 1990, 62.

10. Telmo Martino, "Xuxa: Um xou de xuxexo," 7.

11. Quoted in Julia Preston, "Brazil's Tot-to-Teen Idol," *Washington Post*, 2 Sept. 1991, sec. 2, p. 4.

12. Ferreira dos Santos, "Xuxa: A alegria das crianças."

13. Luciana Barcellos, "Uma revolução na psicologia infantil," *Amiga*, 2 Aug. 1991, 16, 17.

14. Ferreira dos Santos, "Xuxa: A Alegria das Crianças."

15. *Afinal*, 17 June 1986, 77.

16. Ferreira dos Santos, "Xuxa: A alegria das crianças"; Luciana Barcellos, "Uma revolução na psicologia infantil," 18; Magda de Almeida, "Xuxa, menina e mulher, agora no vídeo da Globo," *O Estado de São Paulo*, 23 Mar. 1986, 35.

17. *Folha de São Paulo*, 19 May 1986.

18. Interview with Christine Ajuz, *Istoé*, 2 July 1986.

19. Interview with Ajuz, *Istoé*, 2 July 1986.

20. Interview with Ajuz, *Istoé*, 2 July 1986.

21. The anti-educational attitude is consistent with Xuxa's general approach over the years. For example, when asked in 1987 whether she would advise a child who wanted to get ahead in the world to stay in school, Xuxa answered, "No." (*Folha de São Paulo*, 11 Oct. 1987, sec. 5, p. 1.)

22. Belisa Ribeiro, "Só falta beijinho," 129.

23. Márcia Peltier, "Boneca solitária," *Interview*, June 1991, 22.

24. "Xuxa, dia de 'frisson' na Globo," *O Globo*, 27 Feb. 1986, sec. B, p. 3.

25. " 'Xou da Xuxa' Estréia só depois da Copa," *Folha de São Paulo*, 19 May 1986.

26. *Veja*, 2 July 1986, 86.

27. G. Priolli, "Vinte velinhas para a Rede Globo," Lua Nova, CEDEC, Jan.–Mar. 1985, 48.

28. Gilberto Felisberto Vasconcellos, *Eu e a Xuxa: Sociologia do Cabaré Infantil* (São Paulo: Leia Mais, 1992), 81, 71.

29. Michèle and Armand Mattelart, *O Carnaval das Imagens: A ficção na TV* (São Paulo: Brasiliense, 1989), 28.

30. Regina Festa and Luiz Fernando Santoro, "A Terceira Idade da TV: O Local e o Internacional," in *Rede Imaginária: Televisão e Democracia*, ed. Adauto Novaes (São Paulo: Companhia das Letras, 1991), 194.

31. "Por baixo do pano," *Veja*, 17 June 1992, 98.

32. *Veja*, 21 Aug. 1991, 68–69.

33. Mattelart, *O Carnaval*, 43.

34. Roberto Bahiense, "Vítima e Cúmplice," 258, and "Apêndice," 309, in *Rede Imaginária*.

35. Nico Vink, *The Telenovela and Emancipation: A Study on TV and Social Change in Brazil* (Amsterdam: Royal Tropical Institute, 1988), 221.

36. Bahiense, "Apêndice," 309.

37. Bahiense, "Apêndice," 309.

38. Fábio Konder Comparato, "E possível democratizar a televisão?" in *Rede Imaginária*, 302.

39. Quoted in Helena Tavares, "Memórias de um velho lobo do mar," *Jornal do Brasil*, "TV Programa," 18 Aug. 1991, 38.

40. "Xuxa continua global. Ponto final," *O Estado de São Paulo*, 9 Feb. 1988, sec. 2, p. 3.

41. "Olivia Gonçalves, "Xou da Xuxa. Toda liberdade," *Jornal do Brasil*, 30 June 1986.

42. *Jornal do Brasil*, "TV Programa," 25 Aug. 1991, 38.

43. Maria Rita Kehl, "Eu vi um Brasil na TV," in *Um país no ar: História da TV Brasileira em três canais*, ed. Inimá F. Simões et al. (São Paulo: Brasiliense, 1986), 202.

44. Luci Vasconcelos, "Mulher, o moleque Xuxa," *Afinal*, 17 June 1986, 77.

45. Boni, the vice president of Globo Network Operations, wanted to name the program the "Show da Xuxa," but Xuxa insisted on the "Xou," saying it would tie in with her name, and "leave room for more word games." See Jussara Martins, "Super Xuxa na batalha contra as drogas," *Manchete*, 23 July 1988, 73.

46. See, among other media texts, *Interview*, June 1991, 23, and the "Show de Cristina," on Univisión, 14 May 1992.

47. "Um Xímbolo Xexual," *Ultima Hora*, "Revista," 27 Aug. 1987.

48. Barbara Gancia, "Xuxa prepara as armas para invadir a América," *O Estado de São Paulo*, 4 Mar. 1990, sec. 2, p. 3.

49. "Sem Xuxa," *Amiga*, 24 Aug. 1990, 63.

50. Divane Carvalho, "Recife não quer 'dixionário,' " *Jornal do Brasil*, 16 Oct. 1987.

51. "Xuxa e Pelé, o casamento adiado," *Ultima Hora*, 23 July 1983.

52. Rodney Mellos, *Jornal da Tarde*, 15 Mar. 1983, 15.
53. "O império da Xuxa," *Veja*, 27 Jan. 1988, 99.
54. Vasconcellos, *Eu e a Xuxa*, 13.
55. "Xou da Xuxa," 4 Dec. 1991.
56. "Xou da Xuxa," 2 Oct. 1991.
57. "Xou da Xuxa," 10 Sept. 1991.
58. The Corcovado Christ statue seems especially appropriate for its iconographic role on Xuxa's show: more a tourist site than a true religious icon, the statue appears on travel brochures promoting Rio de Janeiro around the world, even though it, like New York harbor's emblematic Statue of Liberty, is a product of France.
59. Jussara Martins, "Super Xuxa na batalha contra as drogas," 74.
60. Promotional handout, "Materia tirada de revista Chilena," distributed in 1991, 1.
61. 10 Oct., 15 Oct., and 14 Oct. 1991.
62. "Xou da Xuxa," 4 Nov., 21 Nov., and 4 Nov. 1991, respectively.
63. Under pressure at the time from *Playboy* to do a spread, Paula announced about ten days later that she had decided to decline the invitation.
64. Some of the many sources on this material are Luciana Barcellos, "Casar com um homem que ame muito é o único sonho que não consegue realizar," *Amiga*, 9 Aug. 1991, 18; Ana Gaio, Marina Nery, and Tarlis Batista, "Xuxa: Uma estrela contra a solidão," *Manchete*, 24 Feb. 1990, 114; Jussara Martins, "Xuxa acerta no Senna," *Manchete*, 21 Jan. 1989, 100–103; and Theodomiro Braga, "Xuxa no clã dos Kennedy," *Jornal do Brasil*, 15 Feb. 1992, sec. 1, p. 1, and sec. 2, p. 8.
65. On the issue of childbearing, Vink, *The Telenovela*, cites a number of gender studies dealing with the working class. One finding noted is that for working-class women, "motherhood means self-realization" (76). A working-class woman's identity is constructed around the family. One study showed that "if married women again assume a salaried job, they see

it as something belonging to their role as mother, they do it 'because of the children'" (76). Xuxa's reiterated use of the phrase "because of the children," to describe why she works, affirms that maternal role shared by a great many women in Brazil.

66. "Xou da Xuxa," 15 Oct. 1991.

67. Vera Jardim, "Xuxa ganha carrão como presente de aniversário," *Amiga*, 19 Apr. 1991, 12.

68. Edward L. Palmer, *Children in the Cradle of Television* (Lexington, Mass.: D. C. Heath, 1987), 80.

69. In studies done in the United States, the stereotyping of gender roles on television is clearly found to influence the attitudes and behavior of children who watch television. Not only does television "influence children's definitions of the sex appropriateness of activities," but "children who watch more hours of television are more likely to have traditional sex role attitudes than less frequent TV watchers" (Jean Stockard and Miriam M. Johnson, *Sex Roles: Sex Inequality and Sex Role Development* [Englewood Cliffs, New Jersey: Prentice-Hall, 1980], 190). Susan A. Basow cites a number of studies in her book *Gender Stereotypes: Traditions and Alternatives* (Monterey, Calif.: Brooks/Cole Publishing, 1986), which gives a similar assessment: "The amount of time children spend watching TV has been found to be directly and positively related to their degree of acceptance of traditional sex roles as early as kindergarten age. . . . Even among college students and older adults, the amount of TV viewing of stereotyped programs has been found to be significantly and positively correlated with the amount of gender stereotyping in self-descriptions. . . . Frequent viewing is likely to be a powerful reinforcer of gender stereotypes" (139–140).

70. "Xou da Xuxa," 23 Aug. 1991.

71. Cláudio Bojunga, "Xuxa," *Jornal do Brasil*, "Domingo" supplement, 31 Dec. 1989, 14.

72. These include the Ninja Turtles, Scooby-Doo, the Super Mario Brothers (and a series of skits involving the characters), the Ghostbusters, He-Man, Tiny Toons, and, in the early morn-

ing, Popeye. The meaning of cartoon watching for children is a much-debated topic, its greatest virtue usually considered to be its usefulness as a baby-sitting device. While some analysts find value in the superheroes' enactment of empowerment, most warn against excessive television viewing, regardless of content, because of the solitary and passive nature of the activity. Yet Brazil's economic decline in the Xuxa years has made television, and cartoons, all the more important for overworked women responsible for home child care.

73. "Xou da Xuxa," 9 Oct. 1991.

74. Vasconcellos, *Eu e a Xuxa*, 80.

75. *Veja*, 24 June 1987, 87.

76. Maria Rita Kehl, "Eu Vi um Brasil na TV," 202.

77. Vasconcellos, *Eu e a Xuxa*, 23.

78. The connotations of the name "Neguinho" are complex. The diminutive of "nego," which is an affectionate variant of "negro," or, "black," "Neguinho" is widely used in Brazil to mean something like "friend" or "pal." It is not often used as an insult, though it may well sound, to the non-Brazilian, as if it might be offensive.

79. On *pagode*, see Chris McGowan and Ricardo Pessanha, *The Brazilian Sound* (New York: Billboard Books, 1991), as well as Charles Perrone, *Masters of Contemporary Brazilian Song: MPB 1965–1985* (Austin: University of Texas Press, 1989), and, by the same author, the liner notes to the LP *O Samba*, compiled by David Byrne, 1989, which also provide musical examples.

80. The characterization is taken from a valuable article, "Saturday Morning Fever: The Hard Sell Takeover of Kids TV," (*Mother Jones*, Sept. 1986, 39–48, 54) by Tom Engelhardt. The author documents the fate of children's television, and its effect on children, during the Reagan years.

81. Engelhardt, "Saturday Morning," 47.

82. Engelhardt, "Saturday Morning," 46.

83. Xuxa sometimes takes time on her program to make public service announcements, and she has participated in public service campaigns off the show as well. She helped publicize the polio vaccine; performed at "Health Aid," sponsored

by the World Health Organization, in 1989; and joined in a "We Are the World"–style recording to benefit Brazilian street children in 1991.

84. *Istoé*, 27 June 1990, 77.

85. Belisa Ribeiro, "Só falta beijinho," 128.

86. "Glória repartida," *Veja*, 16 Nov. 1988, 127.

87. Edson Engels dos Santos, quoted in "Glória repartida," 127.

88. Quoted in "Glória repartida," 127.

89. Gaio, Nery, and Batista, "Xuxa: Uma estrela contra a solidão," 110.

90. "Glória repartida," 126.

91. Augusto Guilherme, "Globo coloca Xuxa no lugar de Chacrinha," *Contigo*, 1988, 27.

92. The term *babá eletrônica* (electronic baby-sitter) is often used to refer to Xuxa. One example is in an interview by Regina Rito, "As dúvidas da musa dos baixinhos," *Jornal do Brasil*, 29 Sept. 1991, sec. 1, p. 14.

93. Promotional handout, "Xuxamania," 1990, p. 2.

94. This and the following letters were published in *Ultima Hora*, "Revista," 27 Aug. 1987.

95. "Xuxa después del intento de secuestro," *Para Ti* (Buenos Aires), 26 Aug. 1991.

96. "A lourinha alegre," *Veja*, 1 Nov. 1989, 134; "Glória repartida," 127.

97. Text by Milton Belintani, *Cláudia*, Oct. 1990, 140–145; promotional material on pages 138–139 and 146.

98. Fernán Martínez, "Xuxa: Diversión de niños, tentación de padres," *Más*, July–Aug. 1992, 57.

CHAPTER THREE

1. Márcia Peltier, "Boneca solitária," *Interview*, June 1991, 21.

2. The song is "Fã No. 1," by Paulo Massadas and Michael Sullivan.

3. Regina Rito, "As dúvidas da musa dos baixinhos," *Jornal do Brasil*, 29 Sept. 1991, sec. 1, p. 14.

4. Nico Vink, *The Telenovela and Emancipation: A Study on TV and Social Change in Brazil* (Amsterdam: Royal Tropical Institute, 1988), 44.

5. The "Xou" was first aired in Spanish in Argentina, on channel 11, Telefe, on May 6, 1991.

6. Jacqueline Breitinger, "Multinacional brasileira," [*Istoé* or *Veja*], July 1991, 42 (photocopy given to the author with incomplete documentation; from the author's files).

7. The releases on this label include "Carnaval dos Baixinhos," "Lambada da Xuxa," and the Paquita and Paquito LPs.

8. Paula Guatimosim, "Xuxa é hoje marca de sucesso internacional," *Jornal do Brasil*, 24 Mar. 1991, sec. Negócios e Finanças, p. 6.

9. *Amiga*, 16 Feb. 1990, 3.

10. "Entertainment Tonight," NBC, 2 Nov. 1992.

11. "Xuxamania," press release in English distributed in 1991.

12. Interview with Xuxa in promotional material, in Spanish, distributed 1991.

13. Julia Preston, "Brazil's Tot-to-Teen Idol," *Washington Post*, 2 Dec. 1991, sec. 2, p. 4.

14. Gisele Porto, "Xuxa," *O Estado de São Paulo*, 21 June 1987, sec. 2, p. 3.

15. Luis Antônio Giron, "Super Xuxa enfrenta o baixo astral," *Folha de São Paulo*, 22 Sept. 1991, sec. 5, p. 14. Vink observes the tendency for the less educated to identify with dramatic narrative, such as the kind Xuxa constructs around her image, in contrast to the critical distance the better educated are more likely to maintain. This configuration may also figure in the generally sympathetic treatment of the star on issues such as consumerism (Vink, *The Telenovela*, 126). Vink cites Schoenmakers and Bourdieu on the process of identification and the class differences associated with audience proximity to or distance from a dramatic narrative.

16. *Veja*, 2 Oct. 1991, 10. Other criticism of Xuxa surfaced

as well in late 1991. A letter to the *Folha de São Paulo* recommended that an investigation be instituted as to whether Xuxa pays any taxes on the "astronomical" amount of money she makes (Letter from Heráclito De Gubernatis, *Folha de São Paulo,* 2 Oct. 1991, sec. 1, p. 3). Another letter, this time to the *Jornal do Brasil,* complained that Xuxa "de-educated" kids by showing a racist preference for blondes and North American, instead of Brazilian, Indians (Letter from José Arnulfo Alves da França, *Jornal do Brasil,* 9 Oct. 1991, sec. 2, p. 7).

17. Lilia Coelho, "Luiza Brunet declara guerra contra a musa dos baixinhos," *Contigo,* (1988?), 14 (photocopy given to the author with incomplete documentation; from the author's files).

18. Coelho, "Luiza Brunet," 15.

19. *Veja,* 9 Dec. 1987, 78.

20. Laurindo Leal Filho, *Atrás das Câmeras: Relações entre Cultura, Estado e Televisão* (São Paulo: Summus, 1988), 46. According to the same source, in recent years television has become "the most important sales vehicle" in Brazil, showing higher revenues from advertising than newspapers, magazines, or radio (44).

21. Julia Michaels, "Use of In-Program Ads Plays Big Role in Success of Brazilian TV Network," *Wall Street Journal,* 4 Jan. 1989.

22. Alan Riding, "On Brazilian TV, the Subtle Sell Pays Off Big, Too," *New York Times,* 3 June 1988.

23. Quoted in Riding, "On Brazilian TV."

24. Jane J. Sarques, "A magia da publicidade nos programas infantis," paper presented at the 16th Brazilian Social Communications Congress, Londrina, October 28–31, 1988, 7.

25. Sarques, "A Magia," 12.

26. Quoted in Riding, "On Brazilian TV."

27. Two useful books that touch on this topic are Mark Crispin Miller, *Boxed In: The Culture of TV* (Evanston, Ill.: Northwestern University Press, 1988), and Bill McKibben, *The Age of Missing Information* (New York: Random House, 1992).

28. Augusto de Almeida, quoted by Nelson Blecher in "TV mostra comercial simultâneo da Estrela," *Folha de São Paulo*, 15 Oct. 1991, sec. 3, p. 10.

29. According to Tom Engelhardt, it is not until children reach the age of seven or eight that they start to distinguish between ads and shows, and moreover, to "discount the ads," an observation that would be encouraging were it not for the nature of much of the programming between advertisements ("Saturday Morning Fever: The Hard Sell Takeover of Kids TV," *Mother Jones*, Sept. 1986, 47).

Among the products advertised during commercial breaks on the "Xou" on 22 August 1991 were Barbie dolls, Duracell batteries, a record of Italian songs, the Maggi soup with Xuxa-letter noodles, and CIAO cookies. There was also a public service announcement for the August 25 Soldier Day, and three ads for Globo programs—the network's prime time soap opera that season, "O Dono do Mundo," a Globo video featuring the comedy group "Os Trapalhões," and a news break promoting the news program that follows the "Xou." Globo sells a lot of Globo on Globo.

30. Sérgio Miceli, "O papel político dos meios de comunicação de massa no Brasil" (São Paulo: USP-IDESP, 1989), 28. According to the same source, about 25.76 percent of Brazilians five years or older are illiterate. Another source reports that 45 million people, of a population given as 155 million, are illiterate or can only write their names (*Veja*, 20 Nov. 1991, 46).

31. Sarques, "A Magia," 9.

32. Belisa Ribeiro, "Só falta beijinho, beijinho na vida de Xuxa," *Playboy*, Aug. 1987, 69, 125, 128. The following two citations are from the same source.

33. *Jornal do Brasil*, 15 Dec. 1984.

34. "Só para as 'baixinhas,'" *Veja*, 20 May 1987, 70.

35. "Só para as 'baixinhas,'" *Veja*, 20 May 1987, 70.

36. Gisella Bisordi, "Xuxa, atrevida e cheia de graça," *Folha de São Paulo*, 2 May 1982.

37. Jussara Martins, "Super Xuxa: Uma pantera loura

contra o baixo-astral," *Manchete*, 6 Feb. 1988, 112. Xuxa acted in several movies before then, including a number of films with the very successful comedy team the "Trapalhões" (*Super Xuxa* was, in fact, inspired in a way by the "Trapalhões," who had a virtual monopoly on productions aimed at the youth audience). Two early films in which Xuxa acted, before the "Trapalhões" series, were *Love Strange Love* (1982), discussed in Chapter One, and *Fuscão Preto* (1983), a children's film with a theme of love, courtship, and jealousy involving a car (the *fuscão* of the title) and a farmer's daughter (Xuxa). Some of Xuxa's movies with the "Trapalhões" are *O Trapalhão na Arca de Noé* (1983), *Os Trapalhões e o Mágico de Orôs* (1984), *Os Trapalhões no Reino da Fantasia* (1985), *Os Trapalhões no Rabo do Cometa* (1986), and *A Princesa Xuxa e os Trapalhões* (1989).

38. Paulo Adário, "Maria da Graça Meneghel S/A," *Jornal do Brasil*, 18 Nov. 1987.

39. Helena Carone, "O alto astral de Xuxa," *Jornal do Brasil*, 22 June 1988, sec. 2, p. 1. The following citation about the film from the *Jornal do Brasil* is from the same source.

40. Jussara Martins, "Super Xuxa: Uma pantera loura contra o baixo-astral," *Manchete*, 6 Feb. 1988, 113.

41. Press release from Dream Vision, "Xuxa Conquers National Cinema Crisis," originally published in *O Dia*, 17 Mar. 1991.

42. Quoted in press release distributed by Dream Visions, "Lua de Cristal chega ao Brasil, Xuxa estoura no exterior."

43. "Estréia filme da Xuxa," *Folha de São Paulo*, 9 June 1990, "Folinha," sec. 7, p. 5.

44. Richard Dyer, *Heavenly Bodies: Film Stars and Society* (New York: St. Martin's Press, 1986), 44.

45. Two years after the film was released, *Veja*, in its 1991 retrospective issue, commented on sexual harassment and the Clarence Thomas–Anita Hill episode in the United States: "The case is unthinkable in Brazil. Here, a case of sexual harassment would never end up in the Senate with coverage by Globo" (1 Jan. 1992, 62). The mainstream media in Brazil treated the episode, and the subject, as a joke.

46. Press release distributed by Dream Visions.

47. Press release distributed by Dream Visions.

48. Xuxa also contributed cuts on various LPs, starting in 1984.

49. "Discos de brinquedo," *Veja*, 30 Mar. 1988, 76.

50. João Luiz Albuquerque, "Na terra do jabá," *Interview* 142 (1991): 58–59.

51. "Colosso adormecido," *Veja*, 23 Dec. 1987, 92. In Brazil, selling 100,000 copies earns a gold record, while 250,000 represents a platinum. Xuxa's sales are so strong, she would qualify routinely for platinum records in the United States as well.

52. "A subida do balão," *Veja*, 4 Jan. 1984, 73. Mike Biggs, the son of Ronald Biggs, the British mastermind of the 1963 great train robbery who moved to Brazil in 1970, was one of the three members of the group. Mike was nine years old when he was recruited by the president of CBS (Brazil) himself, who was impressed by his "charm and spontaneity" when he appeared on television in 1981 to ask for the return of his father, who had been kidnapped. Of the other two members of the Turma do Balão Mágico, Simony was discovered on an amateur hour television program, and Tob had been a child fashion model and acted in television commercials.

53. "Hino do herói," *Veja*, 26 March 1986, 123.

54. One critic of the new children's music was the well-known composer João de Barros, now in his eighties. He is cited expressing regret at the way rock had replaced Brazilian-rooted sounds on the new children's LPs ("Discos de brinquedo," *Veja*, 30 Mar. 1988, 77).

55. "Discos de brinquedo," 77.

56. "Sexo, som, e ambição," *Veja*, 13 June 1990, 96.

57. *Istoé*, 8 Feb. 1984, 9. Most of the cuts on the first album, "Clube da Criança," by RCA Victor, consisted of performances by other artists. Pelé participated on one tune.

58. "Os donos das paradas," *Veja*, 26 Aug. 1987, 130.

59. Sullivan's real name is Ivanilton de Souza Lima. The name Michael Sullivan, picked at random from a New York

City phone book, was intended to lend commercial advantages to the then budding singer's career. (See "Os donos das paradas," *Veja*, 26 Aug. 1987, 130).

60. "Os donos das paradas," *Veja*, 26 Aug. 1987, 129.

61. "Os donos das paradas," *Veja*, 26 Aug. 1987, 129.

62. Setting the tone for Xuxa's recording history is one of her early efforts, before the annual Som Livre releases. The 1985 album "Xuxa e Seus Amigos" was designed to correspond to a television special celebrating two years of the "Clube" on Manchete. The LP consisted of cuts by some of Brazil's most respected artists and artist-songwriters, including Chico Buarque and Caetano Veloso. Xuxa's voice was added to the original recordings by a remixing procedure performed in the studios of Polygram records. One review called Xuxa's duet with Chico Buarque a "perfectly forgettable moment" in Brazilian popular music ("Perfeitamente esquecível," *Istoé*, 6 Nov. 1985, 46). The album was an obviously contrived effort to take advantage of a television event. The review, however, also noted that the record would likely sell well.

63. " 'Xou da Xuxa' vende 2,5 milhões em meses. Inédito," *O Globo*, 8 Nov. 1986. The following three citations are also from this source.

64. "Xegou o novo Xou," *Jornal do Brasil*, 26 June 1987.

65. Gisele Porto, "Xuxa," *O Estado de São Paulo*, 21 June 1987, sec. 2, p. 3.

66. "Coração Criança," Paulo Massadas and Michael Sullivan, "Xou da Xuxa 3" (1988).

67. "Turma da Xuxa" is by Reinaldo Waisman and Robson Stipancovich; "Amiguinha Xuxa" is by Rogério Enoé and Messias Corrêa.

68. "Meu Cavalo Frankenstein" is by Mario Lúcio de Freitas and Tati; "Meu Cãozinho Xuxo" is by Rogério Enoé and Messias Corrêa.

69. "Amiguinha Xuxa" and "Turma da Xuxa;" see note 69 above.

70. "Peter Pan," is by Rita Lee and Roberto de Carvalho.

71. "She-Ra" is by Joe and Tavinho Paes; "Garoto Problema" is by Frejat and Guto Goffi.

72. "Quem Qué Pão," is by Tuza and J. Corrêa.

73. "Doce Mel" is by Cláudio Rabello and Renato Corrêa.

74. "Os amigos do peito," *Veja*, 24 June 1987, 86–87.

75. Xuxa also released a sing-along album in late 1987 called "Karaokê da Xuxa." It included three new songs she performed in her live show.

76. *Playboy*, Aug. 1987, 35.

77. "Xegou o novo Xou," *Jornal do Brasil*, 26 June 1987, sec. 2, p. 1.

78. Deborah Dumar, "Xuxa vende tudo," *O Globo*, 18 June 1987, sec. 2, p. 1.

79. "Beijinhos Estalados" is by Lincoln Olivetti and Cláudia Olivetti.

80. João Gabriel de Lima, "Festa ensaiada," *Veja*, 27 July 1988, 124. Lima compares Xuxa's LP unfavorably to classics such as Chico Buarque's "Os Saltimbancos" or Vinícius de Morais and Toquinho's "Arca de Noé." The author concedes, however, that since Xuxa is "one of the greatest mass communication phenomena in Brazil and the protagonist of a program that leads absolutely in the ratings," it would be too much to ask her to be a "brilliant vocalist" as well.

81. "Ilariê" is by Cid Guerreiro, Dito, and Ceinha.

82. "Dança da Xuxa," Prêntice and Ronaldo Monteiro de Souza.

83. "Xuxerife" is by Reinaldo Waisman, Alexandre Agra, Fred Nascimento, and Guilherme Jr. The words *bunda* and *bicha* are not clearly articulated on the recording, but they are audible and are included on the lyrics sheet.

84. The song "Arco-Iris" is by Paulo Massadas, Michael Sullivan, and Ana Penido. A 1991 press release in Spanish entitled "Materia Tirada de Revista Chilena" claimed that the name Xuxa means "rainbow" in Korean. In Jussara Martins, "Super Xuxa," *Manchete*, 6 Feb. 1988, 111, the star said her name means "Happy Rainbow" in Chinese. In Renee Sallas,

"Xuxa y el Diablo," *Gente* (Buenos Aires), 8 Aug. 1991, 7, Xuxa reports that someone from Japan told her "xu" means rainbow and "xa" means pretty, "for Orientals."

85. "Apolo" is by Paulo Massadas and Michael Sullivan.

86. The anti-drug song, "Alerta," is by César Costa Filho, Sérgio Fonseca, and Reinaldo Waisman; the arithmetic song is "Conte Comigo," by Prêntice and Ronaldo Monteiro de Souza; the telling-time tune is "Passatempo," by M. Bijou and Guilherme Jr.

87. The original title of "Não Basta" is "No Basta." The song is by Franco de Vita, version by Biafra.

88. Press release, "Xou da Xuxa 6," Sept. 1991.

89. "Hoje E Dia de Folia" is by Nando Cordell.

90. "Meu Cachorrinho Pimpo" is by R. Alexandre.

91. From an ad on the inside back cover of *Revista da Xuxa*, Aug. 1991.

92. *Jornal do Brasil*, 6 Dec. 1991, sec. 1, p. 4. Related information in this paragraph is from the same source unless otherwise noted.

93. *Folha de São Paulo*, 7 Dec. 1991, sec. 1, p. 10.

94. Luzia Salles, "Xuxa adota favelada," *Contigo*, 5 Dec. 1991, 23.

95. Cristiane Costa, "Nova Jerusalém agora tem medo de ser crucificada," *Jornal do Brasil*, 24 Nov. 1991, sec. 1, p. 26.

96. Luzia Salles, "Xuxa adota favelada," *Contigo*, 5 Dec. 1991, 23.

97. Jeb Blount, "Xuxa's Very Big Neighborhood," *Los Angeles Times*, "Calendar" supplement, 19 Apr. 1992, 78.

98. Nancy Scheper-Hughes, *Death Without Weeping: The Violence of Everyday Life in Brazil* (Berkeley: University of California Press, 1992), 473.

99. That October, Xuxa made a public statement lamenting how minor her contribution to children through the Fundação was. She said, "The Fundação is so little," and later in the same interview Xuxa admitted she spent almost as much money on her pet animals as she did on the children at the Fundação

(interview with Xuxa by Ricardo Lombardi, *O Estado de São Paulo*, 1 Oct. 1991, sec. 2, p. 10).

100. Jaguar, "Xuxa ajuda criança pobre," *O Dia*, 16 Oct. 1991, sec. "Opinião," p. 4.

101. Sônia Apolinário, "Xuxa renova com a Globo e entra na linha da denúncia social em 92," *Folha de São Paulo*, 12 Oct. 1991, sec. 5, p. 1.

102. Sarques, "A Magia," 12.

103. "O Xou da Xuxa começou," by Dido de Oliveira.

CHAPTER FOUR

1. "A loirinha chegou lá," *Veja*, 25 Sept. 1991, 106.

2. The first Paquita, Andréa Veiga, was hired to help Xuxa mind the children on her "Clube da Criança" show on the Manchete network. The star explains the origins of the Spanish-language name "Paquita": Xuxa had named a pet parrot Paquito, after a Cuban dentist who once treated her in New York. As Xuxa tells it, her parrot was seeking a girlfriend while she herself was looking for a helper on the television program. When an attractive girl was found, she was named Paquita, the feminine of Paquito. Using the logic of fantasy and cartoons, the Paquitas are thus conceptualized from the beginning as objects of romantic interest (girlfriends), as well as serving Xuxa's needs for baby-sitting aides in the caretaker role.

3. *Contigo* ran an article about one group consisting of an impersonator of Xuxa (Andréia Fabiana) and her "Paquitas." The magazine claimed they were making a lot of money giving performances in "various cities." It is obvious from the photograph of the impostors that they lack the strict training, grooming, and costly outfits of the originals (20 Dec. 1990, 3).

4. Nico Vink, *The Telenovela and Emancipation: A Study on TV and Social Change in Brazil* (Amsterdam: Royal Tropical Institute, 1988), 49.

5. Patrícia Veiga, "Xuxa, rainha da nova moda infantil," *O Globo*, 7 Jan. 1987.

6. "Estilo Xuxa," *Veja*, 9 Mar. 1988, 78.

7. Veiga, "Xuxa, rainha."

8. Patrícia Veiga, "Xuxa total," *O Globo*, 20 June 1987.

9. Ana Gaio, Marina Nery, and Tarlis Batista, "Xuxa: Uma estrela luta contra a solidão," *Manchete*, 24 Feb. 1990, 110.

10. "Vaidade mirim," *Veja*, 12 Oct. 1988, 94.

11. "Estilo Xuxa," *Veja*, 9 Mar. 1988, 78.

12. Jeb Blount, "Xuxa's Very Big Neighborhood," *Los Angeles Times*, "Calendar" supplement, 19 April 1992, 78.

13. "Entertainment Tonight," broadcast on 4 Sept. 1990.

14. "Xuxa invade os Estados Unidos," *Manchete*, 9 May 1992, 102.

15. Maria Luíza Silveira, "Adolescentes: Uma licão de sexo," *Manchete*, 15 Oct. 1988, 103.

16. Silveira, "Adolescentes," 103. The star was supported by other observers of Brazilian culture. Child psychiatrist Christian Gauderer, addressing the topic of children acting as adults on soap operas, said, "The democratization of information, a process in which television is fundamental, opened a new horizon for children. Today's child really is more mature and precocious" ("Soro da maturidade," *Veja*, 13 May 1992, 89). Others, however, see eight-year-olds placed in adult situations in soap opera dramas as unnatural. *Veja* concludes that they become "hybrid beings, more like puppets of adults, or dwarfs" ("Soro da maturidade," *Veja*, 13 May 1992, 88).

17. Contardo Calligaris, *Hello Brasil: Notas de um psicanalista europeu viajando ao Brasil* (São Paulo: Escuta, 1991), 151–152.

18. Naomi Wolf, *The Beauty Myth: How Images of Beauty Are Used Against Women* (New York: William Morrow, 1991), 214–217.

19. Wolf, *The Beauty Myth*, 215.

20. Denise Duhamel suggests in her article "Barbie and Self-Esteem" (*The City of DIS* 2 [1992]: 16–17) that black

women in the United States suffer less than whites and Hispanics from the distortions of self-esteem associated with the presence in childhood of the Barbie doll as a model of ideal feminine beauty. "Black women who had Barbies as girls are more emotionally removed from the activity of playing with them," Duhamel writes, "whereas white baby-boomer women are usually the ones who most relate, convinced that Barbie screwed them up in some profound and fundamentally weird way" (16).

21. Marina Nery, "A Sedução dos Astros-Mirins," *Manchete*, 23 July 1988, 67, 68. The following five citations are from the same source, page 71.

22. *Veja*, 13 May 1992, 62.

23. "Ninfetomania," *Veja*, 11 Sept. 1991, 98.

24. *Veja*, 1 Jan. 1991, 64.

25. Anna Muggiati and Jacqueline Mello Pedrosa, "As Novas Ninfetas," *Manchete*, 28 Nov. 1987, 58.

26. Muggiati and Pedrosa, "As Novas Ninfetas," 60.

27. The Paquitas' male counterparts, called "Paquitos," mainly serve as visual props onto which the teenagers in the audience are encouraged to project their romantic fantasies. The Paquitos escort Xuxa to and from her spaceship at the beginning and end of the program, but have few other roles other than occasionally performing songs (they released an LP in 1990).

28. "O Brasil se liga nas ninfetas eletrônicas," *Manchete*, 24 Feb. 1990, 66.

29. Press release in Spanish, distributed 1991.

30. "Ninfetomania," *Veja*, 11 Sept. 1991, 98.

31. Interview with Regina Rito, *Jornal do Brasil*, 29 Sept. 1991, sec. 1, p. 14.

32. Not only the Paquitas, but almost any young, attractive woman in the public eye in Brazil learns to expect offers to pose nude for men's magazines. The case of athletes Hortência and Paula was noted in Chapter Two. The 28 Sept. 1991 issue of

Manchete mentioned them in an article on the subject of nude posing by well-known female public figures including athletes, actors, and newscasters. The article included a page of photos of women who had agreed to pose nude, and another of those who had refused (112–113).

33. Gerson Vieira, "Ex-Paquita vira megera na novela das seis," *Contigo*, Apr. 1990, 17.

34. *Veja*, 3 Aug. 1988, 79; and Vieira, "Ex-Paquita vira megera," 17.

35. *Playboy*, Sept. 1988, 60–71.

36. The two discussions of racial issues occur in "Modelito ariano," *Istoé*, 21 Dec. 1988, and Arnaldo Jabor, "Choram as quatro damas do baralho nacional," *Folha de São Paulo*, 26 Sept. 1991, sec. 1, p. 14. The first is a one-and-a-half-page examination primarily of white images on Brazilian children's television programs. The second only mentions the question of race in passing, but because of the prominence of the newspaper and of the author, the comments represent a significant departure from the general posture of silence.

37. James Brooke, "Brazil's Idol Is a Blonde, and Some Ask 'Why?' " *New York Times*, 31 July 1990, sec. 1, p. 31.

38. Brooke, "Brazil's Idol," sec. 1, p. 31.

39. Tova Chapoval, "Brazil's Blond Bombshell Explodes Worldwide," *San Diego Union*, 31 Jan. 1992; also published under the headline "Watch Out, Big Bird: Here Comes Xuxa!" in *The Arizona Republic*, 19 Jan. 1992, sec. 8., p. 6.

40. Blount, "Xuxa's Very Big Neighborhood," 78.

41. *Correio Braziliense* (Brasilia), 23 Aug. 1989.

42. Throughout Latin America, white images of beauty predominate on television and in advertising. The host of the "Show de Cristina" is herself white and blond. The reach of Xuxa's image, whose authority has now spread all over the continent, makes her promotion of the white aesthetic particularly pernicious, since her show so clearly represents an unusual opportunity for change. By hiring nonwhite Paquitas, for example, Xuxa could take a step in the direction of ending

negative stereotypes and putting a stop to a system that perpetuates racist thinking. That she does not take such a simple step speaks to racism's powerful appeal.

43. Daniel Cerone, "A Hit in L.A. Latino Homes, Xuxa Is Working on Her English," *Los Angeles Times*, "Calendar" supplement, 19 April 1992, 10.

44. Teodomiro Braga, "Temporada de caça a Xuxa nos EUA," *Jornal do Brasil*, 11 Jan. 1992, sec. 2, p. 1.

45. Ana Claudia Souza, "Paquita, o novo sonho de toda menina-moça," *Jornal do Brasil*, "TV Programa," 8 Sept. 1991, 7.

46. From remarks by Xuxa on the "Show de Cristina," Univisión, 14 May 1992.

47. Mônica Bergamo, "Marlene Mattos: A dona da Xuxa," *Playboy*, June 1990, 55.

48. *Amiga*, 16 Feb. 1990, 13.

49. Bergamo, "Marlene Mattos," 55.

50. *Istoé*, 27 June 1990, 78; and Bergamo, "Marlene Mattos," 55. Mattos has been called Xuxa's opposite, the beast to the star's beauty, dark to Xuxa's white, short compared to Xuxa's height. Mattos is from a poor family in northeastern Brazil. Before she got a job at Globo in Rio, Mattos was an elementary school teacher in the state of Maranhão. Xuxa's manager does not give interviews but sometimes issues dictums representing her philosophy. Some of these reflect the conservative views that inform the Xuxa experience. One of Mattos's sayings, for example, refers to the poverty that characterizes the region where she is from: "People from the Northeast all get lethargy injections when they're born. I got away from my nurse, and he hasn't caught up with me since." Another Mattos quote asserts a belief in hard work and individual effort: "My grandmother used to say going hungry was just a lack of creativity. In Maranhão I ate a lot of dried fish and manioc meal. I never went hungry." One more expression of Mattos's philosophy, a variant on "Where there's a will, there's a way," places her securely within the ideological framework on which the "Xou" is predicated: "You can achieve anything as long as you set goals.

The only thing you can't be is God. Everything else is possible." Here Mattos expresses a kind of American dream belief in the virtues of work and discipline, an ideology that ultimately serves to support the status quo (Bergamo, "Marlene Mattos," 55; quoted in Regina Rito, "Maranhense é quem decide por Xuxa," *Jornal do Brasil*, "TV Programa," 13 Oct. 1991, 33).

51. Wolf, *The Beauty Myth*, 200.

52. In her chapter on "Hunger," in *The Beauty Myth*, Wolf discusses the history and tradition of women eating differently from men, specifically, "less and worse" (190).

53. "Amor Adolescente" is composed by Rubens Alexandre and Vadinho.

54. "Alegres Paquitas" is by Cesar Costa Filho and Sérgio Fonseca; "Fada Madrinha (E Tão Bom)" is by Tito Costa and Borges Machado.

55. These examples are taken from "Trocando Energia," by Cesar Costa Filho, Luiz Sarmanho, and Elizabeth.

56. The song, "Auê," is by Marcos Netto and Teresa Costa; MTV broadcast the video on 20 Nov. 1991.

57. Hermano Vianna, in *O Mundo Funk Carioca* (Rio de Janeiro: Jorge Zahar, 1988), discusses funk and its meaning in Brazil.

58. Lúcia Rego, "Angélica," *Manchete*, 2 Sept. 1989, 112.

59. After hosting the "Nave da Fantasia" on the Manchete network, Angélica took over the "Clube da Criança" when Xuxa left Manchete for Globo. Angélica began hosting "Milk Shake" on Manchete as well, in 1988.

60. Nery, "A Sedução dos astros-mirins," 71.

61. An abundance of media texts use the words "Lolita," "menina-mulher," and "nymphet" to refer to Angélica. The *Folha de São Paulo*, 6 Dec. 1991, sec. 5, p. 2, calls her a "Lolita." "Angélica: A nova musa da TV," *Manchete*, 15 Oct. 1988, 110, labels her a "menina-mulher," and in *Manchete*, 4 June 1988, 55, she is a "sexy nymphet." In another example, on the occasion of the release of an Angélica LP, the vice president of CBS records stated "she is a nymphet" ("A lourinha alegre," *Veja*, 1 Nov. 1989, 137).

62. These three views of Angélica are from: Lúcia Rego, "Angélica," *Manchete*, 2 Sept. 1989, cover; Hélio Contreiras, "Angélica: A nova musa da TV," *Manchete*, 15 Oct. 1988, 110; Muggiati and Pedrosa, "As Novas Ninfetas," 60.

63. "A lourinha alegre," *Veja*, 1 Nov. 1989, 134, 135, and 137.

64. The song, "Angelical Touch," is by Debarros Fo.

65. Other characteristics associated with Xuxa's recordings are found in Angélica's as well, including the participation of Massadas and Sullivan, the studio-produced disco pop sound, and the commercial approach most notable in the song "Angelical Touch," which draws attention both to the singer and to her cosmetic and bath products marketed under the label Angelical Touch. These are pictured beneath the lyrics to the song on the lyric sheet, where they are individually identified as "shampoo," "conditioner," "deodorant-cologne," and "lip gloss."

66. *Manchete*, 6 Aug. 1988, 46.

67. "A lourinha alegre," 137.

68. *Playboy*, May 1989, 140–141.

69. Contreiras, "Angélica," 110.

70. Contreiras, "Angélica," 112.

71. Marilda Varejão, "Angélica: A Estrela Cresce," *Manchete*, 4 June 1988, 52.

72. Angélica has made numerous statements about her wish to be a virgin on her wedding day. The citation here is from an interview by Lilian Viveros in *Contigo*, 18 July 1991, 26.

73. Varejão, "Angélica," 56.

74. Ana Gaio, "Angélica mulher," *Manchete*, 16 Nov. 1991, 113.

75. *Manchete*, 6 Aug. 1988, 46.

76. Interview with Flávio Landi in "Folhateen," *Folha de São Paulo*, 11 Nov. 1991, sec. 7, p. 4.

77. Varejão, "Angélica," 56.

78. Revelations in "A lourinha alegre," 137, about an exhausted Angélica given glucose injections in order to go on stage, also seem to convey the idea of the young star as property.

According to the article, she was rescued from her manager by her father, whom the former in turn accused of exploiting his daughter.

79. Marina Nery, "Angélica: O début de uma princesa," *Manchete*, 10 Dec. 1988, 111.

80. Nery, "Angélica," 109.

81. Marina Nery, "A Sedução dos astros-mirins," 71.

82. Cíntia, a nonwhite child host of the kids' program "Cometa Alegria," is the exception. When Xuxa discussed leaving Brazil in late 1991, Cíntia was one of many show business figures asked to comment. She is quoted saying, "Don't leave Brazil, Xuxa. You are the symbol, the heroine, the idol the whole nation needs" (*Contigo*, 3 Oct. 1991, 25).

83. "Modelito ariano," *Istoé*, 21 Dec. 1988.

84. Ana Claudia Souza, "Paquita, o novo sonho de toda menina-moça," *Jornal do Brasil*, "TV Programa," 8 Sept. 1991, 6.

85. "Racismo no ar: Crianças negras ficam longe das câmaras," *Veja*, 13 May 1992, 89. The *Veja* article describes how a production assistant was fired by the director of the program, who asked, when he noticed there were black youngsters among the group gathered for the recording session, "Foi você quem escolheu aqueles dois negrinhos?" ("Are you the one who chose those two little black kids"?)

86. Eliane Azevedo, "Marcadas pelo tipo," *Veja*, 22 Apr. 1992, 85.

87. Azevedo, "Marcadas," 84.

88. Azevedo, "Marcadas," 85.

89. Azevedo, "Marcadas," 85.

90. "Modelito ariano," *Istoé*, 21 Dec. 1988.

91. "Modelito ariano," *Istoé*, 21 Dec. 1988.

92. Arnaldo Jabor, *Folha de São Paulo*, 26 Sept. 1991, sec. 1, p. 14.

93. Gil's 1992 release is entitled "Parabolicamará."

94. Márcio Nicolosi, *Fetichast: Províncias do Desejo* (São Paulo: Nova Sampa, 1991); the *Playboy* issues referred to are May 1989, 64–71, Oct. 1989, 110–117, June 1985, 60–65; on Tim Maia, see *Jornal do Brasil*, 20 Sept. 1991, sec. 2, p. 2.

95. On Madonna and Xuxa, see Eduardo Mack, "Madonna dá uma de Xuxa," *Jornal do Brasil*, "Programa," 23 Aug. 1991, 36; on M. C. Hammer, see *Jornal do Brasil*, 29 Oct. 1991, sec. 2, p. 6.

96. On the use of Xuxaspell in the larger culture, *Veja* magazine of 19 Oct. 1988, ran an article on page 43 entitled "Xou do Xarney" about President Sarney's withdrawal of a government promotional television spot. An example of Xuxa's trademark kiss as a general cultural reference occurs in the *Folha de São Paulo*, 2 Oct. 1991, sec. 5, p. 2, where a society page photo shot at a luncheon shows a woman with her lips puckered as if to give a kiss. The caption describes the woman giving "a Xuxa." The term "baixinhos" is increasingly used as a synonym for *criança* (child); an example is a brief article on the *"dupla sertaneja"* Chitãozinho e Xororó, in *Amiga*, 8 Nov. 1991, 53, where the words "baixinhos" and "crianças" alternate in the text.

97. It is generally assumed that Angélica is Xuxa's principal imitator, although the younger star has denied it (see Marilda Varejão, "Angélica," 52) and on one occasion, declined to discuss whether she "is or is not a Xuxa clone" (see Marcia Cezimbra, "Angélica S.A.: nova empresa da TV," *Jornal do Brasil*, 13 Oct. 1988).

98. Lúcia Rego, "Angélica," *Manchete*, 2 Sept. 1989, 112.

99. Jacqueline Breitinger, "Multinacional brasileira," [*Istoé* or *Veja*], July 1991, 42 (photocopy given to the author with incomplete documentation; from the author's files).

100. Cláudio Uchôa, "A adolescente Angélica acorda mais cedo para roubar baixinhos de Xuxa," *Jornal do Brasil*, "TV Programa," 2 May 1992, 37.

101. Blount, "Xuxa's Very Big Neighborhood," 9.

102. Marina Ney, "Angélica: O début de uma princesa," *Manchete*, 10 Dec. 1989, 109.

103. Interview with Ricardo Lombardi, *O Estado de São Paulo*, 1 Oct. 1991, sec. 2, p. 1.

104. Márcia Pereira, "Xuxa tem tudo. Menos amor," *Contigo*, 13 June 1991, 29. Pitanguy's fame has brought him international attention. He even surfaces in feminist literature in

the United States, such as Nora Scott Kinzer's *Put Down and Ripped Off: The American Woman and the Beauty Cult* (New York: Thomas Y. Crowell, 1977). In another feminist critique of the beauty industry, *Face Value: The Politics of Beauty*, by Robin Tolmach Lakoff and Raquel L. Scherr (Boston: Routledge and Kegan Paul, 1984), Pitanguy and his approach are invoked to exemplify the "objectification of the subject of medical practices." The authors of *Face Value* describe the Brazilian cosmetic surgeon using women as "laboratory rats" (174).

105. Muniz Sodré and Francisco Antonio Doria, *Jornal do Brasil*, 15 Jan. 1989, sec. 2, p. 1.

106. "Angelical Touch," by Debarros Fo̱, on the LP "Angélica," 1989.

107. Lúcia Machado, quoted in Luis Antônio Giron, "Super Xuxa enfrenta o baixo astral," *Folha de São Paulo*, 22 Sept. 1991, sec. 5, p. 14. Soon after replacing Xuxa on Manchete's "Clube da Criança," Angélica began to be seen as competition for the older star. *Manchete* asked the question "Nasce uma nova Xuxa?" ("Is a new Xuxa emerging?") in its 11 April 1987 issue (p. 57), hoping, no doubt, that Angélica would prove to be serious competition for the star the Manchete network had lost to Globo a year earlier. Angélica was presented as "the new muse of the 'baixinhos' " in 1987, by 1988 it was announced the "copy was beginning to surpass the original," and by 1991, Angélica was the "Vice-Queen of the 'Baixinhos' " (*Manchete*, 7 Nov. 1987, 57; Marcia Cezimbra, "Angélica S.A.," sec. 2, p. 2; *Veja*, 11 Dec. 1991, 75).

108. *Veja*, 18 Dec. 1991, 7; Nancy Scheper-Hughes, *Death Without Weeping: The Violence of Everyday Life in Brazil* (Berkeley: University of California Press, 1992), 157. In Scheper-Hughes's discussion of the phenomenon of the nongenetic dwarfs, or "nanicos," in northeastern Brazil, she cites the Brazilian nutritionist Nelson Chaves's book *Fome, criança e vida* (Recife: Editora Massangana, Fundação Joaquim Nabuco, 1982), in which the author uses the word "pygmies" to describe the population "stunted by chronic hunger, not by genes" (Scheper-Hughes,

144). Referring to Malaquias Batista Filho's book *Nutrição, alimentação, e agricultura no Nordeste Brasileiro* (Recife: Embraer, 1987), Scheper-Hughes writes that "two-thirds of all rural children [in northeastern Brazil] showed signs of considerable undernutrition and stunting, and of these, 40 percent could be classified as nutritionally dwarfed, as 'nanicos' " (153). Scheper-Hughes also observes that "the average [caloric] intake of the Nordestino sugarcane cutter today" is less than that of the food allotment in the Buchenwald concentration camp in 1944 (157).

109. "Xou da Xuxa," 2 Dec. 1991.

CHAPTER FIVE

1. *Veja*, 1 Jan. 1992, 76.

2. "Antes tarde: Xuxa vê o óbvio e se assusta com o país," *Istoé*, 18 Sept. 1991, 15.

3. Ana Gaio, "Xuxa: Por que a estrela chora," *Manchete*, 5 Oct. 1991, 12.

4. Apoenan Rodrigues, "Xuxa cai na realidade," *Jornal do Brasil*, 16 Sept. 1991, sec. 2, p. 6.

5. Rodrigues, "Xuxa cai," sec. 2, p. 6.

6. That version of the story is the one given in the *Jornal do Brasil*, in its second edition of Thursday, August 8. There is another version, in the same newspaper, on August 13, according to which Alves, not Aílton, is the one who dies. The newspaper also has Aílton testifying on August 12 that the Chevette circled the block five times before stopping, and that, as a result, both he and his companion were definitely wary before one of them walked over to the car. In the August 14 issue of *Veja*, it is Aílton who first approaches the car, is shot in the chest by the occupant on the passenger side, and dies. Alves then goes to the aid of his downed fellow soldier and is shot. The armored vehicle happens to pass by at that moment, the Chevette takes off, and a "cinematographic chase" ensues.

7. *Jornal do Brasil,* 2nd. edition, 8 Aug. 1991, sec. Cidade, p. 5.

8. Reported in, among other places, *Jornal do Brasil,* 9 Aug. 1991, sec. Cidade, p. 1.

9. *Veja,* 14 Aug. 1991.

10. *Veja,* 14 Aug. 1991, 80.

11. *Jornal do Brasil,* 9 Aug. 1991, sec. Cidade, p. 1.

12. *Manchete,* 24 Aug. 1991, 14.

13. *Jornal do Brasil,* 13 Aug. 1991, sec. Cidade, p. 5.

14. *Jornal do Brasil,* 10 Aug. 1991, sec. Cidade, p. 5.

15. *Para Ti* (Buenos Aires), 26 Aug. 1991.

16. *Veja,* 14 Aug. 1991, 81.

17. *Jornal do Brasil,* 10 Aug. 1991.

18. *Jornal do Brasil,* 13 Aug. 1991, sec. Cidade, p. 5.

19. Dr. Haim Grunspun is a child psychiatrist, professor at the Pontífica Universidade Católica, and author of several books on child behavior problems. He is quoted in the *Jornal do Brasil,* 10 Aug. 1991, sec. Cidade, p. 5.

20. Quoted in *Jornal da Tarde,* 9 Aug. 1991, 16.

21. *Jornal do Brasil,* 9 Aug. 1991, sec. Cidade, p. 1.

22. *Manchete,* 24 Aug. 1991, 14, 15.

23. *Contigo,* 22 Aug. 1991, 31; *Jornal do Brasil,* 14 Aug. 1991, sec. Cidade, p. 5, and 15 Aug. 1991, sec. Cidade, p. 5.

24. According to the *Folha de São Paulo,* 10 Aug. 1991, Alberto was moved in the afternoon.

25. *Jornal do Brasil,* 13 Aug. 1991, sec. Cidade, p. 5.

26. *Jornal do Brasil,* 14 Aug. 1991, sec. Cidade, p. 5.

27. Luzia Salles and Rosani Alves, *Contigo,* 22 Aug. 1991, 31.

28. *Contigo,* 22 Aug. 1991, 31. As a somewhat curious footnote, both brothers were described as having been "killed by police" in a report about Xuxa broadcast in the United States on "Entertainment Tonight," which aired on NBC, 2 Nov. 1992.

29. When an earlier plan to kidnap Xuxa was discovered, in September 1990, children reportedly tried to organize "patrols" to protect her. The alleged plan was foiled when police shot and

killed a man named Maurinho Branco, who was connected to various criminal activities, and among whose belongings was found a notebook with observations about Xuxa's schedule and movements (*Amiga*, 5 Oct. 1990).

30. *Manchete*, 5 Oct. 1991, 12. The following remark about Wonderwoman is from the same source.

31. *Contigo*, 13 June 1991, 29.

32. *Para Ti* (Buenos Aires), 26 Aug. 1991.

33. *Contigo*, 22 Aug. 1991.

34. Gaio, "Xuxa," 10–13.

35. *Folha de São Paulo*, 10 Aug. 1991, sec. 1, p. 2.

36. Aydano André Motta, "O país perdeu a graça," *Istoé*, 25 Sept. 1991, 23.

37. Renée Sallas and Tarlis Batista, "Xuxa total," *Manchete*, 21 Dec. 1991, 113.

38. *Folha de São Paulo*, 2 Oct. 1991, sec. 7, p. 2, and 21 Sept. 1991, sec. 5, p. 2.

39. *Jornal do Brasil*, 25 Sept. 1991, sec. 1, p. 6.

40. *Istoé*, 25 Sept. 1991, 24.

41. *Istoé*, 25 Sept. 1991, 23.

42. *Istoé*, 25 Sept. 1991, 24.

43. *Istoé*, 25 Sept. 1991, 24.

44. *Folha de São Paulo*, 2 Oct. 1991, sec. 7, p. 2.

45. Laerte, in *Visão*, 2 Oct. 1991, 66.

46. Nancy Scheper-Hughes, *Death Without Weeping: The Violence of Everyday Life in Brazil* (Berkeley: University of California Press, 1992), 422.

47. "Xuxa y el diablo," *Gente*, 8 Aug. 1991, cover.

48. *Folha de São Paulo*, 10 Aug. 1991, sec. 2, p. 2.

49. "Xuxa fez pacto com o diabo," *Amiga*, 6 Sept. 1991, 10. The following rumor, that a Xuxa doll had wept blood, is reported in the same source.

INDEX